STUDENT THINKING AND LEARNING IN SCIENCE

This readable and informative survey of key ideas about students' thinking in science builds a bridge between theory and practice by offering clear accounts from research, and showing how they relate to actual examples of students talking about widely taught science topics.

Focused on secondary students and drawing on perspectives found in the international research literature, the goal is not to offer a comprehensive account of the vast literature, but rather to provide an overview of the current state of the field suitable for those who need an understanding of core thinking about learners' ideas in science, including science education students in teacher preparation and higher degree programs, and classroom teachers, especially those working with middle school, high school, or college level students. Such understanding can inform and enrich science teaching in ways which are more satisfying for teachers, less confusing and frustrating for learners, and so ultimately can lead to both greater scientific literacy and more positive attitudes to science.

Keith S. Taber is University Reader in Science Education, University of Cambridge, UK.

Teaching and Learning in Science Series
Norman G. Lederman, Series Editor

Student Thinking and Learning in Science: Perspectives on the Nature and Development of Learners' Ideas
Taber

Integrating Science, Technology, Engineering, and Mathematics: Issues, Reflections, and Ways Forward
Rennie/Venville/Wallace (Eds.)

Rethinking the Way We Teach Science: The Interplay of Content, Pedagogy, and the Nature of Science
Rosenblatt

Exploring the Landscape of Scientific Literacy
Linder/Östman/Roberts/Wickman/Erickson/MacKinnon (Eds.)

Designing and Teaching the Elementary Science Methods Course
Abell/Appleton/Hanuscin

Interdisciplinary Language Arts and Science Instruction in Elementary Classrooms: Applying Research to Practice
Akerson (Ed.)

Aesthetic Experience in Science Education: Learning and Meaning-Making as Situated Talk and Action
Wickman

Visit **www.routledge.com/education** for additional information on titles in the Teaching and Learning in Science Series

STUDENT THINKING AND LEARNING IN SCIENCE

Perspectives on the Nature and Development of Learners' Ideas

Keith S. Taber

NEW YORK AND LONDON

First published 2014
by Routledge
711 Third Avenue, New York, NY 10017

and by Routledge
2 Park Square, Milton Park, Abingdon, Oxon OX14 4RN

Routledge is an imprint of the Taylor & Francis Group, an informa business

© 2014 Taylor & Francis

The right of Keith S. Taber to be identified as author of this work has been asserted by him in accordance with sections 77 and 78 of the Copyright, Designs and Patents Act 1988.

All rights reserved. No part of this book may be reprinted or reproduced or utilized in any form or by any electronic, mechanical, or other means, now known or hereafter invented, including photocopying and recording, or in any information storage or retrieval system, without permission in writing from the publishers.

Trademark notice: Product or corporate names may be trademarks or registered trademarks, and are used only for identification and explanation without intent to infringe.

Library of Congress Cataloging-in-Publication Data
Taber, Keith.
 Student thinking and learning in science : perspectives on the nature and development of learners' ideas / Keith S. Taber.
  pages cm. — (Teaching and learning in science series)
 Includes bibliographical references and index.
 1. Science—Study and teaching (Secondary)—Great Britain. I. Title.
 Q183.4.G7T33 2014
 507.1'241—dc23
 2013043638

ISBN: 978-0-415-89731-0 (hbk)
ISBN: 978-0-415-89735-8 (pbk)
ISBN: 978-0-203-69508-1 (ebk)

Typeset in Bembo
by Apex CoVantage, LLC

Printed in Great Britain by TJ International Ltd, Padstow, Cornwall

DEDICATION

I would like to dedicate this book to the memory of Prof. Phil Scott (University of Leeds and former coeditor of *Studies in Science Education*): a school teacher, researcher, teacher educator, influential academic, and—above all—a much-missed human being. Phil was a capable intellectual and researcher who never lost sight of the need to communicate his work to teachers as well as other researchers. Moreover, when Phil talked to teachers they recognised him as not only an expert on science education, but also as a fellow science teacher: someone who understood their work, their issues, their perspective, and their classroom priorities. Phil left us much too early, but his work and influence live on, and I would like to think he would have recognised the present book as making some small contribution to communicating research in ways that teachers can engage with, and make use of, in their classroom work.

CONTENTS

Preface ix
Acknowledgments xiii

SECTION 1
Student Conceptions and Science 1

    Introduction. The Things Students Say: Learners' Ideas About Science Topics 3

1 Why Is Learning Science So Difficult for Many Students? 12

2 Characterising and Labelling Learners' Ideas 30

3 Alternative Conceptions of Learning 59

SECTION 2
Making Sense of Student Thinking 73

4 Innateness and Development: Cognitive Biases Influencing Learners' Ideas 75

5 Developing Intuitions About the World 91

6 The Role of Language in Learning Science 106

7 The Influence of Everyday Beliefs 135

8	Thinking About Knowing and Learning: Metacognitive and Epistemological Limitations on Science Learning	145
9	Integrating Knowledge and Constructing Conceptual Frameworks	161

SECTION 3
Diagnosing Student Thinking in Science Learning 175

10	A Provisional Synthesis: Learning, Teaching, and 'Bugs' in the System	177
11	The Science Teacher as Learning Doctor	191
12	Science Teaching Informed by an Appreciation of Student Thinking	210

Index   *219*

PREFACE

One of the common complaints about much educational research is that it seems too far removed from the day-to-day work of practitioners—the teachers and others actually supporting student learning in schools and colleges. Research is often written in technical language, with a strong theoretical framing, with studies often focusing on seemingly esoteric points and published in inaccessible and expensive research journals. Research papers often suggest implications for practice, but usually individual studies contribute iteratively, and sometimes modestly, to a developing research programme. It is the current state of the programme that can best inform teachers—not the discrete research papers scattered around different journals and edited scholarly books.

For research to be effective and contribute to our developing understanding is it important that the individual studies reported in primary research papers continue to be technical and theoretical, and to focus on adding incrementally to knowledge, and on testing and extending esoteric claims made in previous studies. The real problem is not that researchers do write for other researchers, as they need to do that for progress to be made, but that they do not also always write for practitioners. In part this is down to the kind of writing which is valued when academics are appointed, given tenure, or promoted. However, writing for teachers also requires a different style of writing, and a willingness to address issues of a broader scope as writing about one research study in isolation is often of limited value to classroom practitioners. (There is however a well-established review journal in science education, *Studies in Science Education*, which does publish broad reviews of research topics which, though aimed primarily at academics, includes many articles that would be of interest to teachers.)

I have been very lucky in my career to have spent time in a range of roles. I taught science in comprehensive schools (state-funded schools with an open admissions policy) and in a further-education college (a type of institution which offers a broad range of courses from basic literacy and courses developing vocational skills, to degree-level work). During my time as a schoolteacher I got the 'bug' for educational research. My master's thesis project concerned the under-representation of girls in elective physics classes in a school where I taught—a genuine issue of concern for the physics department. For my doctoral research I studied an aspect of students' developing understanding of an area of chemistry. I already appreciated the fascination of talking to learners about their understanding of science from some work I had carried out for an assignment on an earlier postgraduate diploma course, but my doctoral work reinforced this, and I have enjoyed this type of work ever since.

When I first moved to the Faculty of Education at Cambridge I was heavily involved in working with science graduates preparing for secondary teaching. As part of our work with these students we emphasised the importance to effective teaching of appreciating the ways students think about and understand the topics we teach them. We set a course assignment that required students to collect some diagnostic information about student thinking that would inform lesson planning—a type of assignment that is very common in science-teacher education. I was also honoured to be selected by the Royal Society of Chemistry for a year's secondment as Teacher Fellow to work on a project supporting teachers in undertaking diagnostic assessment in their classrooms. One output of that project was materials on 'chemical misconceptions' (Taber, 2002a, 2002b) that were considered by teachers to be very useful in supporting their classroom work (Murphy, Jones, & Lunn, 2004). A related workshop on diagnostic assessment in the classroom, given at various times to both trainee and in-service teachers, also demonstrated how science teachers found it useful to be offered a framework for thinking about the diverse range of ideas students may bring to their science classes.

Since then I have continued to work on various projects that have explored student thinking in different aspects of science. In particular I spent five years visiting one local school to interview a range of students about what they were learning in science classes—and many examples in this book are drawn from that work. I have written two books about this broad area of work that were intended primarily for others working in the field—one reviewing the general field of research into student learning in science (Taber, 2009), and the other arguing that many research papers in the field need to be more explicit in discussing the difficulties of diagnosing what students actually think and understand from what they tell us (Taber, 2013). Those books are relevant to classroom teachers, but are written primarily for academics and research students. The present book is about the same general area of work, but is written very much with classroom teachers, and those preparing for teaching, in mind. My aim here is not only to reinforce well-known messages that (a) learners often have their own ways of thinking about and understanding science topics, and (b) effective teaching needs to take these ideas into account, but also to offer (c) an account of the different sources of learners' alternative ideas, and (d) support to help teachers adopt an approach to diagnostic assessment to inform their classroom work with their own, unique, groups of students. I have found this aspect of the science teacher's work to be fascinating as well as challenging, and I hope something of my enthusiasm is reflected in this volume.

We read a lot about enquiry *learning*—about the need for students to experience science lessons that are enquiry based. The message of the present book is that effective science *teaching* is also enquiry based—teaching is in part a problem-solving activity based on ongoing enquiry into learners' developing thinking. In that sense, the science teacher needs to be a practising scientist in his or her own classroom.

References

Murphy, P., Jones, H., & Lunn, S. (2004). *The evaluation of RSC materials for schools and colleges: A report*. London: The Royal Society of Chemistry.

Taber, K. S. (2002a). *Chemical misconceptions—prevention, diagnosis and cure: Classroom resources* (Vol. 2). London: Royal Society of Chemistry.

Taber, K. S. (2002b). *Chemical misconceptions—prevention, diagnosis and cure: Theoretical background* (Vol. 1). London: Royal Society of Chemistry.

Taber, K. S. (2009). *Progressing science education: Constructing the scientific research programme into the contingent nature of learning science*. Dordrecht: Springer.

Taber, K. S. (2013). *Modelling learners and learning in science education: Developing representations of concepts, conceptual structure and conceptual change to inform teaching and research*. Dordrecht: Springer.

ACKNOWLEDGMENTS

Thanks are due to many people for their support in this work. As always, thanks and love are due to my wife, Philippa, for tolerating the kind of commitment a book project requires. I am grateful for the enthusiasm and encouragement offered by the series editor, Norman Lederman, when I proposed my initial ideas for this book, and the patience of Naomi Silverman, my publisher at Routledge when it was delayed by unanticipated events. (As John Lennon suggested, life is what happens to you while you are busy making other plans.) As a science educator who is a chemist and physicist, I very much appreciate two colleagues who are biologists and biology education specialists—Professor Michael Reiss of the Institute of Education, University of London, and Dr. Mark Winterbottom of the Faculty of Education at the University of Cambridge—for reading the text and offering comments on my treatment of biology topics. Any remaining mistakes are of course my own.

Special thanks go to all the students who have talked to me or otherwise provided research data, and the teachers who have helped facilitate this. Particular thanks go to the unnamed school that provided coffee and organised a schedule of volunteers to talk to me over a period of five years.

SECTION 1
Student Conceptions and Science

INTRODUCTION

The Things Students Say: Learners' Ideas About Science Topics

A Book About Student Thinking . . .

This book is about the way learners think and learn about science topics. There is now a good deal of research into these topics (for example, reviewed in Taber, 2013), although much of it is reported in technical literature that is not readily available to classroom teachers and others working directly with young learners (Duit, 2009). This book draws on that research literature, with a particular focus on informing those, such as teachers, supporting the learning of students. In particular, this book is intended to help teachers and others when they seek to make sense of students' thinking by interpreting what students say (and write) about science topics.

. . . To Inform Teaching

There was a time when in some educational systems a science lesson would comprise largely of the teacher presenting information for students to learn, interspersed with occasional tests which would allow the teacher to see which students had learnt most of the set material, and which students had learnt less. Often it was accepted that some students were 'brighter' than others, or some had more of a 'bent' or aptitude for science, and the familiar experience of many teachers was that a fair proportion of students in many classes seemed to fail to learn (and by implication perhaps failed to make much sense of) a lot of what they were 'taught'.

Such a situation was perhaps seen acceptable if school science was understood to be part of a system to select the best science students for university courses and ultimately careers in science, technology, and engineering. That notion of curriculum designed as a kind of filter to identify an intellectual elite is now—rightly—recognised as being unacceptable, and today science education is considered centrally important to all young people (Millar & Osborne, 1998; Reiss, 2007)—both as part of their own education and for the benefit of the technologically advanced societies in which they will become consumers and voters.

Perhaps there still are contexts where science teaching is based on the idea of the transmission of the teacher's notes to the student's notes—as it is sometimes said, without bothering the minds of either—with the expectation that 'good' students will then learn the notes for regurgitation in an examination. However, increasingly notions such as 'active learning', 'dialogic teaching', 'individualised learning', and 'assessment for learning' have become referents for good teaching.

Something like forty years ago there was something of a shift in the focus of the science education research community, which started to look in more detail at how students spoke and wrote about the science topics that they were studying to see how the learners were making sense of what they were being taught (Gilbert, Osborne, & Fensham, 1982). Rather than simply considering students responses that did not match the canonical answers as 'wrong', it was recognised that it was important to try to understand how and why students came away from classes with alternative interpretations of science topics. Answers that might formerly have been dismissed as simply the student 'getting it wrong' came to be seen as important diagnostic clues to how teaching was proving ineffective.

The Things Students Say

Indeed any science teacher who has given any thought to the 'wrong' or 'alternative' explanations and suggestions of their students will know these are often quite intriguing, sometimes mystifying (given what we know we have taught), and on occasions quite impressively creative. As part of my own work over the years—firstly as a school and college science teacher, later as a teacher educator, and as a researcher—I have taken a strong interest in the comments students make that can offer indications of their understanding and thinking about science topics. Textbox 0.1 presents a small sample of things students have said (or written) about science topics in the school curriculum.

The examples given in Textbox 0.1 represent just a small sample from data I have collected over a number of years. As will become clear later in the book, it is sometimes inappropriate to read too much into an isolated comment—sometimes students are struggling to find something to say in response to a question, and occasionally they are intentionally mischievous or intend to be humorous. Much of my data comes from extended interviews with students that allow opportunities to probe and test students' understanding (many more examples are included on a website intended to inform teachers—see the further reading that follows). But even then, there is always an act of interpretation involved in drawing inferences about student thinking and understanding from how they express their ideas (Taber, 2013).

> **Textbox 0.1: A selection of students' comments on a range of science topics.**
>
> **Apples fall from trees because** *"it is the intension (intention) of the tree that the pips have their own source of nutrients as they start to grow . . ."*
>
> *"I don't know what Physics is . . . you study like things you can't see and things you can see in Physics."*
>
> *". . . I think the sodium atom would realise that it could form a more stable configuration by giving one of the electrons to the chlorine and forming a bond . . ."*
>
> *"I think the stars, some stars, are closer, maybe, than planets."*
>
> *"It could have been like evolution, like . . . the atoms evolved so that they could hold on to each other."*
>
> **People age because** *"they get worn out. Eventually the vital parts of the body become unrepairable and the limbs slowly become more useless. Cells diminish over the years and eyes become over-used . . ."*
>
> *"[Plants] respire more at night, because—they do it then instead of in the day because they do photosynthesis during the day."*
>
> **Some animals sometimes eat their own young because** *"they . . . feel that there [their] young are not capable of handaling [handling] the style of life and don't want to make them suffer."*
>
> *"The gases, their particles try to stay as far away from each other as possible . . . because they are trying to spread out into the whole room."*
>
> These examples are revisited in later chapters.

Indeed one of the criticisms of some of the early research in science education was that some researchers seemed to focus on collecting examples of students comments about particular science topics, but without having any clear indication of what the real significance of the students' comments were for teachers. This is linked to wider criticism of what is sometimes called 'constructivism' in science education. Constructivism is a theory about how people learn, which has great deal of evidential support, and which offers insights that can support teachers in their classroom work (see Chapter 3). As a research programme, constructivism in science education has now progressed considerably beyond the 'natural history' stage of simply collecting and cataloging 'misconceptions' (Taber, 2009), and this book draws upon different perspectives on learning to consider the various sources of learners' ideas in science.

As a basis for teaching science, constructivism has a more checkered history. In New Zealand/Aotearoa, for example, constructivism was adopted as a basis for curriculum reform (Bell, Jones, & Car, 1995), but not without some opposition (Claxton, 1996). In the United Kingdom, constructivist pedagogy was adopted as the basis for a 'National Strategy' of guidance on how to teach science

(Key Stage 3 National Strategy, 2002), but arguably in a form that made challenging learners' alternative ideas appear so straightforward that it trivialised the potential significance of those ideas as impediments to learning science (Taber, 2010b). In the United States, there has been a long-standing and quite vigorous—indeed, sometimes somewhat vicious (Cromer, 1997)—debate around constructivism (Berube, 2008; Tobias & Duffy, 2009).

For most of those working as researchers, teacher educators, and experienced science educators, the basic principles of constructivist teaching (which involves taking into account what the learner already thinks) are widely accepted, and indeed sometimes seem as so obvious now that they are considered passé. Yet, in the United States in particular, constructivism has become embroiled in arguments about the relative merits of 'direct instruction', 'enquiry teaching', 'student-centred learning', 'progressive' education, and so forth. Unfortunately most of these terms mean different things to different people, and in particular the versions of these approaches presented by their critics are often unrecognisable to their advocates. So opponents of direct instruction may identify it with the teacher simply *talking at* students; and opponents of enquiry teaching may suggest that it involves the teacher refusing to reveal scientific knowledge and expecting learners to *rediscover it all by themselves*. Clearly no one who knows about science teaching would advocate either of these caricatured approaches, so this does not make a very good basis for a productive debate. (It certainly does not follow the constructivist approach of seeking to move understanding forward by taking into account the other person's thinking, and presenting your own arguments informed by how the other person understands the issues.) As a result much of the debate about constructivism consists of clever people talking past each other (Taber, 2010a).

Opponents of constructivism in teaching often label it as 'unguided' or 'minimally guided', implying that the teacher largely lets the learners take their own path to knowledge (Kirschner, Sweller, & Clark, 2006). Yet teaching which is genuinely informed by constructivist theory is *very* different from that—seeking to find the *optimum* level of guidance to best support learners: sometimes this means giving learners time and space to explore the implications of their own current thinking, but often it involves high levels of support and structure, and it always involves the design of learning activities planned to guide learners towards scientific understandings (Taber, 2011).

Readers should be assured that the version of constructivism informing this book (see Chapter 3) derives from research showing that simply telling learners the scientific account is often an ineffective way of teaching, and that rather the teacher has to carefully 'scaffold' learning, taking into account learners' current knowledge and understanding. We may not yet always know exactly how best to do this kind of optimally guided instruction for all science topics, but the basic constructivist idea that effective teaching is contingent upon learners' existing ideas is very well established.

An Invitation to Become a Science Learning Doctor

In this book I discuss examples of things students have said or written that give insight into their thinking and offer research-informed perspectives of how learners come to have these ideas. This is used as a base to argue for the importance of diagnostic assessment to inform teaching, and in particular of the value to science teachers of acting like medical practitioners in paying attention to the 'signs and symptoms' of science teaching that is going wrong: when learners say or write things that suggest they do not understand the teaching, or that they have managed to understand teaching quite differently from how we intended.

The latter parts of the book will revisit some of the examples readers met earlier in the book in the context of a simple model of where science teaching can go wrong in engaging with learners' thinking. Teachers can adopt this model as a useful heuristic tool for thinking about teaching and learning in their own classes. It is suggested that classroom teachers who are reading this book to support their own classroom work might also consider starting to keep a file of their own examples of 'the things students say' when they come across examples of questions, comments, written responses, and so on which suggest that students are thinking along very different lines from the scientific account being presented in class. For example, a simple log in the form of a table such as Table 0.1 would be sufficient.

The suggestion is that when reading about the model (in Chapter 11), the reader may wish to consider how the examples they have collected from their own teaching make sense in terms of the ideas discussed in the book. Teachers who have been introduced to this model in teacher development sessions have reported that they find it a helpful tool to think about student learning, and I hope that many readers will also find that this model is useful, whether applied directly as a formal tool to support diagnostic assessment in the classroom, or simply as a perspective to inform thinking about your day-to-day work.

Technical and Ethical Notes

The examples of student comments used in the book are all authentic examples provided by real students studying science subjects in various contexts. Written comments have been copied and typed into my records. Interview data has been transcribed from recordings. Transcribing always involves an element of interpretation,

TABLE 0.1 A table for recording signs of learners' thinking inconsistent with science teaching.

Student/class	Context	Student comment	Notes

as natural spoken language is seldom entirely clear when a recording is listened to forensically. Recordings often reveal hesitations, false starts, mixed tenses, missing subjects, and so forth that we do not actually notice in 'real time' during a conversation. (For an example of how our brains process and make sense of sensory data, and present a polished version of what we see or hear to consciousness, see Chapter 5.) In transcribing speech we need to decide how much of this detail that is filtered out as noise during the actual listening experience should be included in the written record. When we use extracts in our writing we then have further decisions to make about how much tidying up of language is sensible. Hesitations may reflect uncertainty, for example, but too much 'um'-ing and 'ah'-ing can make for difficult reading. The judgment to be made is to tidy up extracts to aid readability without distorting the essence of the original speech. I have always tried to limit such editing and use it to enhance the communication of the original meaning rather than distort it. Of course, it is possible to get this wrong. I have done my best to present authentic reports of what students actually told me, but the reader should bear in mind that my interpretations of what students have told me can be fallible, just as can those students' interpretations of what their science teacher told them.

'Informed consent' was obtained from students when collecting data. That means students understood why I was talking to them, and knew the kind of things I might do with the information—such as use it in talking to or writing for teachers—and they were happy to provide the 'gift' of an interview on that basis (Limerick, Burgess-Limerick, & Grace, 1996). In most cases (with students under 16 years of age) permission was also obtained from the students' parents and/or their schools. In interviews, students were reminded that they could decline to answer questions or stop the interview at any time. Assumed names are used to stand for students' own names, as is the common practice in this kind of work.

Often researchers use member checking to confirm their interpretations of data. So for example, in one project I interviewed a head teacher, and later asked him to check he was happy with the interpretations I made from the data. This is often appropriate when research concerns people's views or opinions. It is more problematic if we are exlporing students' understandings during teaching both because these shift (we hope), and because students are not in a position to judge our interpretation of how their thinking differs from canonical scientific accounts. However, semistructured interviews of the kind used in much of my work provide opportunities to test the researcher's interpretation of students' comments—using techniques such as seeking reiteration, reflecting interpretations back for confirmation or otherwise, and revisiting ideas at different times or in slightly different contexts. More extensive interview extracts relating to many of the examples included in the book (as well as other examples) can be viewed at the ECLIPSE project website (see Further Reading).

I certainly cannot be sure of the veracity of all my interpretations of student comments (and indeed the theme of how to best interpret such comments runs through the book), but I am generally confident that where I draw on in-depth interviews I am able to offer reasonable interpretations. Sensibly, however, I seek to adopt an approach I would also recommend to my readers. This is to both (a) make efforts to ensure that one forms interpretations based on a dialogue that gives students full opportunity to clarify their thinking, and then to (b) always consider our interpretations as—like science itself—provisional: our current best understanding, but always potentially open to revision.

Further Reading

There are many books that report or discuss aspects of learners' ideas in science, as well as a vast literature in the form of journal and conference papers and book chapters (Duit, 2009). Two books that are quite old now, but remain of considerable interest, are:

Black, P. J., & Lucas, A. M. (Eds.). (1993). *Children's informal ideas in science.* **London: Routledge.** This book provides a very useful introduction to some of the perspectives taken on the nature of learners' ideas, although it does not encompass some of the perspectives that have been developed in more recent scholarship.

Driver, R., Squires, A., Rushworth, P., & Wood-Robinson, V. (1994). *Making sense of secondary science: Research into children's ideas.* **London: Routledge.** This book offers a survey of common alternative conceptions across most of the topics included in secondary science courses. Whilst it is not completely comprehensive, it provides key reading for any teacher planning the teaching of a science topic and looking to find out what ideas learners are likely to bring to class.

Three recent books commissioned by the *Association for Science Education* offer guidance to teachers in the three main science subjects in teaching core secondary science topics. These books are informed by research into student thinking and science pedagogy.

Reiss, M. (Ed.). (2011). *Teaching secondary biology* **(2nd ed.). London: Hodder Education.**

Sang, D. (Ed.). (2011). *Teaching secondary physics* **(2nd ed.). London: Hodder Education.**

Taber, K. S. (Ed.). (2012). *Teaching secondary chemistry* **(2nd ed.). London: Hodder Education.**

ECLIPSE (Exploring Conceptual Learning, Integration and Progression in Science Education, accessed from www.educ.cam.ac.uk/research/projects/eclipse/). The website of this project reports examples from the author's own research projects, and is updated with new examples regularly. The ECLIPSE project website includes links to examples of students' comments about a wide range of science topics. Many of the examples reported in the book are explored in more detail on the project website.

I also list here two of my other books for any reader who wishes to explore the topics and issues in this book in more detail. The present book is informed by a good deal of research literature, and cites key work, but the focus here is on offering an account that I hope is readable for busy readers such as classroom teachers and those setting out to prepare for teaching. Both of my books listed should be accessible to science teachers, but are written in a style that makes them especially suitable for those who are carrying out research, or studying for graduate degrees in science education.

Taber, K. S. (2009). *Progressing science education: Constructing the scientific research programme into the contingent nature of learning science.* **Dordrecht: Springer.** This book offers a scholarly account of constructivism in science education and considers common criticisms of constructivism, and the nature and progress of research into learning in science, in some detail.

Taber, K. S. (2013). *Modelling learners and learning in science education: Developing representations of concepts, conceptual structure and conceptual change to inform teaching and research.* **Dordrecht: Springer.** This book discusses many of the issues discussed in the present volume, but from a more technical standpoint and with a particular focus on how researchers can make sense of research data—often of the form of student comments such as those in Textbox 0.1—when exploring student thinking and learning in science.

References

Bell, B., Jones, A., & Car, M. (1995). The development of the recent National New Zealand Science Curriculum. *Studies in Science Education, 26,* 73–105.

Berube, C. T. (2008). *The unfinished quest: The plight of progressive science education in the age of standards.* Charlotte, NC: Information Age.

Claxton, G. (1996). A SMER campaign: Combating creeping constructivism. *Studies in Science Education, 27,* 157–165. doi: 10.1080/03057269608560081

Cromer, A. (1997). *Connected knowledge: Science, philosophy and education.* Oxford: Oxford University Press.

Duit, R. (2009). *Bibliography: Students' and teachers' conceptions and science education.* Kiel: Leibniz Institute for Science and Mathematics Education. Retrieved from www.ipn.uni-kiel.de/aktuell/stcse/stcse.html

Gilbert, J. K., Osborne, R. J., & Fensham, P. J. (1982). Children's science and its consequences for teaching. *Science Education, 66*(4), 623–633.

Key Stage 3 National Strategy. (2002). *Misconceptions in Key Stage 3 science.* London: Department for Education and Skills.

Kirschner, P. A., Sweller, J., & Clark, R. E. (2006). Why minimal guidance during instruction does not work: An analysis of the failure of constructivist, discovery, problem-based, experiential, and inquiry-based teaching. *Educational Psychologist, 41*(2), 75–86.

Limerick, B., Burgess-Limerick, T., & Grace, M. (1996). The politics of interviewing: Power relations and accepting the gift. *International Journal of Qualitative Studies in Education, 9*(4), 449–460.

Millar, R., & Osborne, J. (1998). *Beyond 2000: Science education for the future.* London: King's College.

Reiss, M. J. (2007). What should be the aim(s) of school science education? In D. Corrigan, J. Dillon, & R. Gunstone (Eds.), *The re-emergence of values in science education* (pp. 13–28). Rotterdam: Sense.

Taber, K. S. (2009). *Progressing science education: Constructing the scientific research programme into the contingent nature of learning science*. Dordrecht: Springer.

Taber, K. S. (2010a). Constructivism and direct instruction as competing instructional paradigms: An essay review of Tobias and Duffy's constructivist instruction: Success or failure? *Education Review, 13*(8), 1–44. Retrieved from www.edrev.info/essays/v13n8 index.html

Taber, K. S. (2010b). Paying lip-service to research? The adoption of a constructivist perspective to inform science teaching in the English curriculum context. *Curriculum Journal, 21*(1), 25–45.

Taber, K. S. (2011). Constructivism as educational theory: Contingency in learning, and optimally guided instruction. In J. Hassaskhah (Ed.), Educational theory (pp. 39–61). New York, NY: Nova. Retrieved from https://camtools.cam.ac.uk/wiki/eclipse/Constructivism.html.

Taber, K. S. (2013). *Modelling learners and learning in science education: Developing representations of concepts, conceptual structure and conceptual change to inform teaching and research*. Dordrecht: Springer.

Tobias, S., & Duffy, T. M. (Eds.). (2009). *Constructivist instruction: Success or failure?* New York, NY: Routledge.

1
WHY IS LEARNING SCIENCE SO DIFFICULT FOR MANY STUDENTS?

The introduction highlighted how it is commonplace for many students to fail to learn what was intended in science lessons. No doubt this experience is shared to some extent by teachers in other areas of the curriculum, but science is often recognised by students themselves as 'harder' or 'more difficult' that most other school subjects. Those working as specialist science teachers often did not share this experience when school students, and indeed sometimes may have found much that other students considered incomprehensible or counterintuitive to make perfect sense. This chapter is meant as a reminder to subject experts, that learning science can actually be a demanding challenge for most of our students—making teaching itself a challenging activity.

Introduction: Why Should Science Be Difficult?

Teaching can be challenging for all sorts of reasons. Perhaps the ideal scenario for many teachers is being faced with groups of students who attend regularly, and are motivated to learn from classes that take place in well-maintained and resourced classrooms. Most real teaching contexts fall short of this ideal to some extent, and sometimes considerably so. There are all kinds of reasons why students may be distracted from focusing on learning, and may miss classes or fail to concentrate when they do attend. Those that do attend may not all value academic learning, or may not see the relevance of particular subjects, or simply may not find science very interesting. Whilst there are certainly things teachers can do to make classes more relevant and interesting, science is likely to remain a difficult curriculum area for many learners. Of course it certainly helps if learners find it interesting and relevant, as then they are more likely to feel the effort involved is worthwhile.

However, even when the students are present and attentive and wish to learn, teaching science is seldom straightforward.

Understanding the World

At one level science is about the world we experience. Science seeks to explain why trees grow, and why rivers flow (and sometimes change their course), why there are changes in the weather (and changes in weather patterns), why some materials are springy, why some materials can be used as fuels, and so on. That is, science relates to phenomena in the world. In the natural sciences there is a strong emphasis on objectivity—the notion that different observers should be able to agree on what is being observed—so we should be able to find ways to agree that a tree *is* growing or that weather patterns *are* shifting. This does not imply agreement will always be easily reached, but science does involve a commitment to a belief in an objective external world (in the sense of not just being in our minds) that is stable enough to be observed and described. This may seem rather obvious—as we might think that people are only able to live their everyday lives and go about their business with others because they do live in and experience the same physical world. However some theorists argue that we should consider reality as socially constructed (something that may be sensible when dealing with social phenomena), and others consider the observable world to be to some extent illusionary and obscuring a deeper reality. These are respectable alternative philosophical positions, but cannot support progress in the natural sciences.

Even if we find the assumption of a stable objective reality unremarkable, there is another fundamental assumption underpinning science that we also tend to take for granted, and that is that we (people) are able to understand the world. We tend to assume that by doing science we will be able to make sense of the world—to uncover nature's 'secrets' or to find out its 'mechanisms'. Metaphorical language is being used here: nature—although often personified poetically—cannot actually have secrets, and a term such as 'mechanism' is being used metaphorically when we talk about (for example) the biochemical mechanisms of cell division, suggesting that something is 'like clockwork'—and therefore works through simple causes and effects that we can reverse engineer with enough effort. As will be suggested later in the book we should be careful to treat all poetic language with caution (see Chapter 6). Metaphors and other such literary devices can be very valuable, and there is no suggestion here that they should be excluded from either science or science education, but rather that we should always keep in mind that they have the potential to be persuasive and give the impression we understand more than we do.

As science teachers we are charged with helping our students understand the scientific accounts of the world, and this presupposes that human beings are actually capable of understanding the world. It is worth therefore asking on what basis we might think we can understand the world. There are probably many possible arguments, but here I consider three that might have some merit.

Argument: We Can Understand the World Because the Universe Was Deliberately Created

Many of the figures who are considered among the first modern scientists—people like Newton, Hooke, and Faraday—were influenced by a notion known as 'natural theology'. William Whewell, who coined the term 'scientist', wrote a treatise on astronomy, physics, and natural theology, which began by stating that 'the examination of the material world brings before us a number of things and relations of things which suggest to most minds the belief of a creating and presiding Intelligence' (Whewell, 1833, p. 1). These scientists believed in a God who had created the Universe and had deliberately put people into that Universe. They tended to believe that God had created people to have minds in some ways like God's Himself. They saw the study of nature as the study of God's works, and for many of them science was inspired by faith as much as curiosity—the idea that reading the book of God's work would complement the book of his Word (that is, religious scripture). The general mindset here was that God probably wanted man to study his creation to better know God, and that as God's creation was perfect He would have created man to be up to the job. Science ('natural philosophy' as it was known) was not seen so distinct from other areas of thought, and scientists such as Newton certainly did not feel they needed to avoid mention of God in their scientific writings.

This perspective is much less common among scientists today. For one thing, it is generally understood among scientists that scientific work needs to stand apart from any prior assumptions brought from religious convictions, and there are few explicit references to God in modern scientific writing. Where Whewell saw the stability of planetary orbits as most unlikely to occur without deliberate intent from the Creator, and Newton was prepared to consider orbital motion as *nearly* stable, and perhaps needing God to tinker from time to time to keep things in order, it is widely accepted today that supernatural influences are not admissible in scientific explanations. Indeed, teleological arguments (that things are as they are because of some greater purpose or plan) are treated with distrust (see Chapter 6). Science is multinational, and multicultural, and so even if a scientist believes that the world is created by God, he or she cannot assume that others reading their work will share that commitment. There are certainly very many scientists of religious faith, and many of them do still see their scientific work in part at least in terms of studying the works of their creator. However, it seems less clear that the creation (if the universe is understood that way) can readily be interpreted by human minds. So there may be a *personal* conviction held by some scientists that God has set the world up so we will be able to understand and explain it, but that is certainly not a shared commitment of the scientific community as a whole (Taber, 2013a), and it is not an explanation that can be drawn upon in science education.

Argument: We Have Evolved to Understand Our Environment

From a scientific perspective, a more admissible argument draws upon evolution and natural selection. This argument would suggest that human beings have evolved over many millions of years to fit their environment, and that our survival, and indeed—in population terms at least—success to date, shows that natural selection has fitted us to our environment. In particular we have evolved the most complex brains known, and that these brains allow us to build mental models of the world that we can mentipulate, in turn allowing us to manipulate and control our environment. This is only possible because we are able to understand the world, and so act in it intelligently.

There is certainly something in this argument—but it also has some rather major flaws. For one thing there are other highly successful species which presumably do not understand the world in the depth we do: ants and termites seem to be doing well in the population stakes, as for that matter do grasses and bacteria. This certainly suggests these organisms are well fitted to their niches in this world, but is not strong evidence that they share a good understanding of the nature of the world.

It is true that humans have found ways to live comfortably in a wide range of environments, many of which are quite different from those experienced by our early ancestors, but we also know that some very simple organisms have evolved through natural selection to survive in even more extreme conditions such as Arctic ice sheets and deep ocean vents. This is all leaving aside the very real concerns that human populations may not be sustainable at current and projected levels given demands upon resources, and that if we have triggered major climate change it is quite possible our apparent success and fitness could be coming to an end relatively soon. That we so far cannot agree on the extent of shifts in weather patterns we are observing, and the extent to which any ongoing climate change is anthropocentric rather than part of natural geological cycles, suggests that there is a limit to how well we have evolved the cognitive apparatus necessary to understand the world.

Argument: The Evidence Is That We Do Understand the World

That said, we clearly *seem to* understand a great deal about the world. We can build tall buildings that, usually at least, do not fall down. We can send probes to other planets that, sometimes at least, land intact and send back interesting data. However, whilst there may be some evidence we often understand the world, there is no basis for complacency or smugness. For one thing, we do not have any independent measure of whether we really or fully understand things we think we understand. One test is that we can apply our knowledge to achieve things technologically—but we also know that many technologies have developed more by trial and error than by theoretical reasoning, and so success in applications is only an operational measure of understanding. We could sometimes be getting the right outcomes due more to luck than good understanding. Moreover, there are many species of animals that regularly achieve incredible feats of construction or navigation, yet we would not consider this to be based on conceptual understanding of the world.

Of course in science we test our ideas through experiment—but we know that is not an assurance of understanding. Experimental tests are useful indicators, but experiments always underdetermine theory. That is—as with technological applications—our experimental predictions can sometimes be right for the wrong reasons. An important guide to scientists in evaluating new ideas is that they are consistent with existing well-established theories—but again this cannot be seen as a sufficient basis for accepting an idea, both because wrong ideas can sometimes be consistent with right ideas, and because well-established ideas are themselves sometimes found to need adjusting. So in science even our most well-established knowledge is formally considered provisional and open to review in the light of new evidence.

However, it is certainly reasonable to argue that science seems to offer us reliable (if not certain) knowledge of the world where our ideas fit into well-integrated, consistent conceptual frameworks (see Chapter 9) that have been rigorously tested through a series of experiments, and where those ideas can be adopted in technological applications that work. The evidence is that we do seem to have a pretty good understanding of at least some aspects of our world.

Scientific Knowledge Is Often Hard Won

What is equally clear, however, is that scientific knowledge of the world is often not easily attained. We celebrate scientists like Galileo, Newton, Darwin, Einstein, and Meitner because we recognise their intellectual achievements. Many of the major breakthroughs of science have involved individuals who have found a new way of looking at things that others had not considered. Sometimes scientific breakthroughs are not even recognised by others in the field, who may not easily shift their way of thinking (Kuhn, 1996). It has sometimes taken years or decades to persuade scientists to accept new ideas—even when in retrospect we now consider the new ideas obviously better. For example, modern scientists explain combustion in terms of a chemical reaction with (nearly always) oxygen. The notion that combustion concerned the release of a mysterious substance or essence called phlogiston now seems rather bizarre to most of us. Yet the oxygen theory only slowly replaced the phlogiston theory, which continued to be championed by some otherwise successful scientists (and in particular the chemist, theologian, and political theorist Joseph Priestley).

Anyone expecting to contribute to science in significant ways today is expected to be educated to doctoral level, and many areas of science now rely on very specialised apparatus. Indeed in some areas of science such as high-energy physics, progress depends upon the development of labs the size of small towns, and budgets that match. Whilst the notion that scientists are all ultra-intelligent and dedicated to their work to the exclusion of anything else is a caricatured stereotype, it is true that in most scientific fields major developments depend upon clever people who are highly educated and well equipped, and are able to commit to spending much of their time working on a problem over extended periods. Indeed, it has been suggested that extended engagement is needed to develop true expertise within any field (Gardner, 1998).

This brief consideration of scientific work suggests that producing scientific knowledge can often be hard work. It seems that what is learnt from science is not usually obvious until one already has a lot of background knowledge, and is able to collect data that is not readily available to most people. Moreover, the history of science tells us that even having the background knowledge and the data does not always make the conclusions obvious to the scientists themselves! Understanding the world in scientific ways can be challenging—even for highly trained scientists.

Why Is Science Difficult?

The task of the science teacher is to help learners understand something of the scientific accounts of the world. Those learners will not always be considered highly intelligent, and indeed school teachers will often be charged with explaining science to learners across a broad attainment range. Moreover, this task usually has to be achieved in a few hours per week to young people who often have as many as a dozen other subjects they are being asked to study at the same time. The science teacher will usually have available lab facilities, and perhaps some access to opportunities for fieldwork, but will lack direct access to many of the tools of modern science—mass spectrometers, electron microscopes, radio telescopes, and high-energy particle accelerators being well beyond the budget of most educational establishments. Colleges and universities will fare better than schools here, but will expect their students to have already understood a good deal of science before reaching that stage in their education.

None of this is seeking to excuse science teachers from doing our jobs, but it is useful to reflect on why science teaching is so challenging, and so how teachers can best respond to the challenges. Doing science can be difficult, and for many students learning science is also often difficult. Understanding why this is can help us consider how best to teach *for understanding* in our science classes.

A Note on Knowledge Construction

Before proceeding it is worth briefly addressing a key point that may have occurred to some readers. Science is accumulative in part because scientists build upon one another's discoveries and ideas. Isaac Newton famously wrote to his scientific colleague, the 'vertically challenged' Robert Hooke, to suggest that if he (Newton) had seen further than others it was because he had stood on the shoulders of giants—that is, he had built upon the work done by others.

This raises the question of whether it becomes easier to understand material that someone else has already made the effort to understand. Only when teaching research students at postgraduate level do we need to enable students to actually produce 'new' scientific knowledge. Science teachers at the school and college level are not expected to enable their students to make major new scientific breakthroughs in class, but rather 'just' to take on board what others have already worked through.

This is a very important point. It *is* going to be easier to acquire a scientific idea when someone else has already carefully formulated the argument for that idea and can furnish the necessary evidence. Yet as we have seen, even when the scientific evidence and arguments are published other scientists are not always immediately persuaded. Sometimes it has taken decades for the scientific community to come to a consensus on whether the available arguments and evidence do, or do not, sufficiently support a particular idea. This might seem odd: presumably all scientists accept the same logic, so why should they come to different views from the same evidence base?

This is a question that is addressed through this book, although with a focus on science learners rather than scientists themselves. Research into how people learn and come to knowledge shows us that even when knowledge is represented in a public forum (a textbook, a documentary), it cannot just be absorbed and adopted by others in a straightforward way. Acquiring knowledge is more akin to acquiring nutrition than it is to building up a music collection. I can add to my music library in straightforward ways by buying discs or downloading music I do not have. Usually I buy CDs when available, but then import them into my computer. The process of transferring the music to the computer is actually a process of re-representing information coding for music on the CD (.aiff files) to information coding for the same music in a different form (.mp3 files) in a different place. The .mp3 files are a 'lossy' version of the originals on the disc (that is, they are like a reproduction of an image in a lower resolution), but they provide a pretty good copy of the original when I play the tracks.

We are often tempted to think of learning a bit like building up a music library (or a library of books, or a collection of stamps, coins, or baseball cards)— something that involves incremental additions to our stock. We might consider viewing a documentary, reading a magazine article, or attending a class as allowing us to make copies of someone else's knowledge and add it to our library of things known and understood—ready to be pulled out of the collection when needed. Yet there is a great deal of research evidence that suggests learning is not like this—and any science teacher will have plenty of experience suggesting that what students learn often seems quite different from what we thought we had taught.

In some ways nutrition offers a better analogy for how we acquire new knowledge. A good meal comprises some very complex materials, sometimes structured in very intricate ways. Yet to make use of the available nutrition we need to physically decompose the structures, puree the contents, and selectively extract the sugars, proteins, vitamins, and lipids. Moreover, we will chemically deconstruct complex carbohydrates into simpler sugars, and we will deconstruct complex proteins into simpler amino acids that can be used to build quite different structures—akin to scavenging from a ruin for bricks to make a new structure (what archaeologists refer to as 'robbing out'). Indeed sometimes we will even modify the amino acids chemically to get different shaped 'bricks' to fit our current requirements.

Learning is a bit like this process of ingesting and digesting food. Just as the gut membranes which act as protective barriers between us and the non-us of ingested material are impermeable to large complex molecules, so our cognitive apparatus has filters that select which incoming sensory information is processed and attended to. Human working memory can only mentipulate a modest amount of new material at any time, and this might (metaphorically) be considered to be acting like the gut membranes in protecting our existing models of the world from the sudden admission of highly complex new information that could disturb our mental equilibrium (Sweller, 2007). We may take something from the meal of a lecture or a textbook chapter, but by the time is has been selectively absorbed, modified to fit, and used to contribute to our ongoing building projects, it may have limited resemblance to the source materials. This is a theme that will be considered in more depth in Chapter 3.

Complications in Learning Science

Given this nature of human learning, there are a number of reasons why students might find science difficult to learn. For one thing science is a conceptual subject that often deals with abstract ideas. Moreover the evidence supporting scientific ideas is not always straightforward and accessible. These reasons relate to the science itself, but as well as these 'intrinsic' factors, the science teacher often has to deal with the challenge of not being able to teach a topic to a 'neutral' audience, as often students come to classes with existing ideas about science topics, and these ideas may be quite different from, or even in direct contradiction to, the scientific accounts themselves.

Scientific Concepts Are Abstract

It was suggested previously that 'at one level science is about the world we experience'. By this I meant that the starting point for scientific enquiry is a phenomenon—something we experience—to be understood and explained. Rainbows must have seemed pretty mysterious to people at one time, and it is understandable why they might have been considered having some special significance being commonly observed when rain gives way to sunshine (perhaps explaining religious and folk associations), but scientists are now able to explain the phenomenon of a rainbow as a physical process. However, the explanation of the rainbow calls upon theoretical constructs that are not themselves phenomena, such as refraction, refractive indices, wavelengths, and electromagnetic radiation.

One Example of an Abstract Concept: Refraction

To a science teacher it may seem odd to say that refraction and light wavelengths are not phenomena; after all we commonly demonstrate these notions in school science, shining beams of light from ray boxes into prisms of glass or Perspex. We show students how rays of light change direction and sometimes split into the colours of the spectrum—or rather we demonstrate with *beams* of light that we model in abstraction *as* rays. We may also demonstrate refraction with the bent appearance of a pencil or glass rod in a beaker of water, or show how a coin can seem to disappear from sight as we raise the water level in a beaker. We may draw representations with ray diagrams showing how spearfishing involves aiming the spear somewhere other than where the fish appears to be.

Yet refraction does not describe the phenomena themselves. What students observe are beams of light and pencils that seem to bend, coins that seem to vanish, and fish that appear to be in the wrong place. Indeed, from the perspective of our observations, and how people would naturally talk about what they have experienced in everyday life, we see a bent pencil just as we see a bent light beam. A term that is sometimes used here is that of the 'life-world' (Schutz & Luckmann, 1973)—the world as experienced—and in the life-world a pencil bends when we put it in a beaker of water.

'Refraction', on the other hand, is a technical term that describes a physical process where waves change speed and wavelength at the interface between media, and often (that is, when not travelling perpendicular, 'normal', to the interface) also change direction. Refraction can explain the bending of light, and the apparent bending of pencils, the technique needed for successful spearfishing, and the disappearance of the coin. (It is temping to write the 'apparent disappearance' of the coin, as we know it has not gone anywhere—but of course disappearance *means* to no longer appear to be there.) So refraction is a theoretical construct which scientists use in their explanations of a range of phenomena. Refraction is an abstract idea—and the scientist, or science teacher, can *abstract* from the range of distinct phenomena (rainbows, bent pencils, disappearing coins, and misplaced fish, etc.) that what these have in common is that light is being refracted.

Part of the wonder and power of science is the way it can offer such abstract theoretical accounts that can be applied across a wide range of phenomena (see Chapter 9). Yet that makes scientific discourse quite different from the life-world, the world as directly experienced, and the way people naturally tend to talk about those experiences. Scientists and science teachers come—over years—to adopt a very different discourse, and they actually come to be able to *see* the world differently.

Why Is Learning Science So Difficult? 21

A Demonstration to See Refraction

A science teacher might set up a ripple tank with light shining through the tank to produce a pattern on the floor below or ceiling above. By placing a suitable object in the tank (which makes the water at that point shallower) the image will show a series of evenly spaced lines spreading across the tank, and then changing their separation when they pass over the object (see Figure 1.1). The science teacher may suggest that the class are 'seeing diffraction', and probably believes that is the case—because that is what the teacher *has learnt* to see.

Of course, what is *actually* seen is a shifting pattern of lighter and darker areas on the surface used as a screen, and not refraction (the change in speed of the water waves) itself. For any reader who has never thought much about this demonstration (and especially those readers who use this in their classroom teaching),

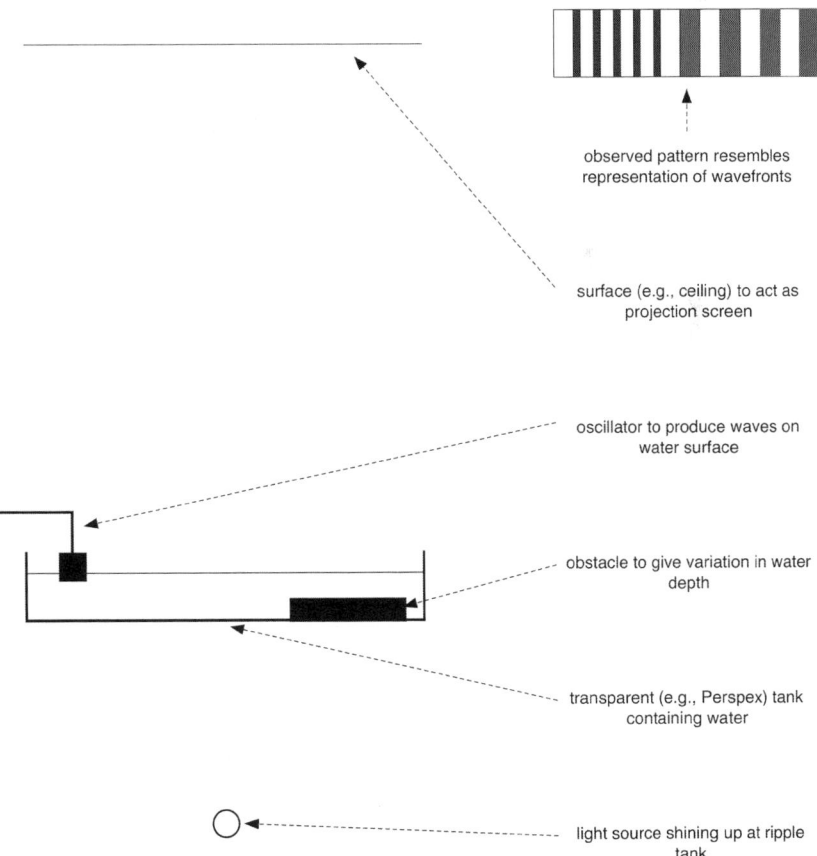

FIGURE 1.1 Setting up a ripple tank to demonstrate refraction: do students appreciate what they are seeing?

it is interesting to consider why this apparatus for producing a shifting pattern of darker and lights areas on a screen is considered to be a good way of demonstrating refraction to learners: what science do we expect students to understand here in accepting that this set-up demonstrates refraction in water waves?

The image that students observe in this demonstration is a series of lines or bands, where light passing through the tank of water falls upon the ceiling (acting as a screen) at greater intensity in some places than others. Because we often represent wavefronts as a series of lines, the teacher may feel this is a good demonstration as we can 'see' the wavefronts. Yet this is just a representation of wavefronts, not what they really 'look like'. If students could see the waves (and often only those close to the demonstration will be able to actually see this), they would actually see the water surface is uneven—as a series of waves pass across it.

The image that is presented as evidence of refraction does indeed show how the waves change wavelength as they pass over the obstacle, but this relies on a second refraction event. The image on the screen is formed because the water surface with its sequences of waves acts like a series of lenses, so that the light from beneath the tank changes direction, being focused towards some parts of the screen and away from others. It is the shape of the water surface causing refraction of light that leads to the banding pattern. Should teachers explain this—or is it more sensible to simplify the demonstration by just ignoring this as long as students are persuaded that they can 'see' the wavefronts in the banding pattern on the ceiling? There is a case here for not overcomplicating matters, at least when using the demonstration with younger learners—but this could also be seen as something of a sleight of hand because the teacher knows that the students do not understand how the evidence being presented can logically be argued to demonstrate refraction in the water. Is it acceptable to rely on such a 'trick'?

A Teaching Analogy to 'Explain' Refraction

If that is acceptable (after all, the demonstration is logically defensible, just perhaps overcomplicated for many secondary students to appreciate in detail) then what about the teaching model sometimes used to 'explain' why refraction often causes a change in direction. Light changes direction when it moves from a medium of one refractive index to another of different refractive index, unless it is 'normally' incident on the interface (that is, it arrives 'straight on', perpendicular to the surface). A common teaching model of this is a vehicle (or marching band) that passes from one surface to another. It is argued that if a car, for example, drives across a hard surface and then passes onto a very different surface—perhaps from tarmac to sand—it is likely to change direction unless it crosses the boundary such that the front wheels change surface at the same time. If the car hits the boundary at an angle, then one wheel will move from the surface with good grip to a much-less-suitable driving surface before the other. So one side of the car slows before the other side, and the car accordingly turns for a moment until both wheels are on the new surface.

This analogy, or variations on it, is commonly used by teachers, and sometimes by textbook authors, to compare with light passing from one material to another. However for analogies to be useful they have to offer structural similarity between the two situations. The car changes direction because one side of the car changes surface before the other side—so for this to be a useful analogy light should be doing something similar. But light is electromagnetic radiation—an oscillating coupling of magnetic and electrical fields propagating through space. Is it meaningful to consider light to have a finite thickness such that one 'side' of it passes into a new medium before the other? If not, then the analogy with vehicles or people marching only has value as a way of thinking about or remembering what is going on, but not for explaining it. If this is so, and a student already clearly remembers that light changes direction, there seems little value in making an analogy with a situation that relies upon a mechanism that does *not* apply in the situation we are trying to understand.

Deciding when a teaching model is needed, or is appropriate, is never simply a matter of considering the science—as we always also have to consider how students will make sense of the model, and how it might influence their future thinking. Teachers can only make these judgments when they have a good understanding of common ways of student thinking in the topics they teach.

Abstract Ideas Are Integral to Science

This is not an isolated example. Many of the big ideas in science, the ideas that are considered central to understanding key areas of science and mooted as suitable foci for planning learning progressions, are similar abstractions (Alonzo & Gotwals, 2012). Indeed because of the intellectual work they are intended to do, scientific concepts tend to take this nature.

Magnetic fields, chemical bonds, food webs, natural selection, electric current, the second period of elements, electromagnetic induction, genetic mutation, nuclear fusion, continental drift, black holes, transpiration, oxidation, the big bang, centripetal force . . . none of these terms describes phenomena in the normal sense of things people might observe and wonder about as they go about their everyday lives. Science produces a toolkit of abstract concepts that are used to explain processes by referring to classes of things (for example, acids) or processes (for example, photosynthesis) that can *indirectly* be used to explain phenomena people experience in the world. Science seeks to help us understand the world and explain phenomena. However, whilst science certainly is indeed about the world, modern science has shifted far from phenomena themselves.

The Scientific Argument and Evidence May Be Complicated

Scientific work centrally involves the interpretation of evidence to support the production of new scientific knowledge. That knowledge is generally of the form of theories and models and provides scientific accounts suitable for understanding and explaining aspects of the world. Usually the interpretation process, by which data collected come to be considered as evidence for some idea or other, itself depends upon previously established theories. For example, much science today uses complex apparatus (nuclear magnetic resonance spectrometers, electron microscopes, gas chromatograms, etc.), such that the interpretation of readings or scans relies upon the theory of how those instruments work.

This is one reason why a simplistic notion of falsification—that one negative result invalidates a scientific hypothesis—is invalid. A negative result may mean the theory is wrong, or perhaps just needs development as it does not yet reflect the complexity of the world, so does not yet apply to all cases within its apparent range; or maybe that there was some human error in the collection of data; or perhaps the theory of instrumentation does not apply. Given the complexity of much front-line science, negative results are often taken under advisement—but then put to one side and in effect ignored for the time being. The philosopher of science Imre Lakatos (1970) argued that putting such anomalies into a kind of intellectual 'quarantine' was often the sensible approach within an area of science otherwise making good progress, even if in principle such anomalies *could sometimes* imply a major flaw in the theoretical framework being adopted (Kuhn, 1996).

Often the actual logical chain of argument that persuades scientists to accept some new idea is complex and nuanced. Current scientific understanding may represent the outcome of several phases of development, perhaps undertaken by a range of scientists over quite a number of years. Sometimes it may be appropriate to offer suitable simplifications in teaching, which ignore some of the complexity of actual scientific evidence to convey core ideas. For example, Millikan's oil drop experiment used falling oil drops—but it is easier to explain the general principle of his work by assuming the oil drops were held stationary by the balance of gravitational and electric fields. A teacher has to balance opposing considerations: *'how much complexity are the students in this class ready to deal with?'* versus *'to what extent is simplification reducing the authenticity of the account provided?'*

We have to be careful not to oversimplify such as to offer misleading accounts—especially where these may conflict with ideas the learner may meet later in their science education. For example, Mendel's laws of inheritance were derived from atypically 'cooperative' traits in (some of) the organisms he chose to study. Teaching a model based on Mendel's laws offers students an entry point to appreciating genetic inheritance, but with the danger that students assume these simple laws can be generalised to other traits that have more complex dependence on many genes (Dougherty, 2009).

Ultimately we have to accept that the argument for some scientific ideas is complicated. For one thing an argument will often depend upon already understanding and adopting other scientific ideas (which means that teaching has to be sequenced carefully). The most powerful scientific ideas are often of the form of theories that provide a framework for thinking about some topic area: a framework that is constructed by coordination of a range of different principles and/or sources of evidence.

The Case for Natural Selection

A particular case in point would be the theory of evolution by natural selection. Most readers will be aware that this is considered a foundational theory in modern biology. One noted biologist famously claimed 'nothing in biology makes sense except in the light of evolution' (Dobzhansky, 1973). Readers will also be aware that teaching evolution can be very challenging. In some cases students may be minded to reject evolution for reasons that have little to do with the scientific evidence and arguments (this is considered further in Chapter 7)—but even when learners have no initial bias against the idea of evolution at all, they often fail to appreciate key aspects of the theory (Taber, 2013b). For example, Textbox 1.1 reports comments of a student talking to me about work he had being doing in his science classes about adaptation.

Bert was calling upon a notion of inheritance of acquired characteristics, akin to the kind of model proposed by Jean-Baptiste Lamarck. This seems a reasonable idea: after all, if we accept that offspring tend to share their parents' characteristics, and that we can change some of our characteristics by behaviour, then is it not reasonable that the body builder might pass on her physique, or the acrobat his finely developed sense of balance? Unfortunately the scientific evidence does not (generally) support this reasonable idea.

It is sometimes suggested that natural selection is a simple idea once it is understood, but actually appreciating how natural selection can lead to the diversity of life on earth requires the coordination of a number of quite abstract ideas (Taber, 2009, pp. 287–288). Students have to understand how the pool of genes within a particular population allows variation within the population—whilst the limited gene pool leads the members of a single species to be basically the same type. All chimpanzees are different—but all chimpanzees are much the same. Students have to appreciate that the genetic material is stable enough to allow parent organisms to pass on their genes to their offspring, yet open to sufficient mutation to introduce some new variety in the gene pool. Students have to appreciate how

---

Textbox 1.1: A student suggests inheritance of acquired characteristics.

". . . they breed dogs, they breed them to be like retrievers. Because they've like been taught over and over to retrieve. And so when they have puppies then they automatically have already got that sense."

(Bert, c. 15 years old)

Source: ECLIPSE project website; see www.educ.cam.ac.uk/research/projects/eclipse/.

> Textbox 1.2: Natural selection made simple: a student's account of the long necks of giraffes.
>
> *"Before giraffes had long necks they had short necks, and they ate all the trees, and they ate all the leaves on the bottom of the trees, but there was this like a couple of mutant giraffes that had really long necks so they could reach the top [of] trees as well. And then, when they've eaten all the bottom trees and there were no leaves left, all the short giraffes, short-necked giraffes, died, but only the mutant ones with long necks could reach the upper ones so they survived, and they passed on their mutant genes to their children. And so all of them have long necks now."*
>
> (Jilly, c. 15 years old)
>
> Source: ECLIPSE project website; see www.educ.cam.ac.uk/research/projects/eclipse/.

fitness in a particular environmental niche relates to characteristics that vary in the population but are inheritable due to—sometimes quite small—differences in likely survival rates. This is of course a statistical matter: being in the wrong place when predators are around or when there is a major flood or forest fire or volcanic eruption can prove fatal to any individual even if they are slightly taller or stronger or faster or darker or whatever than most of their cospecifics who were lucky enough not be there that day. So students need to appreciate the kinds of timescales and numbers of generations involved in speciation, as well as the need for some kind of reproductive separation into distinct groups that separately experience selection pressures.

Given such complexity, this is an topic where at secondary level we might be grateful enough if we feel students have begun to grasp at least some of these major ideas, even if we know that a strong, robust understanding is likely to rely upon coordination of the various ideas into one coherent theoretical framework. For example, Textbox 1.2 presents one 15-year-old's explanation for how giraffes developed long necks.

Even though Jilly's explanation is an evolutionary one based on the notion of natural selection, it is a naively simplistic account that seems to involve one type of mutation event occurring between two successive generations, and bringing about long necks in one step. By comparison, an expert view of the same process is considerably more complex:

> Consider, for example, the causal processes involved in bringing about the long neck of giraffes. In no particular order, these include, at least, features of ancestral giraffes' environment, including the presence of nutritious leaf matter high up in tall trees; various genetic influences of giraffe

morphology; developmental processes, including additional regulator genes, involved in giraffe neck-development; certain genetic mutations arising; competition for resources such that giraffes with a greater reach enjoyed increased rates of survival; and changes in developmental processes resulting in longer necks. (Potochnik, 2013, p. 54)

Just as natural selection is a complex theory, the evidence base for evolution is diverse in type (anatomical, biochemical, etc.) and often complicated to interpret. A key issue for policymakers, curriculum developers, and teachers is how much complexity should students at different ages be expected to make sense of, and what kinds of simplification of complex ideas still allow teaching that is both authentic to the science, and not likely to make it more difficult for learners to make further progress later. This issue will be revisited at various points later in the book.

Our Minds Do Not Offer a 'Level Playing Field'

The abstract and complex nature of many scientific ideas is probably sufficient grounds for many learners to find learning science challenging—in turn making teaching challenging for many science teachers. One way to respond to these issues would be through careful analysis of the material to be taught which identifies the optimum level of simplification of concepts (simple enough to be understood by learners at the particular stage, without distorting key scientific ideas) and carefully sequencing teaching so that prerequisite learning is always met before it is needed for understanding more advanced concepts.

Of course there are many complications here: scientific developments have often involved an element of boot-strapping with advances in related areas being iterative and occurring in parallel, so that it is not always clear which ideas are more foundational. In addition, learning in science does not take place in a vacuum—for example, mathematical skills may be needed for certain topics, and without coordination with other teaching areas some science topics may need to be deferred until teaching has taken place in other school subjects. Moreover, teaching in the most 'logical' order may not offer the best route for process skills development; and may not offer the best way of motivating learners by connecting with their interests; and offers limited scope for being topical by responding to current issues in the news. So logical sequencing may be important, but it can never be the only consideration for planning science teaching.

Even if it were possible to plan teaching to give the most rational sequence according to the internal logic and structure of science, the teacher would soon find a rather significant additional complication—learners' own ideas. The science teacher's task would be much more straightforward if we could assume that students already know all the things that they were intended to learn from previous lessons on relevant topics, and nothing else about the topics we teach. In reality, as a good deal of research—and most science teachers' own classroom experiences—tell us, more often than not, learners in our classes:

- do not know a lot of what we think they should already have been taught;
- recall incomplete and often distorted versions of what they do remember studying;
- often bring to a class a good many other existing ideas that *they* think are relevant to topics we teach but which are not consistent with the 'target knowledge' that they are expected to learn in our lessons.

Experience suggests that ignoring this complication, and teaching students as though they know nothing about a topic outside of what is taught in school, often leads to the students retaining existing scientifically incorrect ideas and misinterpreting our teaching in accordance with previously established ways of thinking (see the examples in Textbox 0.1 in the introduction). A good deal of scholarship and research in science education has been undertaken on the basis that *effective science teaching means taking learners' ideas into account*. It is probably fair to say that the vast majority of experts on science education around the world would acknowledge this principle and recognise it as central to developing effective pedagogy in science subjects (and probably other academic curriculum subjects as well). This present book then concerns a topic of great importance to all science teachers—learners' ideas about science.

There has been a good deal of research, undertaken in many parts of the world, to explore the nature of students' ideas in science topics, and to develop and test approaches to teaching science topics in the light of learners' ideas (Duit, 2009). However, it is fair to say that there is not always consensus about how to best go about this, nor even a single preferred approach. Indeed in many regards the research literature is itself inconsistent with different experts recommending quite different things. One possible response to that situation is to take the view that if the experts do not all agree, then there is little point in teachers taking too much notice until they do.

That response seems both defeatist and optimistic. It is defeatist because it implies teaching in suboptimal ways until such time as researchers can agree a simple system that all science teachers should adopt. It is also optimistic in assuming that it is just a matter of time before researchers agree and clarify how to best respond to learners' ideas in science. Researchers have described and characterised learners' ideas in very different ways (as will be outlined in the next chapter). However, a careful consideration of the range of findings in the literature relating to learners' ideas in science subjects and how they respond to teaching suggests that the different research outcomes often actually reflect the varied nature of learners' ideas. It seems that learners' ideas can vary in a number of ways (something which is not obvious from the use of a general and familiar term such as 'ideas') that are significant for how best to respond to them. This is the theme of the next chapter.

References

Alonzo, A. C., & Gotwals, A. W. (Eds.). (2012). *Learning progressions in science: Current challenges and future directions.* Rotterdam: Sense.

Dobzhansky, T. (1973). Nothing in biology makes sense except in the light of evolution. *American Biology Teacher, 35*(3), 125–129.

Dougherty, M. J. (2009). Closing the gap: Inverting the genetics curriculum to ensure an informed public. *American Journal of Human Genetics, 85*(1), 6–12.

Duit, R. (2009). *Bibliography: Students' and teachers' conceptions and science education.* Kiel: Leibniz Institute for Science and Mathematics Education. Retrieved from www.ipn.uni-kiel.de/aktuell/stcse/stcse.html

Gardner, H. (1998). *Extraordinary minds.* London: Phoenix.

Kuhn, T. S. (1996). *The structure of scientific revolutions* (3rd ed.). Chicago, IL: University of Chicago Press.

Lakatos, I. (1970). Falsification and the methodology of scientific research programmes. In I. Lakatos & A. Musgrove (Eds.), *Criticism and the growth of knowledge* (pp. 91–196). Cambridge: Cambridge University Press.

Potochnik, A. (2013). Biological explanation. In K. Kampourakis (Ed.), *The philosophy of biology: A companion for educators* (pp. 49–65). Dordrecht: Springer.

Schutz, A., & Luckmann, T. (1973). *The structures of the life-world* (R. M. Zaner & H. T. Engelhardt, Trans.). Evanston, IL: Northwest University Press.

Sweller, J. (2007). Evolutionary biology and educational psychology. In J. S. Carlson & J. R. Levin (Eds.), *Educating the evolved mind: Conceptual foundations for an evolutionary educational psychology* (pp. 165–175). Charlotte, NC: Information Age.

Taber, K. S. (2009). *Progressing science education: Constructing the scientific research programme into the contingent nature of learning science.* Dordrecht: Springer.

Taber, K. S. (2013a). Conceptual frameworks, metaphysical commitments and worldviews: The challenge of reflecting the relationships between science and religion in science education. In N. Mansour & R. Wegerif (Eds.), *Science education for diversity: Theory and practice* (pp. 151–177). Dordrecht: Springer.

Taber, K. S. (2013b). Representing evolution in science education: The challenge of teaching about natural selection. In B. Akpan (Ed.), *Science education: A global perspective* (pp. 65–91). Abuja, Nigeria: Next Generation Education.

Whewell, W. (1833). *Astronomy and general physics considered with reference to natural theology.* London: William Pickering.

2
CHARACTERISING AND LABELLING LEARNERS' IDEAS

This chapter introduces the different terms that have been used to describe students' ideas in science, and offers an account of the significant differences underpinning these various terms. Whilst the chapter is organised around terminology, in seeking to explain why researchers have used such a range of terms, the chapter will introduce key themes about the nature of learners' ideas that will be developed in the second section of the book ('Making Sense of Student Thinking'). It has long been argued that terminology in this area of science education is confused and unhelpful (Abimbola, 1988). Common terms are introduced here both because (a) teachers and others will come across many of these different terms in their reading, and because (b) despite the lack of consistent usage, the choice of these terms often reflects assumptions about the nature and origins of learners' ideas that are relevant to teachers.

So this chapter takes the form of a survey of terms, but its key messages for teachers are not in the particular nomenclature, but rather concern how different researchers and scholars have understood the nature of learners' ideas themselves.

Introduction: The Research on Students' Ideas

As suggested in the previous chapter there has been a considerable research effort over some decades to characterise, and to some extent to catalogue, learners' ideas in science. One bibliography of references to work on this topic—books, journal articles, chapters, and so on—lists well over eight thousand studies in this general area (Duit, 2009). That is clearly many more studies than any one person could learn about in any detail, and vastly more reading than is viable for a busy classroom teacher looking to inform his or her teaching. Of course there are reviews and surveys that offer a more succinct overview of the field, and of findings in particular topics, and these can make valuable reading for any science teacher.

Anyone setting out to read some of the work in this area will likely soon run into a problem of vocabulary, and wonder about the range of terms that are used to categorise learners' ideas in different studies. The phrase 'students' ideas' has been commonly used, and has been seen as a somewhat neutral term that does not carry too much baggage in terms of what it might imply (Black & Lucas, 1993). Another very common term used in many reports is 'misconceptions' (Key Stage 3 National Strategy, 2002)—which is also a term commonly used in everyday talk. Yet the reader will soon come across a range of other, less familiar terms such as 'alternative conceptions', 'preconceptions', 'alternative frameworks', 'intuitive theories', 'p-prims', 'knowledge facets', 'implicit knowledge elements', and so forth.

It seems reasonable to ask what these terms mean, and why they are all needed. Indeed, we might wonder whether such a range of terms is required to highlight important distinctions between the different types of ideas learners have—or whether perhaps there has been a proliferation of terms without a strong rationale. This latter view certainly has some substance, especially as there is no consistency in the way different researchers have reported their findings. Although there have been a number of attempts to clarify terminology in this area, these have not to date been very successful—and the historical legacy of several decades of studies will remain with its diversity of terminology. It is important to realise that the work that describes learners' ideas in science has developed in many countries over a long period—and has been undertaken by researchers with different disciplinary backgrounds (some from science departments in universities, some from education departments, and some from psychology and cognitive science backgrounds). This is not to excuse the confused terminology in the literature, but it does help explain why research into this area lacks the relative orderliness that tends to be found in many research fields in established sciences.

The terminological confusion is unfortunate, but does reflect how the phrase 'learners' ideas' is misleadingly simplistic because there *are* important differences reflected by the diverse terms used in research. The approach taken in this book is to advise readers not to allow themselves to get too bogged down in the terminology itself, but to remain aware that we do need to make some important distinctions if we wish to understand the nature and significance of learners' ideas in science. The work of this chapter will be to set out what the important distinctions are, and to explain the ways some of the most important terms are commonly used. This chapter will also act as a useful primer for themes that will be discussed in further detail in the second section of the book. The approach taken here draws upon analysis presented in two earlier books (Taber, 2009, 2013b). The present volume is intended to offer an introductory guide to this area of research, but readers looking for a more in-depth discussion of this area may find those earlier volumes useful.

Terms Commonly Used to Describe Learners' Ideas

Here a brief account of the most common terms that have been used to describe learners' ideas in science is presented to explain the terms that anyone reading around this topic is likely to come across. Science teachers certainly do not need to adopt all of these terms themselves. As you read through this section you might wish to consider whether these different terms relate to useful distinctions that teachers should keep in mind in their classroom planning and teaching.

Concepts

Concepts have traditionally been considered as central to teaching and learning science, as is reflected in the quote presented in Textbox 2.1. As the authors of that quote (Sadler & Zeidler, 2009) point out, it is now widely recognized that science education needs to have broader aims, reflecting the way schooling needs to support the encounters all of us make with science in our everyday lives—nonetheless, scientific concepts remain a core focus of science teaching.

The word 'concept' itself is used in various ways (Gilbert & Watts, 1983), but often denotes ideas in abstract. So, for example, we might refer to the concept of natural selection, the concept of magnetic fields, the concept of combustion, or the concept of a black hole. The implication is that these scientific concepts have an abstract existence in their own right (without reference to how any individual understands them). Perhaps these concepts exist in the minds of 'scientists', or can be found in definitive textbooks or in research journals, or are spelt out in curriculum documents.

Actually, a little thought suggests it may prove to be quite difficult to track down a definitive version of a scientific concept—any written definition or explanation, for example, is really just a representation of someone's understanding of the concept and so the words then need to be interpreted by the reader before they can understand the idea being represented (Taber, 2013b). We will see in the next chapter that ideas cannot be readily transferred from one mind to another—otherwise teaching would be a much easier profession.

There are often also *many* experts who we might consider should know the scientific concept, and *many* articles, books, and reference sources where we might hope to find a definitive account, but in reality we often find the experts tell us something slightly different from each other, and the available published accounts often do not agree on all details. This might suggest that perhaps we can know scientific concepts, but cannot clearly communicate them—or perhaps there are

---

Textbox 2.1: A traditional notion of the aim of science education.

"the idea that the primary aim of science education ought to be the promotion of scientific concepts and processes, thus helping students develop robust understandings of scientific findings and formalisms as well as the skills and processes used within the sciences"

Source: Sadler & Zeidler, 2009, p. 910.

multiple versions of scientific concepts and no single definite version to which we can refer. We might even come to the conclusion that in a sense definitive scientific concepts do not really exist at all, and that they are just a fiction!

Anyone who is familiar with the debates about the nature and philosophy of science, and what is known as 'postpositivism' is unlikely to be surprised by any of this. After all, it is now generally accepted that scientific knowledge, whilst potentially powerful and reliable, is always considered provisional and open to revision in the light of new evidence. In many national contexts, this is the perspective that teachers are expected to present in school science, and it is considered important as part of scientific literacy that citizens should know something of the processes by which science produces knowledge and the status of scientific ideas (for example, National Academy of Sciences, 2013).

So scientific concepts are certainly hard to pin down, but even if we were to consider them as fictions, they are useful fictions we commonly refer to in science education. Whilst science education is in important parts about teaching students about scientific values (so, for example, they develop a 'scientific attitude' that leads them to be sceptical and question things), and about enquiry skills, it is also usually considered that students should also be introduced to some of the conceptual 'products' of science—some of the key principles, theories, and models that scientists have suggested help us understand the world.

So the notion of canonical scientific knowledge—a corpus of scientific concepts that are generally accepted in science—is important in guiding curriculum authorities and teachers in setting out target knowledge for learners. There are two useful terms here that may be worth highlighting:

- *canonical knowledge*: the accepted understanding of concepts among those working in a scientific field
- *target knowledge*: what we hope learners will come to understand

Target knowledge is unlikely to match canonical knowledge precisely; scientific ideas can be quite nuanced and complex (as suggested in the previous chapter), and beyond the grasp of young learners. The curriculum therefore often presents simplifications—curricular models *of* the scientific knowledge itself. This target knowledge should be accessible to learners at a certain grade level or age. When the curriculum models are well designed they should lead to teaching that, whilst simplifying the science, remains true to the essence of the canonical knowledge itself (see Figure 2.1). The educational theorist Jerome Bruner used the term 'intellectually honest' in a famous aphorism about simplifying academic knowledge: that 'any subject could be taught effectively, in some intellectually honest way to any child, at any stage of development' (Bruner, 1960, p. 33). Whether we are entirely convinced by Bruner's claim or not, we would probably all agree that we would hope to teach science in an intellectually honest way. (This does not always happen, as will be considered later in the book—see Chapter 11).

34 Student Conceptions and Science

```
┌─────────────────────┐
│ canonical knowledge │
│ the scientific      │
│ account             │
└─────────────────────┘
         │                  transformed          represents
         │                     into
         │ are often
         │ inconsistent                                    ┌──────────────────┐
         │                                                 │ target knowledge │
         │                                                 │ the taught       │
         │                                                 │ curriculum       │
         │                                                 └──────────────────┘
         │                  should inform
         │                  teaching of       interacts
         ▼                                    with
┌─────────────────────┐
│ student conceptions │
│ personal knowledge  │
│ and beliefs         │
└─────────────────────┘
```

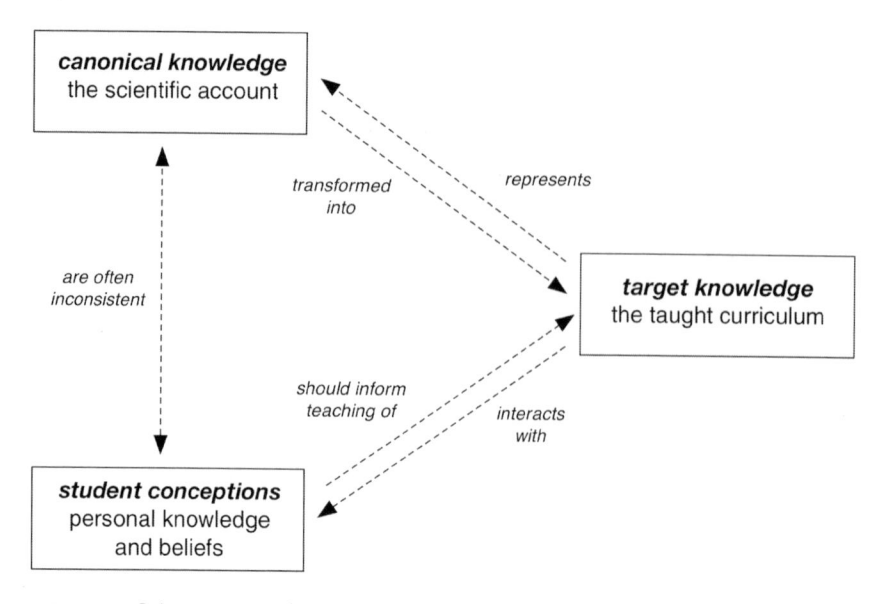

FIGURE 2.1 Science, curriculum, and learners: three distinct forms of knowledge.

Whether we see scientific concepts as useful fictions, or simply as being rather hard to pin down, it is worth noting that the processes of deciding what the canonical knowledge in some area of science actually is, and then how this should be represented in curriculum documents as target knowledge for particular groups of learners, are not always straightforward. This theme will be revisited in Chapter 10.

Conceptions

The term 'conception' is related to the notion of concept, and can be understood as someone's take on a concept. Even if a definitive version of the scientific concept of a black hole may seem elusive, individuals will have formed their own conceptions related to the concept. So we might expect the American theoretical physicist Steven Weinberg to have formed a conception of a black hole, and the British mathematical physicist Roger Penrose to have also formed his own conception. It seems likely these conceptions would be similar in important ways, although we might also suspect they may not be entirely identical.

A high school physics teacher is also likely to have a conception of a black hole, although we might expect their conception to be less extensive than those of Professors Weinberg and Penrose. Many secondary-age students will also have their own conceptions of a black hole (even though in many cases they have never been taught about the concept—an issue that will be picked up later in the book, see Chapter 7). We might expect school students' conceptions of a black hole to

> Textbox 2.2: Reference from a research report to a conception held by learners (15–21-year-old students in Brunei, Darussalam).
>
> *"A large percentage of the students (54%) seem to hold the conception that the Plasmodium parasites that cause malaria are found in the mosquito blood instead of in the mosquito saliva, and that they are transferred to the human blood directly from the mosquito blood system (14%)."*
>
> Source: Cheong, Treagust, Kyeleve, & Oh, 2010, p. 2511.

generally be less sophisticated than that of their teachers or physicists, and possibly to also potentially be quite at odds with the canonical version of the scientific concept. (Note, as suggested previously, that being able to *refer to* definitive versions of scientific concepts is very useful, even if we might doubt whether such things can really be found!) This is a hypothetical example, but the vast research literature in science education includes many examples of accounts of students' (and sometimes teachers') 'conceptions' of scientific concepts—see, for example, Textbox 2.2.

Misconceptions

So the term 'conception' refers to a person's understanding, which may or may not align well with other people's understanding of the 'same' concept area, and may or may not reflect what is considered canonical knowledge. The term '*mis*conception', however, has a more specific meaning in suggesting that someone's conception of some topic is flawed. So the term 'misconception' implies a conception which is seen as deficient in relation to the expected or desired understanding of a topic—see, for example, Textbox 2.3.

Indeed the term 'misconception' implies a misunderstanding, so is often used when we think someone has misunderstood something they should have learnt. There are many studies that refer to misconceptions, even though some researchers in the field suggest it is not an ideal term to use. One reason to be critical of the term is that it may be seen to imply that misconceptions are somehow the learner's fault—if only they had paid more attention in class or studied harder, then perhaps they would not have misconceptions. That may indeed sometimes be so, but as this book will show this is not a fair criticism in many cases. Perhaps

> Textbox 2.3: A claim in a research report about a 'persistent' misconception.
>
> *". . . our findings indicate that we have uncovered a persistent misconception. Students have difficulty understanding that DNA is a chemical and is not alive."*
>
> Source: Witzig, Freyermuth, Siegel, Izci, & Pires, 2013, p. 1368.

more significantly, the notion that misconceptions are about misunderstanding oversimplifies the nature of learning. Many reports of misconceptions seem to refer to ways learners have come to understand things that do not involve any misunderstanding of teaching, again suggesting that misconception could be a misleading term. The term 'misconception' is also seen as suspect because it is often too simplistic to consider misconceptions as just wrong, as a better question to ask is how they can provide a starting point for science learning that moves understanding closer to target knowledge.

Despite this, the term 'misconception' is still widely used. In part it is seen as a term which is widely understood in the teaching profession where other terms commonly used by researchers may be less familiar. Mea culpa, in this regard. When I prepared a book for the UK Royal Society of Chemistry (RSC) about students' ideas in chemistry its main title was *Chemical Misconceptions* (Taber, 2002). The book was to be sent to all the secondary schools and sixth-form colleges in Britain to support classroom teachers. A more appropriate title might have been something like *Alternative Conceptions in Chemistry*, but it was felt that the term 'misconceptions' was more likely to be understood, so that when the materials arrived in schools the teachers would immediately recognise what the book was about and appreciate why it might be useful to them. The term 'misconceptions' was also adopted when a government-funded national strategy to support teaching science was introduced in England which made the idea of students' misconceptions in science a key feature (Key Stage 3 National Strategy, 2002).

One difficulty with adopting terms which are part of the everyday language to describe research is that we may take for granted that we understand the ideas behind them, and fail to sufficiently problematise them. This can be so in the case of the term 'misconceptions', and some (but certainly not all) of the research literature reporting misconceptions does little more than list 'wrong' ideas elicited from learners, without offering reflection on the nature of those ideas, and their significance for further learning. The choice of the term 'misconception' in the title of the RSC materials certainly did not indicate the adoption of a simplistic and superficial account of learning and learners' ideas, as our aim was to produce materials that were accessible to teachers who may not be familiar with the research, but provided enough information to be genuinely useful in the classroom. The evaluation of those materials suggested we were successful in that aim (Murphy, Jones, & Lunn, 2004), and the present book is written in the same spirit: to be comprehensible to classroom teachers, or those preparing for teaching, who have not had an opportunity to explore the research literature in any depth, without oversimplifying what is actually quite a complex area of research. Arguably the use of the familiar term 'misconceptions' in the English National Strategy did reflect oversimplification—certainly in the way it implied to teachers that the process of responding to learners' misconceptions was relatively straightforward (Taber, 2010). Sadly, this is not always so, as some of the examples discussed in this book illustrate.

> Textbox 2.4: Reference to a common preconception in a research report.
>
> *"Many people have a preconception that we do less work when we use simple machines, whereas, in fact, simple machines do not change the amount of work done; they allow us to do work with less effort but over a longer distance."*
>
> Source: Marulcu & Barnett, 2013, p. 1827.

Preconceptions

One of the particular disadvantages of the term 'misconceptions' is the implication that it involves a misunderstanding. All science teachers are probably familiar with times when we know we taught them X, but somehow they seem to have learnt Y instead, and in these cases 'misconception' may seem appropriate. However, a good many of the conceptions that learners hold which are at odds with what we teach in school or college science do not seem to be misunderstandings of teaching at all. Often students seem to come to classes with either existing ideas about a topic before any formal teaching (for example, see Chapter 7), or at least tendencies to think about topics in certain ways that are likely to lead to the formation of misconceptions regardless of how well sequenced, and clear, our teaching is (see Chapters 4 and 5).

Where the term 'misconception' seems to imply misunderstanding something we have been told, '*preconception*' implies developing an understanding about something before we have the information or evidence needed to reach an informed view. An example of the use of this term in a research report is presented in Textbox 2.4. The term may be associated with ideas of bias or prejudice. In a sense these associations may be quite appropriate as a preconception may bias how we come to understand something, such as a teacher's presentation, and does imply having reached a view—or at least an impression—before formal instruction in the matter. However, the terms 'bias' and 'prejudice' can also carry their own associations of something unethical (such as allowing a prejudice about an ethnic group to bias our views of another person's work or opinions) that are unhelpful when considering preconceptions about scientific topics.

Alternative Conceptions

A term that has been widely adopted by science education researchers who have looked at learners' ideas relating to science topics is that of '*alternative* conceptions' (for an example, see Textbox 2.5). Often this term is preferred because it does not obviously suggest a deficit model of learner knowledge—learners' ideas are noted to be *different from* canonical knowledge rather than being labelled as inherently flawed. This also avoids a label that might imply (cf. preconception) that the learner's conception was in place before teaching, or (cf. misconception)

> Textbox 2.5: A claim of student alternative conceptions from a research report.
>
> *"... the findings of this study have identified various alternative conceptions a sample of grades 7 and 8 students has about gravity. These conceptions include that there is no gravity in space, that there is no gravity on the Moon or other bodies (such as Jupiter and the Sun) and that gravity is caused by the atmosphere or composition of the body."*
>
> Source: Lelliott, 2013, p. 15.

is a result of misunderstanding teaching. The term 'alternative conception' covers both these cases, as well as cases where we may not be sure whether the conception was present prior to teaching or developed during it, and indeed the cases (perhaps most!) where such distinctions are themselves oversimplistic. For, as will be argued later in the book, learners' conceptions often develop iteratively over time under a range of influences.

Some in science education have reservations about terms such as 'alternative' conception because they feel it underplays how such ideas may be problematic from a scientific perspective. Moreover, for some the use of such terminology represents a *relativistic* stance that seems at odds with the spirit of science. Science is intended to be an objective enterprise, in that it is expected that scientific processes should allow us to come to agree on the way things are (see Chapter 1), whereas relativism suggests there can be no objective truth as all perspectives are inevitably biased by subjective factors. Scientists present arguments (based on the interpretation of evidence) to support the adoption of particular laws, theories, models, and so forth as part of the accepted canon of science. In practice this is seldom straightforward, but *in principle* scientists certainly look to develop objective knowledge. We expect that if scientist A carries out a particular procedure, and makes a certain observation, then another scientist B following precisely the same procedure should, within limits of experimental error, make the same observations.

In practice science is seldom so simple, and there are all kinds of reasons why it is sometimes difficult to define conditions such that other scientists can reproduce results. So, for example, when a pair of distinguished scientists claimed they had managed to produce excess energy from a simple test tube scale apparatus due to a process of cold fusion, there followed a period of some months where various laboratories reported either replicating, or failing to replicate, the results. Sadly (as cold fusion would have proved very useful), the eventual virtual consensus some years on is that the original claims were not supported.

Such periods of dispute are not so surprising given the myriad factors that could be defined in any experimental set up, and it is not always obvious—especially with a new phenomenon—which need to be specified. Usually there are many potential factors that will be readily discounted (the colour of the lab coat, the need to say a prayer before turning on a power supply), but many others that conceivably could make a difference (does it matter how the test tube is aligned in relation to the earth's magnetic field; could ultraviolet emissions from strip lights be having an effect?) Scientists who work over extended periods of time with particular experimental set-ups often find that they are using tacit knowledge (Polanyi, 1962), that is knowledge of what to do that they have acquired without being explicitly aware of it (see Chapter 5). We all have knowledge of this type (try to explain to someone precisely how you use your muscles to go upstairs—if you walk upstairs your brain must have this knowledge available at some level, as it is sending instructions through your nerves to the muscles) but we tend to think that *in science* we should be able to specify all the relevant information about how to carry out an experiment or procedure. In practice it is not unusual for scientists to visit each other's labs to learn new techniques when the written account in scientific papers is insufficient to allow others to repeat the work (Collins, 2010).

Whereas an objectivist approach at least aspires to objective knowledge that we can all agree about (even if acknowledging that in practice this may just be an ideal), relativists will argue that in principle there cannot be any truly objective knowledge. Rather, they consider that all knowledge is necessarily grounded in a particular standpoint or perspective, and when different people from different standpoints examine the same evidence they will inevitably sometimes fail to agree on what inferences or deductions can be made. Traditionally, science has been understood to be objective, and relativist interpretations of science are sometimes seen as undermining conventional science (Laudan, 1990). After all, if there can be no neutral objective knowledge, and all knowledge claims are inevitably coloured by subjective factors, then there is no absolute reason to prefer, say, astronomical knowledge from astrological knowledge, or to believe that babies are brought into our lives by intimate relations rather than passing storks. As science educators we would claim that there are very good reasons to consider that science can offer us reliable knowledge, even if that knowledge is never absolute.

It is fair to say that the widespread adoption of the term 'alternative conception' does reflect something of a relativist view of knowledge—emphasising how children's ideas are different from accepted science rather than simply being wrong—although this need not be seen as questioning the merits of scientific knowledge. Science educators who have preferred the term 'alternative conceptions' do *not* argue that these alternatives should be considered on par with the scientific alternatives, but rather want to emphasise that it may be inadvisable to simply dismiss alternative conceptions as flawed as this may underestimate their status and significance to the learners who hold them. For one thing, ideas that are scientifically inadequate may still sometimes have considerable utility value in some contexts. This can be illustrated with examples from two areas where research suggests learners often hold ideas that are 'alternative conceptions' when compared with scientific accounts of the world.

Life-World Thinking

One such area is the way people think about energy. Energy is a very abstract idea (something that it was suggested in the previous chapter often makes scientific ideas difficult for learners), but the term 'energy' is widely used in everyday discourse. So it is commonly accepted that food can give you energy. This is an idea that fits with scientific ideas (if not worded in the way a science teacher may prefer). However, research also suggests that children will also commonly suggest that exercise can help you build up energy (Solomon, 1992). This is more difficult to fit with a scientific perspective—which would suggest instead that exercise involves processes that deplete a body's energy supplies. During exercise, carbohydrates are oxidised and energy is transferred through heat to the surroundings.

However, although the conception that exercise builds up energy is scientifically flawed, it is a notion that is not entirely without credit. Regular exercise helps people feel more energetic (by strengthening their cardiovascular system, for example) and builds up muscle strength that then allows them to work harder and undertake more powerful exercise (and so transfer energy from chemical stores at a faster rate). Regular exercise can build up muscle tissue, providing greater stores of glycogen to support strenuous exercise. So there is certainly a sense in which *it is meaningful* to suggest that exercise helps you build up energy, even if the phrasing is likely to make physics teachers cringe!

The point is that in everyday life, when students are talking to each other and their families—rather than to their physics teachers—the idea that exercise can build up energy has 'currency' as it makes sense to most people (see Chapter 7 which discusses what might be termed 'folk science'). That means, of course, that in everyday conversations such ideas are likely to be communicated and reinforced. Some researchers have referred to such ideas being adopted in the life-world (Solomon, 1983), meaning in the way people naturally experience and talk about things when not being influenced by scientific accounts. Consider for example the meaning of sugar in different contexts highlighted in Textbox 2.6.

Textbox 2.6: An example of how the same label refers to different things in life-world and technical contexts.

"Let us consider the focal event of DNA research and the focal event of preparing ice cream in a daily life setting. In both focal events, the mental maps contain the same labels, for example sugar. This label, however, is connected to a completely different focal event, with a completely different behaviour environment, and a completely different meaning of the label: a specific group of carbohydrates (biochemical research) and a sweet white substance (in daily life/kitchen). 'Sugar' in a life-world focal event consists of white grains that taste sweet, while 'sugar' in food chemistry refers to a class of carbohydrates with a related molecular structure."

Source: Gilbert, Bulte, & Pilot, 2010, pp. 831–832.

The important point here for science teachers is that because such ideas carry status and are reinforced in everyday life, they are unlikely to be easily extinguished by a teacher pointing out that they are scientifically suspect. The term 'alternative conception' is sometimes considered to recognise the educational significance of such ideas whereas the label 'misconception' might seem to imply something that can readily be corrected.

Intuitive Theories

Another term that has been used to describe learners' ideas is 'intuitive theories' (Pope & Denicolo, 1986), and an example of a recent study framed in those terms is quoted in Textbox 2.7. Again there has been debate about the merits of this term—whether learners' intuitive ideas really can be considered theory-like.

An idea (or alternative conception) that might be considered to take the form of an intuitive theory would be that an object only moves whilst it is acted upon by a force. This idea proves problematic when force and motion is studied in school science. Newtonian physics—the canonical scientific account taught in school and college—suggests that:

- an object that is moving will continue to move indefinitely if no force acts upon it;
- applying a force to a moving object changes its mode of movement—that is, accelerates it.

However, many learners hold the conception that if a moving object is not acted upon by a force it will decelerate and come to a stop. This is one of the most researched areas of student conceptions (Alonzo & Steedle, 2009), and the research suggests that a clear majority of people (something like four-fifths or more) adopt this alternative conception before formal teaching about force and motion—and that many of them retain this way of thinking regardless of what they are then taught in school.

It is generally considered that the physics here (Newton's first two laws of motion) is counterintuitive—that is, it goes against the way the world seems to

---

Textbox 2.7: Considering conceptions about disease as based on intuitive theories.

"A cold weather theory of infectious disease was invoked by more than half of the children studied here to explain colds and by about a quarter to explain flu in response to open-ended questions . . . the intuitive theories approach illustrated here can readily be extended to other diseases about which people hold mistaken beliefs."

Source: Sigelman, 2012, pp. 73–74.

work for us. The alternative idea—sometimes called an impetus notion after the Aristotelean idea of impetus, or F-v thinking because force is associated with speed rather than acceleration (F-a thinking) as in the scientific account—has been labelled an intuitive theory. Intuitive does not necessarily mean something that is instinctive (that we are born with), but can just be something has become intuitive to us over time because of our experiences. This theme will be explored more in Chapter 5.

It is easy to see why our experience of the world might lead us to expect that objects only keep moving if a force is applied, and soon come to stop otherwise. That is pretty much what seems to happen if we focus only the forces we apply to objects and do not take into account such factors as air resistance and friction. From the physics perspective it makes no difference whether a force is due to a person pushing or resistive forces acting in the environment—but people are obviously more aware of the pushes and pulls they themselves apply, whether directly or using machines such as a car engine. We could argue that the alternative conception makes perfect sense and is a useful way of thinking for many everyday purposes.

Indeed, I have suggested that this alternative conception is not really wrong, but more a different formalism for examining motion than that used in science (Taber, 2009). There are good reasons why scientists adopt the approach they do, but the alternative formalism is pretty self-consistent and offers a good guide on how to move objects about in everyday life. Where ideas like exercise building up energy may be reinforced by social discourse outside the classroom, the F-v alternative conception is reinforced just about every time we move ourselves or other things around.

The claim that this idea is intuitive is generally accepted, but the use of the term 'theory' in the phrase intuitive theory is more controversial among researchers (Keil, 2010). In science a theory is something of high status because it is more than just an idea or guess (although students often equate 'theory' with 'hypothesis' or 'hunch'), but rather a framework of related ideas, offering explanatory and predictive power, and having been tested and shown to be consistent with empirical evidence. Scientific theories are usually developed over time, in a deliberate way, drawing upon accepted scientific principles, and being tested at different stages in the process. The outcome of this process, a scientific theory, is therefore considered to carry some intellectual weight—even if we accept that theories are always conjectured accounts, and do not compose a certain description of how the world actually works.

Those researchers who prefer the term 'intuitive theories' for students' ideas emphasise how such ideas are not simply whims that people adopt on the spur of the moment, but are rather ideas to which they are committed, because they are consistent with their experience of the world. We can certainly imagine how the notion that a pushed or thrown object will soon come to a halt (but will get a bit further if we push or throw harder) is supported by many empirical tests—most of which it will pass with flying colours. The use of the term 'theory' in intuitive theory is intended to indicate to teachers and others that these are ideas that are well grounded in experience, and so will not be readily put aside by learners.

Critics of the term 'intuitive theory' have two lines of argument for not liking the term. One area of contention has been the claim that children do commit to the informal ideas they develop prior to meeting topics in science teaching. Some researchers have argued that actually many of the ideas reported in the research literature are little more than guesses. Indeed, it has been suggested that often researchers ask children, including quite young children, about things they may never have had reason to think about. Some will shrug their shoulders or indicate they do not have an answer—others will make something up on the spot. That is quite normal behaviour, and was noticed by the great pioneer of asking children about their ideas, Jean Piaget. He called this 'romancing' an answer. There are many situations where someone will ask us about something we have given no thought to, and sometimes his or her question provokes us to think up an answer. Often we will give it our 'best shot', and we may even be quite pleased with ourselves—feeling that we came up with a strong answer. Once we have thought of that answer, we may actually keep it in mind for future purposes—it may become part of our knowledge base (this kind of process will be considered more in Chapter 6)—and we may even start to strongly commit to it. However it is also possible that we may have no reason to think further about the issue and soon forget our suggestion. Perhaps if we are asked a similar question a few months later we might come up with a similar response—but perhaps not. Perhaps we just came up with something that seemed feasible at the time—and there was no real commitment to our response.

This is clearly a major issue for those who do research into learners' ideas in science education. Much (although by no means all) of the research has been undertaken by researchers who do not know the young people they interviewed, met them once, interviewed them on that occasion, and never spoke to them again. There are techniques that can be used in interviews to explore the level of commitment students have to their ideas, but often the research does not make it clear if these were used. Sometimes the need to interview a sample of students means there was limited time for each interview. These types of 'survey' approaches can build a reasonable sample size helping us to identify common ideas, but offer limited scope for finding out about the nature of students' thinking.

The critics have a very valid point here, and it certainly seems that a proportion of the ideas researchers have elicited from those they interview are little more than guesses made up in response to the questioning. Those kinds of responses can still be of interest, as they give us insight into the ways people can think about topics, but they do not necessarily reveal the kinds of strongly committed ideas that are well-established ways of thinking (such as F-v thinking). However, we also know from studies that use more in-depth approaches with students over extended periods that learners' alternative ideas can be stable and attract strong commitment (Helldén, 2005; Taber, 1995, 2000).

The second strand to the criticism of the use of the term 'theory' for children's ideas relates to deliberation. Scientists consciously frame and develop their theories, thinking carefully about their merits and limitations. It is less clear that the ideas children develop about the world are the result of deliberation in this way. One leading researcher, Ros Driver, popularised the notion of the pupil as scientist—although her very readable book (1983) on the topic included a telling question mark in its title: *The Pupil as Scientist?*

A related issue concerns the range of application of a theory. Scientific theories tend to have well-bounded ranges of application. Newton's laws of motion refer to all situations concerning force and motion—but cannot be directly applied to questions about how fast a chemical reaction will occur. Darwin's theory of natural selection concerns the origin of species on earth and can be related to considerations of species distribution, behaviour, anatomy, biochemistry, and so forth, but strictly does not apply to the competition between businesses in the marketplace. We might test a theory outside its range of application (for example, can we consider chemical kinetics in Newtonian terms, or can we understand the marketplace in Darwinian terms?), and indeed many useful scientific discoveries have been based on drawing analogies from one field to another, but a theory itself has a clear range of application.

Research suggests that where learners have alternative conceptions to scientific ideas these are often not applied over the same range as the scientific concept. So the learner may seem to apply their alternative conception in some contexts where a scientific principle should be used, but not in others (Teichert, Tien, Anthony, & Rickey, 2008). Some have interpreted that as suggesting that learners' ideas are not theory-like (Claxton, 1993), as they are not applied consistently, but clearly this could just mean that the learners' ideas have a different range of application to the scientific concept. After all, if learners understand the world in alternative ways, there is no reason to assume they will be recognising the same distinctions and divisions as scientists. However, even if learners' ideas do have consistent ranges of application, they may not be fully aware of what these are, as they may often be making 'gut' responses rather than applying principles in a deliberate way as we expect in scientific thinking.

It seems clear that at least some of the ideas that researchers have elicited from learners in their studies do refer to well-established notions that are theory-like in some senses, in that they may consistently apply particular ideas across a wide range of contexts (an example of this is discussed under 'Alternative Conceptual Framework'). However, critics raise an important point that in a sense an intuitive theory is an oxymoron—theories are applied deliberately, where intuition works at a preconscious level. If we do read or use the term 'intuitive theory' we should bear in mind that the 'theory' aspect of an intuitive theory should be taken metaphorically, to imply that our intuition acts as if we are operating with tacit theories of the world.

P-prims—Implicit Knowledge Elements

Indeed another term that has become widely used by some researchers to refer to implicit knowledge—knowledge we have without being consciously aware of it—is 'p-prim', which is an abbreviation for 'phenomenological primitive'. P-prims are considered to be implicit knowledge elements—that is, they act as things we know, without us being aware we know them. This is not as strange as it may sound, as a similar principle operates in language learning. In some school systems students are taught formally about grammar, and technical concepts about the way sentences are formed and can be decomposed. Yet we all tend to learn to use most of the rules involved without any formal instruction at all—we acquire them up through our frequent everyday engagement in using language. The author attended school in England at a time when there was not a strong emphasis on teaching formal grammar in state schools. This did not seem to be a major constraint on my production and comprehension of language—at least until I reached university. I studied chemistry, and at one point was expected to take a short 'German for chemists' course. Unfortunately, the German was explained in terms of technical grammar terminology that meant nothing to me, and so I had little basis for understanding much of the course!

Indeed, young children commonly learn the basics of their mother tongue pretty effectively before reaching school age. There is even a well-recognised phenomenon where children commonly reach a point where they begin to start making regular systematic mistakes. It seems they shift from largely using constructions they have heard to applying rules that they have—at some level—deduced. A language like English has lots of irregularities, where the general rules are not followed in particular cases, but children will apply the rules in these cases as well so making systematic mistakes in the irregular cases.

We could say that the children have learnt and know the rules—but they would not be able to explain to us how they form language as they do. This language learning occurs at an implicit level rather than being explicit to consciousness. The child is using language automatically (in the sense of without conscious attention to how the constructions are put together), and not in a reflective way. They have knowledge of grammar in the sense of know-how, but they can no more explain how they do it than they can explain how they coordinate muscular action in walking.

Researchers suggest that we have a wide range of implicit knowledge elements ('p-prims', although other terms may sometimes be used) that we draw upon in making judgments about the world (diSessa, 1993). The p-prims reflect our experiences of how the world seems to be—see, for example, Textbox 2.8. So when we ask a student a question about something they have not been taught about and have never consciously thought about, they may often produce an answer 'out of the blue' because they can imagine the situation and have an intuition about what might be going on. This is considered to be the operation of the p-prim being

> Textbox 2.8: One of a number of proposed 'p-prims' influencing student thinking about how substances behave.
>
> *"Our final theme (things have a (natural) predetermined configuration) indicates an intuitive sense that substances will spread out. . . . there is obvious scope for the genesis of a primitive notion that things spread out abstracted from common experiences of spreading smells and spilled liquids and the general entropic tendency for the contents of any orderly toy cupboard to become disorderly."*
>
> Source: Taber & García Franco, 2010, p. 135.

activated. This explains how people can 'romance' answers when they would seem to have no relevant knowledge base; actually, we have all built up a store of implicit knowledge elements that represent our intuitions about how things are and how they work.

We are not usually aware of this kind of 'thinking' as it occurs at preconscious levels, although we all rely on it. Sometimes we say we will 'mull things over' or 'let things ruminate', or even that we will 'sleep on' things—we are in effect drawing upon thinking we are not consciously aware of and hoping that by the time we come back to consciously address the matter we will have done some useful thinking in the background! The 'Eureka! moment' of discovery may often come to us when we are (consciously) thinking about something else entirely. Most of us have experienced the 'tip of the tongue' moment when a forgotten name or the answer to a crossword clue is being sought: we are pretty sure we have almost got to the answer, but it has not yet been presented to consciousness (Brown & McNeill, 1966/1976). Probably our conscious thinking is only a small part of the mental processing we do, although as the reflective part where we have control of our thoughts it is especially important to us. (And in many senses our conscious thoughts *are* our mental lives, and in effect our lives themselves.)

Schemata

The term 'schemata' is commonly used in psychology where a schema is a preexisting knowledge structure that allows the automatic organisation of thought. Schemata, then, are similar to p-prims in acting preconsciously so that by the time we become consciously aware the information being considered has been organised into a schema.

For example, if I am presented with the information:

potassium hydroxide + phosphoric acid . . .

I will immediately recognise (a) this as a chemical reaction, (b) that it is a neutralisation reaction, (c) that the products will be a salt plus water, and (d) that the

Characterising and Labelling Ideas

```
  acid    +    alkali    →    salt    +    water
_____ acid        _____ hydroxide     _____      _____
```

phosphoric acid + potassium hydroxide → potassium phosphate + water

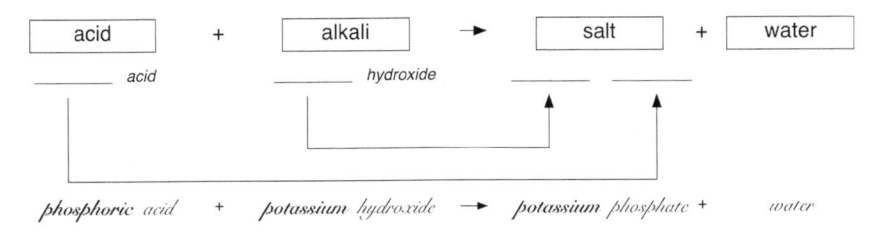

FIGURE 2.2 Representation of a schema for one class of chemical reaction.

salt in this case will be potassium phosphate. This has in effect become automatic, so that I no longer have to make any conscious effort to 'work this out'. It is as though there is a template available in my mind for neutralisation reactions, into which this particular pattern fits (see Figure 2.2).

Of course *a novice*, such as a student who has been taught about neutralisation reactions but has had limited experience of classifying and representing reactions, will only be able to identify the products of the reaction by conscious mentipulation of the information provided in relation to learnt material recalled from memory (Taber & Bricheno, 2009). Only with time and experience does a schema develop to allow us to immediately 'know' answers in these situations, rather than having to consciously work through examples step by step.

Alternative Conceptual Frameworks—or Alternative Frameworks

Another term that readers of the research literature will find commonly used to describe learners' ideas is alternative frameworks or alternative conceptual frameworks. Some researchers have made efforts to distinguish between what is meant by an alternative conception and what is meant by an alternative conceptual framework (or simply alternative framework), but often these terms have often been used interchangeably.

One approach, preferred by the present author, is to use the term 'alternative conception' to refer to fairly limited specific ideas, and to keep the term 'alternative conceptual framework' for more extensive conceptualisations. That is, conceptual frameworks are structures of conceptions—where learners' individual conceptions do seem to be coordinated into more extensive patterns of ideas that might seem more akin to theories.

So, as an example, in some of my own research I reported what I described as an alternative conceptual framework from chemistry education, the octet framework (Taber, 1998, 2013a). The framework, which is discussed in Chapter 9, represented a pattern of conceptions that are related, where there was logical network of ideas built around a central explanatory principle. The range of application of this 'full-outer-shells principle' was extensive—students attempted to apply the principle to the wide range of different examples presented to them.

The term 'alternative conceptual framework' is useful here because students clearly developed a series of related conceptions about an area of knowledge that were logically linked together. The octet framework does not simply involve one alternative conception, but many, and it is not simply a series of discrete conceptions, but rather an extended conceptual structure. Findings of this kind seem to offer very good evidence that learners' alternative ideas can indeed sometimes be theory-like in important senses.

However, this is not to suggest that all ideas elicited from learners are of this kind. This octet framework was developed by interviewing older students (mostly 16–18-year-olds), studying at what is called 'advanced level' in England—these were students who mostly hoped to go on to university—often to study science-related subjects. My argument here is that learners' conceptions *can be* built into extensive and coherent frameworks—but this is certainly not always the case. For this reason I prefer to use the term 'conception' for individual ideas, and to reserve talk of frameworks for those cases where there is clear evidence of learners building up structures of such conceptions. Yet, as noted earlier, there is no clear consensus on how terms are used in the literature. The message again, for those who delve into the primary research literature, is not to read too much into the particular choice of terminology authors use.

Mental Models

Another common term used in research literature concerns learners' mental models. As with many of the terms discussed in this chapter, there have been scholarly treatments suggesting how the terms should be used (Gentner & Stevens, 1983; Johnson-Laird, 1983), but in practice researchers have often been much more flexible in how they have applied the term. Again, then, in practice, it is not always clear that papers that refer to mental models are reporting anything different in nature to those papers that describe alternative conceptions or frameworks.

However, the term 'mental model' *should* imply something more than just an isolated conception (see, for example, Textbox 2.9). In particular the term is useful when it refers to how we model processes in our mind. So, for example, we can visualise processes in our imagination, and to do this we must have a mental model of the situation being simulated (Gilbert, 2005).

Epistemological Beliefs

Epistemology is about how we come to knowledge, and is particularly important in science. When we think about scientific method(s), or enquiry skills, we are thinking about epistemology. A major aspect of the nature of science (NOS), or 'how science works', relates to how scientists develop new knowledge and what status that knowledge is considered to have (that is, such judgements as scientific knowledge not being absolute and certain, but rather being provisional, yet generally reliable).

Textbox 2.9: Characteristics of a mental model described in a research report.

"*What mental models of sound propagation do students use?* . . . *we have identified what we called the 'Entity' model as the dominant alternative model* . . . *According to students using the Entity model, sound is a self-standing unit different from the medium through which it propagates.* . . . *We have identified four sound properties that we uniquely associate with the Entity model. These are:*

1 Sound is independent—sound propagates through the vacuum, i.e., it does not need a medium,

2 Sound passes through the empty spaces between the medium particles a property we called seeping,

3 Sound is a material unit of substance or has mass, and

4 Sound is propagation of sound particles that are different from medium particles."

Source: Hrepic, Zollman, & Rebello, 2010, pp. 2–4.

One area of research into learners' ideas has concerned their epistemological beliefs (Hammer & Elby, 2003)—their ideas about how we come to know something—what counts as evidence, or indeed proofs, and what status we should give to scientific laws, theories, and models. Arguably we are here simply dealing with learners' conceptions, but their conceptions about the NOS (for example, see Textbox 2.10) rather than about particular areas of scientific content. For example, there is research suggesting that school-age students commonly have unsophisticated understandings of what and how scientific models represent (Treagust, Chittleborough, & Mamiala, 2002), and that for many students theories are seen as hunches that have not yet been tested (but which can be promoted to laws or facts if they are proved through experiments).

Textbox 2.10: A research claim of differences in typical epistemological beliefs between students studying in different cultural contexts.

"*the scientific epistemological beliefs of the two groups [Taiwanese and Chinese students] were significantly different for the dimensions of 'the invented and creative nature of science,'* . . . *'the theory-laden exploration,'* . . . *'the cultural impacts,'* . . . *and 'the changing and tentative feature of science knowledge'* . . . *Taiwanese students were more likely to believe that science involves human imagination and creativity, changes with progression, and is influenced by culture than were the students from China. However, the Chinese students tended to consider that science involves personal values and assumptions (i.e., 'the theory-laden exploration').*"

Source: Lin, Deng, Chai, & Tsai, 2013, pp. 42–43.

These are then alternative conceptions about NOS, but it is interesting that they are sometimes labelled as 'beliefs' as this raises the question of how knowledge, conceptions, and beliefs are related. Traditionally, philosophers have reserved the term 'knowledge' for justified true beliefs—things that we think are so, that we have good grounds for thinking are so, and which are so. On this basis very little can be considered knowledge as there is very little we 'know' which we can be sure is correct, and which can feel fully justified in believing—*cogito ergo sum*, as Descartes suggested, perhaps—especially when the NOS teaches us that all knowledge claims should be seen as open to revision in the light of new evidence (McCain & Weslake, 2013).

So the use of the term 'belief' in the term 'epistemological beliefs' does not seem to signify some major distinction from other types of conceptions. However, this does link to the important issue of *levels of commitment* to ideas. Some ideas elicited from learners in research represent well-established notions that the learner is strongly committed to, where others may just represent 'romanced' suggestions in response to an unexpected researcher question. The former types of response may be highly significant for science teaching, but the latter type less so.

Multiple Frameworks and Manifold Conceptions

The research literature also refers to students having manifold conceptions or multiple frameworks where students seem to hold several different conceptions of the 'same' concept area—different versions of how they understand some topic (Pope & Denicolo, 1986). There has been some debate about the validity of such claims, and suggestions that a student may seem to have several alternative conceptions of the same concept area only because of limitations in the research process.

This is quite possible, as researching other people's ideas is actually very challenging: especially when we realise that some important aspects of the knowledge they hold that informs their thinking may be implicit, so often even the people themselves are not really aware of the basis of their thinking. Our ideas are subjective experiences, and the best we can do is represent them to others—through talk, gesture, drawing, and so forth—and the other person then has to interpret those representations and try to reproduce the original thinking (Taber, 2013b). Yet, as the next chapter will suggest, all our interpretations of what we see and hear are somewhat subjective and idiosyncratic, so we can never be sure we are really thinking *precisely* what someone else is thinking.

It is quite possible that some reports of students holding multiple alternative conceptions may actually be a result of the limitations of the communication of the learner's ideas, or the limited imagination of the researcher in making sense of someone else's ideas when they do not match the canonical version of a scientific concept. However, from my own research I am confident that not all reports in the literature of this kind reflect limitations in the research process. In one case I interviewed the same student over 20 times over many months, and was able to obtain very convincing evidence both that he operated with manifold conceptions of chemical bonding, and that over time his use of these alternatives shifted (Taber, 2000).

Indeed, this is what we would hope for as teachers! Given that learners hold alternative conceptions and that sometimes these are not readily abandoned, we would hope to be able to encourage them to consider an alternative way of thinking closer to the scientific account. So a shift from a single alternative conception to manifold conceptions that included a more scientifically acceptable version reflects progress towards adoption of the scientific view.

When students hold manifold conceptions, their answer to a single question will not reveal the full range of their thinking on a topic, as one particular conceptions will be triggered. Sometimes this will be the currently most dominant way of thinking about a topic, but this need not be the case. Aspects of context may cue a particular response, and different forms of context may operate. So a learner may answer a question differently to her friend in a playtime discussion compared to how she would answer the same question to the teacher in a lesson—for example, drawing upon folk-biological categories of living things in the playground and formal taxonomic groups in class. Or a learner may answer the teacher's question differently if his or her question is posed in technical terms (a mass on a spring) rather than in an everyday context (the drum of a washing machine). Sometimes it may be the internal mental context of the learner that is important—what the learner has recently been thinking about may make it more likely that one of the alternative concepts is accessed rather than another. In each of these cases the student is unlikely to be making a conscious decision—but is rather answering in terms of 'what comes to mind', whichever conception is activated in that context.

It seems students' ideas about scientific concepts can get quite complex, and the literature makes reference to knowledge facets—considering conceptions to be multifaceted (Redish, 2004)—and to layers within conceptual structures (Petri & Niedderer, 1998). We should be aware that to some extent we are using metaphors here in trying to describe and explain the complexity of other people's cognition using models that make sense to us—the facets of a crystal, or the layers in something like geological formations. The whole area of research into learners' ideas in science can be seen as a model-building enterprise, seeking to model aspects of student cognition in ways that can ultimately inform teaching (Taber, 2013b).

Making Sense of the Diverse Terminology Used to Describe Learners' Ideas

This brief survey of terminology used in science education to describe learners' ideas suggests the following key points:

- A range of labels have been used in reporting learners' ideas about science and scientific concepts.

- These different labels do reflect some important dimensions of learner cognition that can be significant to teachers in taking into account learners' ideas (these are summarised shortly).
- Unfortunately, the use of terminology across the research literature is not consistent, so readers need to look beyond the labels used by authors in reporting particular studies.

The treatment here is necessarily at an introductory level, and readers interested in delving deeper into the distinctions operating here, and the challenges involved in research to explore learners' ideas in science, are referred to my book *Modelling Learners and Learning in Science Education* (Taber, 2013b). However, it seems clear:

- Learners present ideas which are at odds with scientific accounts (alternative conceptions).
- Sometimes these conceptions are longstanding, and they may be well-established in thinking. (However this is not always the case.)
- Sometimes these conceptions may be generated in situ in response to a researcher's or teacher's question, in which case they may not be strongly committed to.
- The ideas people have may be informed by implicit knowledge elements—cognitive resources they are not even aware of having.
- Learners' conceptions may be somewhat discrete, or they may be linked to others in more extensive conceptual frameworks, or built into mental models that allow them to mentally simulate and visualise complex processes.
- Learners' ideas are not always beliefs—we can all entertain ideas that we have very different levels of commitment to.
- Often learners have more than one way of thinking about the same scientific concept area; sometimes one of these alternatives approximates well to target knowledge, but this need not be the case.

Key Characteristics of Learners' Ideas: The ACME Model of Conceptions

Taken together it seems there are at least four dimensions over which learners' conceptions vary in ways that might be significant for teachers. This is shown in Figure 2.3.

Figure 2.3 shows these four dimensions in parallel, but we might better think of them as occupying some kind of four-dimensional conceptional phase space where any particular idea that a learner has could be represented by coordinates along each dimension. (These four dimensions are perhaps not strictly 'orthogonal' in the sense of being entirely independent of each other, but as always in dealing with aspects of cognition, we are trying to represent something complex in ways simple enough to be useful.)

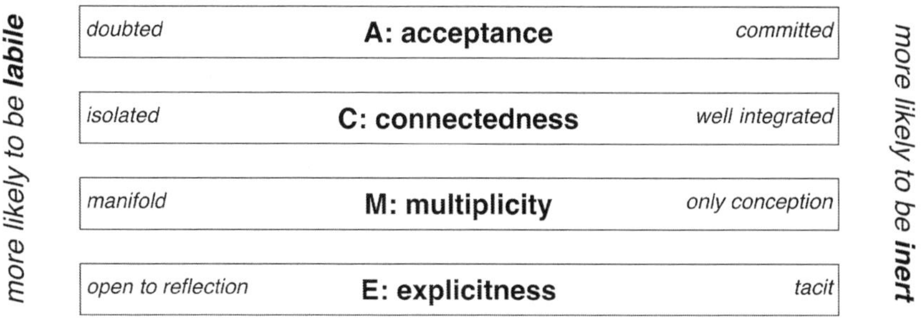

Characterising and Labelling Ideas 53

doubted	**A: acceptance**	committed
isolated	**C: connectedness**	well integrated
manifold	**M: multiplicity**	only conception
open to reflection	**E: explicitness**	tacit

more likely to be labile ← → *more likely to be inert*

FIGURE 2.3 Key dimensions of learner's ideas in science.

In particular, Figure 2.3 suggests that these four dimensions relate to something very important to science teachers: the extent to which an idea is likely to be inert (and so not readily abandoned) or labile (and so easily given up). This ACME (Acceptance-Connectedness-Multiplicity-Explicitness) model is not the only way to think about this issue, but it offers a useful way of thinking about key factors.

A: Acceptance

We are all able to come up with ideas when asked questions without being limited to answers to which we are strongly committed. We have some ideas to which we *are* strongly committed, and we entertain others as viable possibilities. In considering a particular issue we might entertain several possibilities, and at any time evaluate their relative merits. Over time, as the evidence available to us changes, the degree of commitment to particular ideas can shift. Our grounds for committing to or doubting an idea, as will be discussed later in the book, often includes what those around us seem to think as well any more direct evidence.

C: Connectedness

It was suggested previously that sometimes the ideas elicited from learners form parts of more extensive conceptual schemes. This is reassuring to science teachers, as a key feature of scientific knowledge is its highly connected nature (see Chapter 9). In science we look for general principles of wide applicability, and expect new scientific knowledge to fit with what is already established. So if a biochemist were to suggest a new biochemical pathway that involved processes that did not conserve energy, her work would be considered suspect—even though it is presented as new biochemical knowledge and not physics.

The extent to which the many different learners' ideas in science reported in the research literature are integrated into wider conceptual schemes is difficult to judge. Some research certainly demonstrates this can be the case. There are also many studies that present evidence of particular conceptions as though isolated knowledge elements—but often the research methodology used or the information offered in the report does not provide a basis for making judgments about the extent to which an elicited idea may be linked to other ideas.

All other things being equal, a relatively isolated conception that is not strongly linked to other ideas is likely to be more labile—more readily modified or abandoned—than a conception which is one part of a more extensive and coherent knowledge structure. Moreover, when a particular idea is part of a larger conceptual framework it may either occupy a relatively peripheral position within that framework, or be central and strongly connected to a wide range of other conceptions. Highly connected conceptions are therefore likely to be more inert as they cannot readily be put aside or substantially changed without consequences for other related ideas (Thagard, 1992).

M: Multiplicity

As suggested previously, when we find that a student has a certain idea about a scientific concept, we cannot assume that they do not also entertain alternatives. This is particularly important to remember when our questions seem to elicit the right responses from our students—perhaps on another day, or with a slightly different wording to what we think of as the 'same' question, we might have received a very different answer. Multiplicity of conceptions is especially important in terms of progression in learning. A person who only has one viable way of thinking about a topic is unlikely to abandon it until they are offered or discover an alternative.

The presence of manifold conceptions also makes the way we need to think about learning more nuanced. Often as teachers we are not simply concerned with providing learners with the correct scientific idea, or persuading them of the inadequacy of an alternative conception, but rather attempting to encourage learners to shift in their pattern of application among a number of alternative ways of thinking. Ideally we might wish to 'replace' an alternative conception with the scientific alternative, but a good deal of research into conceptual change suggests that this is often not a straightforward process, and shifts towards adopting scientific ways of thinking may take months or years—and apparently abandoned alternative ideas may still be activated by particular cues or contexts long after the student seems to have accepted and adopted the target knowledge we are teaching.

E: Explicitness

The final key dimension included in Figure 2.3 concerns the degree of explicitness of a learner's thinking about a topic. Although we would probably reserve the term 'learner's ideas' for their conscious thoughts, our conscious thinking is constantly being resourced by all the preconscious thinking that goes on 'in the background' of our minds.

In terms of this tacit-explicit dimension it is actually our tacit knowledge that is likely to be more inert. We are aware of our explicit conceptions, and we can reflect upon their strengths, limitations, and overall adequacy in explaining the world. We can sometimes decide that they are not up to the job, and that we need to think further about a topic (and perhaps do some reading or ask a teacher) as we do not really understand it very well.

Our implicit knowledge, however, is more insidious. It informs our thinking without us even being aware it exists. This is possible because it is the source of our intuitions—so it makes up the things that we take for granted and do not stop to question (perhaps until someone challenges us—'why do you think that?') We do not notice the learning process by which we acquire this implicit knowledge (see Chapter 5), and it is often said to be 'encapsulated' so that it operates as unit, like a black box that we have no conscious access to (Carey, 2009).

An analogy that works for me here is the contrast between the circuits on modern electronic chips, and the older types of circuits used before modern semiconductor technology. If an old-fashioned radio was not working well one could open it up and take a look. Someone who knew about circuits would recognise the resistors and capacitors and other components, and could clearly see how they were linked together. Often the radio was not working well because a valve had burnt out—so one of the glass bulbs would have a coating of metal inside the glass, rather than being clear and showing a glowing orange wire inside. The valve could be unscrewed (when it had cooled), and a replacement fitted. Our conscious knowledge is a bit like that. We can set it out in a systematic manner (for example, we can draw a concept map; see Chapter 8) and reflect on the different components, and perhaps identify a weak link where we are not sure we fully understand.

Our tacit knowledge, however, is much more like a modern appliance fitted with a chip. Looking at the chip it is not possible to identify discrete components or see how they link together—it just seems to be one coherent object. Moreover, because there are no user-serviceable parts in the circuit, the modern appliance may not even be built so we can readily open it up and find the chip; we just know there must be something inside allowing the appliance to work. Our implicit knowledge structures are like this: we cannot locate them, and we certainly cannot ascertain their structure, but there must be something there that is leading us to have intuitions about how the world works. Just as we have no conscious awareness of constructing them, we cannot remove or modify them simply by reflecting on them and deciding to change our minds.

Generally these aspects of cognition are inert. This is clearly important for the science teacher as we might be able to challenge learners' consciously accessible alternative conceptions, but a different approach is needed when students' thinking is directed by their implicit knowledge of the world. We need to engineer ways to help learners understand scientific concepts in terms of subsets of their available intuitions about the world (diSessa, 2008).

References

Abimbola, I. O. (1988). The problem of terminology in the study of student conceptions in science. *Science Education, 72*(2), 175–184.

Alonzo, A. C., & Steedle, J. T. (2009). Developing and assessing a force and motion learning progression. *Science Education, 93*(3), 389–421. doi: 10.1002/sce.20303

Black, P. J., & Lucas, A. M. (Eds.). (1993). *Children's informal ideas in science*. London: Routledge.

Brown, R., & McNeill, D. (1966/1976). The 'tip-of-the-tongue' phenomenon. In J. M. Gardiner (Ed.), *Readings in human memory* (pp. 243–255). London: Methuen.

Bruner, J. S. (1960). *The process of education*. New York, NY: Vintage Books.

Carey, S. (2009). *The origin of concepts*. Oxford: Oxford University Press.

Cheong, I. P.-A., Treagust, D., Kyeleve, I. J., & Oh, P.-Y. (2010). Evaluation of students' conceptual understanding of malaria. *International Journal of Science Education, 32*(18), 2497–2519. doi: 10.1080/09500691003718014

Claxton, G. (1993). Minitheories: A preliminary model for learning science. In P. J. Black & A. M. Lucas (Eds.), *Children's informal ideas in science* (pp. 45–61). London: Routledge.

Collins, H. (2010). *Tacit and explicit knowledge*. Chicago, IL: University of Chicago Press.

diSessa, A. A. (1993). Towards an epistemology of physics. *Cognition and Instruction, 10*(2/3), 105–225.

diSessa, A. A. (2008). A bird's-eye view of the 'pieces' vs. 'coherence' controversy (from the 'pieces' side of the fence). In S. Vosniadou (Ed.), *International handbook of research on conceptual change* (pp. 35–60). New York, NY: Routledge.

Driver, R. (1983). *The pupil as scientist?* Milton Keynes, England: Open University Press.

Duit, R. (2009). *Bibliography: Students' and teachers' conceptions and science education*. Kiel: Leibniz Institute for Science and Mathematics Education. Retrieved from www.ipn.uni-kiel.de/aktuell/stcse/stcse.html

Gentner, D., & Stevens, A. L. (Eds.). (1983). *Mental models*. Hillsdale, NJ: Lawrence Erlbaum Associates.

Gilbert, J. K. (2005). Visualization: A metacognitive skill in science and science education. In J. K. Gilbert (Ed.), *Visualization in science education* (pp. 9–27). Dordrecht: Kluwer Academic.

Gilbert, J. K., Bulte, A. M. W., & Pilot, A. (2010). Concept development and transfer in context-based science education. *International Journal of Science Education, 33*(6), 817–837. doi: 10.1080/09500693.2010.493185

Gilbert, J. K., & Watts, D. M. (1983). Concepts, misconceptions and alternative conceptions: Changing perspectives in science education. *Studies in Science Education, 10*(1), 61–98.

Hammer, D., & Elby, A. (2003). Tapping epistemological resources for learning physics. *Journal of the Learning Sciences, 12*(1), 53–90.

Helldén, G. (2005). Exploring understandings and responses to science: A program of longitudinal studies. *Research in Science Education, 35*(1), 99–122. doi: 10.1007/s11165-004-3435-0

Hrepic, Z., Zollman, D. A., & Rebello, N. S. (2010). Identifying students' mental models of sound propagation: The role of conceptual blending in understanding conceptual change. *Physical Review Special Topics—Physics Education Research, 6*(2), 020114.

Johnson-Laird, P. N. (1983). *Mental models: Towards a cognitive science of language, inference and consciousness*. Cambridge: Cambridge University Press.

Keil, F. C. (2010). The feasibility of folk science. *Cognitive Science, 34*(5), 826–862. doi: 10.1111/j.1551-6709.2010.01108.x

Key Stage 3 National Strategy. (2002). *Misconceptions in Key Stage 3 science*. London: Department for Education and Skills.

Laudan, L. (1990). *Science and relativism: Some key controversies in the philosophy of science*. Chicago, IL: University of Chicago Press.

Lelliott, A. (2013). Understanding gravity: The role of a school visit to a science centre. *International Journal of Science Education, Part B*, 1–18. doi: 10.1080/21548455.2013.818260

Lin, T.-J., Deng, F., Chai, C. S., & Tsai, C.-C. (2013). High school students' scientific epistemological beliefs, motivation in learning science, and their relationships: A comparative study within the Chinese culture. *International Journal of Educational Development, 33*(1), 37–47. doi: 10.1016/j.ijedudev.2012.01.007

Marulcu, I., & Barnett, M. (2013). Fifth graders' learning about simple machines through engineering design-based instruction using LEGO™ materials. *Research in Science Education, 43*(5), 1825–1850. doi: 10.1007/s11165-012-9335-9

McCain, K., & Weslake, B. (2013). Evolutionary theory and the epistemology of science. In K. Kampourakis (Ed.), *The philosophy of biology: A companion for educators* (pp. 101–119). Dordrecht: Springer.

Murphy, P., Jones, H., & Lunn, S. (2004). *The evaluation of RSC materials for schools and colleges: A report*. London: Royal Society of Chemistry.

National Academy of Sciences. (2013). Understanding the scientific enterprise: The nature of science in the next generation science standards. In *Next generation science standards: For states, by states* (pp. 96–102). Washington, DC: National Academies Press.

Petri, J., & Niedderer, H. (1998). A learning pathway in high-school level quantum atomic physics. *International Journal of Science Education, 20*(9), 1075–1088.

Polanyi, M. (1962). *Personal knowledge: Towards a post-critical philosophy* (corrected ed.). Chicago, IL: University of Chicago Press.

Pope, M. L., & Denicolo, P. (1986). Intuitive theories—a researcher's dilemma: Some practical methodological implications. *British Educational Research Journal, 12*(2), 153–166.

Redish, E. F. (2004). A theoretical framework for physics education research: Modeling student thinking. In E. F. Redish & M. Vicentini (Eds.), *Research on physics education* (pp. 1–63). Bologna/Amsterdam: Italian Physical Society/IOS Press.

Sadler, T. D., & Zeidler, D. L. (2009). Scientific literacy, PISA, and socioscientific discourse: Assessment for progressive aims of science education. *Journal of Research in Science Teaching, 46*(8), 909–921. doi: 10.1002/tea.20327

Sigelman, C. K. (2012). Age and ethnic differences in cold weather and contagion theories of colds and flu. *Health Education & Behavior, 39*(1), 67–76. doi: 10.1177/1090198111407187

Solomon, J. (1983). Learning about energy: How pupils think in two domains. *European Journal of Science Education, 5*(1), 49–59. doi: 10.1080/0140528830050105

Solomon, J. (1992). *Getting to know about energy—in school and society*. London: Falmer Press.

Taber, K. S. (1995). Development of student understanding: A case study of stability and lability in cognitive structure. *Research in Science & Technological Education, 13*(1), 87–97.

Taber, K. S. (1998). An alternative conceptual framework from chemistry education. *International Journal of Science Education, 20*(5), 597–608.

Taber, K. S. (2000). Multiple frameworks? Evidence of manifold conceptions in individual cognitive structure. *International Journal of Science Education, 22*(4), 399–417.

Taber, K. S. (2002). *Chemical misconceptions—prevention, diagnosis and cure: Theoretical background* (Vol. 1). London: Royal Society of Chemistry.

Taber, K. S. (2009). *Progressing science education: Constructing the scientific research programme into the contingent nature of learning science*. Dordrecht: Springer.

Taber, K. S. (2010). Paying lip-service to research? The adoption of a constructivist perspective to inform science teaching in the English curriculum context. *Curriculum Journal, 21*(1), 25–45.

Taber, K. S. (2013a). A common core to chemical conceptions: Learners' conceptions of chemical stability, change and bonding. In G. Tsaparlis & H. Sevian (Eds.), *Concepts of matter in science education* (pp. 391–418). Dordrecht: Springer.

Taber, K. S. (2013b). *Modelling learners and learning in science education: Developing representations of concepts, conceptual structure and conceptual change to inform teaching and research*. Dordrecht: Springer.

Taber, K. S., & Bricheno, P. A. (2009). Coordinating procedural and conceptual knowledge to make sense of word equations: Understanding the complexity of a 'simple' completion task at the learner's resolution. *International Journal of Science Education, 31*(15), 2021–2055. doi: 10.1080/09500690802326243

Taber, K. S., & García Franco, A. (2010). Learning processes in chemistry: Drawing upon cognitive resources to learn about the particulate structure of matter. *Journal of the Learning Sciences, 19*(1), 99–142.

Teichert, M. A., Tien, L. T., Anthony, S., & Rickey, D. (2008). Effects of context on students' molecular-level ideas. *International Journal of Science Education, 30*(8), 1095–1114. doi: 10.1080/09500690701355301

Thagard, P. (1992). *Conceptual revolutions*. Oxford: Princeton University Press.

Treagust, D. F., Chittleborough, G., & Mamiala, T. L. (2002). Students' understanding of the role of scientific models in learning science. *International Journal of Science Education, 24*(4), 357–368. doi: 10.1080/09500690110066485

Witzig, S., Freyermuth, S., Siegel, M., Izci, K., & Pires, J. C. (2013). Is DNA alive? A study of conceptual change through targeted instruction. *Research in Science Education, 43*(4), 1361–1375. doi: 10.1007/s11165-012-9311-4

3
ALTERNATIVE CONCEPTIONS OF LEARNING

This chapter considers the nature of learning, and summarises some key ideas and perspectives on learning. There is a good deal of research on different aspects of learning, and, although there is much that is not yet well understood, there are now some widely accepted principles that can inform lesson planning and classroom science teaching.

Introduction

There are different kinds of things we can learn. The Russian scientist Pavlov is known for having trained dogs to salivate when they heard a bell. Pavlov's dogs learnt to associate the sound of a bell with food. However, this does not mean that we think the dog has learnt to make a *conceptual* connection between food and the bell: "What's that sound? Oh yes—that's the bell that I often hear when they bring my dinner. I guess that means dinner is on its way—yummy, I'll start salivating ready to chew my food". That might be how dogs' thinking is represented anthropomorphically (that is, as though nonhuman animals think much like people, see Chapter 6) in some cartoons, but in most of the animal kingdom such deliberate, reflective thinking is not the norm. Salivation is an instinctive behavioural response to certain stimuli—the sight, and probably especially the smell—of food. But this is not mediated by conscious thought just as our blink reflex does not require us to recognise a hazard and respond (which would take much longer than the reflex response). Pavlov discovered that given that dogs will instinctively salivate in response to certain stimuli, he could train them by regularly presenting a new stimulus in tandem with the existing stimulus (ringing the bell as the food was presented) and in time the dogs would respond to the new stimulus alone as they had originally responded to the food. We might say that the dogs learnt to *associate* the bell with food, but this was a purely automatic type of learning that required no deliberate effort or studying on the part of the dogs! Yet this was certainly a type of learning.

As human beings we all normally learn to walk—something that requires quite impressive coordination of the muscular-skeletal system—and we seem to manage this through trial and error and without any academic study of the concepts that would be needed to understand how a person is able to walk. Just like Pavlov's dogs, we learn some things with little or no conscious effort or reflection.

Even in school or college science we learn skills that are primarily manipulative, rather than conceptual. Some students have a good understanding of the principles of titrations, yet are not very good at stopping a titration at the end point of the reaction, or filling a burette without pouring solution all over the laboratory bench. Others have very fine manipulative skills without being able to explain clearly why the process can enable us to, for example, deduce the oxidation state of the cation present in solution. Both aspects of the technique can be improved through learning, but the kind of learning involved in understanding conceptually how titration readings relate to oxidation states, percentage purity, or molecular masses is rather different from the kind of learning that improves skills in carrying out the practical technique. A certain level of understanding must help us know what we are doing during the manipulation (and I once observed a student carrying a filled burette across a laboratory with the tapped end held uppermost—the burette was no longer filled on reaching the destination), but generally the kind of learning involved seems quite different.

Learning of skills—manipulative skills, accurate graph plotting, clear sketching—is important in science, but is not the principal focus of this volume. Rather this book is concerned with learners' ideas and their understanding of science concepts—and how conceptual learning can be supported by taking into account their existing ways of thinking.

An Aufbau Principle of Learning

The perspective on learning informing this book is constructivist. In chemistry there is an 'aufbau' or building-up principal which is used to determine the ground state electronic configurations of atoms: so sodium is $1s^2\ 2s^2\ 2p^6\ 3s^1$ for example. The constructivist perspective on learning suggests that conceptual learning involves an aufbau or building-up process as well. Constructivism has been widely discussed in education, and in science education in particular, over many years (Matthews, 1998; Osborne, 1996; Solomon, 2000; Taber, 2006; Tobin, 1993). Unfortunately, as with so many of the terms met in the last chapter, the term *constructivism* has been used to mean rather different things by different authors. The term has also been qualified by references to personal constructivism, social constructivism, radical constructivism, psychological constructivism, and a range of other variants. There are some interesting debates in the scholarly literature about the merits of these different terms, and the ideas they reflect (Bickhard, 1998; Bodner, Klobuchar, & Geelan, 2001). These discussions and the points they raise are not needed for the purposes of the present volume, but it is only fair to point out that the take on constructivism offered here is not the only version available.

Constructivism has its roots in a number of thinkers, mostly working in areas related to psychology, during the 20th century, but became widely adopted in science education in the late 1970s and during the 1980s. There have been quite vigorous debates about the nature and merits of constructivism in science education (Matthews, 1998; Tobias & Duffy, 2009), but I think it is fair to suggest that the account offered here is not especially contentious. Indeed, many would suggest that the perspective discussed here is now so widely accepted that it is largely taken for granted in science education. That is probably true in many countries as far as researchers and teacher educators are concerned, but I am less sure this is generally the case among science teachers themselves.

The (Discredited) Xerox Model of Teaching

Some wit once proposed a definition of teaching as the transfer of information from the teacher's notes into the students' notebooks without passing through the minds of either. Like many such witticisms it can make us smile because we recognise it has tapped into a significant truth at some level. Yet research into teacher thinking before constructivist models of learning became widely influential suggested that for many teachers the process of teaching *was* seen as one of transfer or copying of information from the source (the teacher's mind, the textbook) to the learners' minds, with a focus on clarity of communication. The teacher was responsible for presenting a full, accurate, and clear account of the subject matter, and the students were responsible for being attentive and learning (which might be understood as memorising) what was taught.

Such an approach can work quite well (at least in the sense of students demonstrating recall of material) where the students concerned have been selected to be especially good at working in this way, but we would not now think of this as good teaching. *Most* students do not learn a great deal when teaching is restricted to clear authoritative expositions, and even for those that can manage to reproduce much of the presented material understanding is often limited. If we are teaching for the benefit of all our students, and we want them to understand the ideas of science—not just reproduce a few definitions and be able to use algorithms to do standard exercises—then teaching needs to engage more than just an ability to record and memorise information.

Most readers of this book will recognise that many students will only achieve limited learning through being the audience of a teacher's presentation, no matter how well sequenced and explained. Yet even today, decades after constructivist ideas have regularly been taught in teacher preparation courses, new teachers often feel that their main job is to give little lectures, and indeed curriculum documents may be stuffed full of so much content that teachers feel that teaching has to focus on 'covering' subject matter. Teachers may even sometimes feel guilty on the occasions when we can observe our class of busy students all engaged in relevant learning activities—apparently doing very well without needing our input for the moment. We may even feel an imperative to interrupt them anyway to say something 'helpful'—as that is what a teacher does. Perhaps it is just as well that with many classes this tends to be an occasional and short-lived situation!

Teaching People Is Not Like Updating Computers

Imagine someone is working with a file on a computer, and that file can be considered to represent information of some kind—perhaps the ongoing manuscript of this book. Perhaps there is a desire to transfer the information from this computer to another computer. These days this is usually a very straightforward process. The manuscript file is being prepared using a software application (called Pages) on a computer running a particular operating system (a version of Mac OS X) that relies on the computer containing a certain kind of chip. I am typing this halfway down my garden (on a rare sunny day in England!), but later on I need to go out. Before I do, I will save the file on my laptop. I will also then save a copy of the file onto a disk that is only connected to the laptop through the wireless network in the house. That disk is wired to the desktop computer in my study. Later I will be able to open up the copy of the file on my study computer, and (I hope) I will find that file contains all the information being typed into this computer. I will have transferred a virtually identical copy of the information from one computer to another.

A few years ago the process would have involved an intermediate medium, like a pen drive or a floppy disk, but the general principle would have been the same—that a high-fidelity copy of the information would have been transferred from one computer to another. Quite often we compare our minds to computers, and think that we process information in a similar way to a computer system. That is true in principle, although there are some major differences between digital electronic computers and brains that we should keep in mind. (A major one is the ability of the brain to upgrade its architecture without any external engineering input; another is the lack of what we might call 'read-only memory' in a human brain. More on that later.) It is worth considering why it is possible to transfer complex information in high fidelity between different computers.

The computer I am using to write this sentence and the computer on my study desk look superficially quite different. However they share similarities at several levels. For one thing they contain compatible processing chips, produced by a company that sells clones of the same chips in the millions. A few years ago the company that produces the computers I buy changed their choice of chip manufacturer, leading to their new computers supporting a different range of applications from previously. Updating the computer meant losing some familiar applications. Secondly, the two computers concerned are running versions of the same operating system (OS X). They are able to do this because the OS is provided centrally by the manufacturer, so that the same system can be installed on myriad machines. Thirdly, both the computers I am using to write this book have copies of the relevant application (Pages) so that files written on the laptop can be opened correctly by the desktop computer and vice versa.

Both the OS and the applications of a computer can be updated, but this is possible because the design of the computer allows the copying from external sources of enormously complex sets of instructions—so it is possible to import perfect copies of the information that will remain identical to the source code. This is important as any small errors in transferring the files are likely to prevent them functioning at all. Often 99.9% of an application download is only as much use as 0.1%—that is, none at all.

Human cognition works quite differently. In particular there appears to be a major limitation on how much new information we can keep in mind at any one time (in what is called working memory). Whether this is an unfortunate consequence of some limitation in our evolution, or simply that this was sufficient during most of human/prehuman evolution, or whether perhaps there is even a selective advantage of having such a limited working memory is not known for sure, but the limitation has been investigated and seems to be something we all share.

It seems we have evolved to base our understandings of our environment largely on models we have previously developed, with the ability to just complement that with a trickle of new information from our senses. If computers were like us, it would take millions of successive downloads to update a single software application! Unlike computers, our specifications do not make us suitable for acquiring extensive amounts of new information at a single sitting—well certainly not when packaged as a discrete unit to be assimilated in one go. Yet many traditional lectures and classroom presentations might seem to be very much of that form.

Intuitive 'Theories' of Mind and Folk Psychology Informing Teaching

If this is so, then this raises the question of why teaching was traditionally (and sometimes still is) organised in a form that seems more suitable for updating computers than teaching human beings. If we cannot transfer large amount of data in high fidelity from one person's mind to another's, then why do we all tend to behave as if we can?

There are two types of answer here. The positive answer is that if we teach according to constructivist principles then we can—at least in some circumstances—make a form of lecturing work. Some teachers are able to teach well using a good deal of teacher presentation, addressing the whole class and working through quite complex amounts of information. However even when this *looks like lecturing* it is only effective because it engages with learners' existing ideas (Millar, 1989), and that does not happen without a good deal of effort and/or teacher sensitivity to learners' thinking. I will have a lot more to say about this later in the book.

The negative answer is that, in terms used in the previous chapter, our thinking as teachers is often influenced by our own alternative conceptions. Teachers' thinking is no different in principle to learners' thinking—teachers are learners too of course, and have come to be teachers through their own learning. Teachers' thinking is subject to the same affordances and constraints as learners' thinking.

A key factor here is what is known as theory of mind (TOM). Humans acquire a TOM as children through normal developmental processes (Wellman, 2011). Indeed when this occasionally does not occur we consider the result to be a deficiency and use labels such as autism or Asperger's syndrome to describe the resulting 'conditions'. As children we come to consider that some of the regularities in our environment are like ourselves, in that we are aware of our environment and may act in it deliberately. This awareness may not originally be conceptualised in such terms, but children start to act as though mummy and daddy, and perhaps a cat, and possibly their teddy bear, can know things, and can act to bring about certain ends, whereas other regularities in their environment—their cot, their rattle, their chair, and so forth—do not have these properties. That is, children start to make an ontological distinction between active agents and passive objects.

By the time we are adults we take this TOM for granted—we talk to other people as though they are as aware of the surroundings as we are, and are capable of having similar ideas to us, and experience similar feelings as we do. We get sad or happy, or annoyed, or scared, and we read similar emotions in the words and body language of others. We get a joke, or detect an insult, and expect others to do the same. By this stage we have probably come to realise that the cat may only have access to something that's a bit like our experience of the world, and we may have sadly had to admit that teddy's apparent ability to share our joys and disappointments was more to do with what was going in in our own heads than in his. So we have refined our TOM to something that seems to work pretty well most of the time.

Yet the common development of a TOM that becomes taken for granted by us individually (so it can be considered an intuitive 'theory' in terms of the terminology discussed in the previous chapter) and then built into the shared structure of our everyday discourse with others is based on a rather limited and not technically accurate understanding of the nature of mind. In particular, the facility of memory is seen as some kind of storehouse of experiences and information (Claxton, 2005). We 'keep' things in mind, or put them 'out of' mind, or at least to the 'back of our minds' where we might later need to 'dig them out'. We 'take in' information, and some people may even be said to be able to 'soak up' information 'like a sponge'. This language is of course metaphorical—but metaphor can be very influential (see Chapter 6) which is why simile, metaphor, and analogy are major tools for teaching and learning (Haglund, 2013).

This language is largely based on spatial metaphor—the mind, or at least our memory, is considered to be a place where we can put things for safekeeping, and then later take them out when we need them. Research suggests that this is a misunderstanding of how our minds actually work. Our brains have not actually evolved to be especially good at preserving information in high fidelity, and research even suggests that it may be a mistake to think that there are parts of the cortex that store memories, and other parts which do the thinking for us. It seems that our memories are not stored away safely for future reference, but rather are treated as if drafts—like drafts of this book manuscript—to be constantly updated and modified as we work. For example, eyewitness accounts (in court cases for instance) are notoriously unreliable as memory is a reconstructive process. That is, remembering is not generally a process of finding something we have safely stored away, but rather a process of putting together what seems a feasible account from the fragments that can be accessed.

We are usually not aware of this, as the reconstruction process occurs preconsciously ('out of mind') and often an apparently complete memory appears in our consciousness. Components of what we recall that are accurate recollections may be joined seamlessly with filling out that is based on preconscious best guesses. So we have no way of knowing how much of what we think we remember is valid, and how much is imaginative patching up, drawing upon other available resources (recollections of other similar events, things we have seen in films, things we have read or been told about, etc.). We may only start to suspect our version of events when other trusted witnesses start to cast doubt on what seem reliable memories.

So our common ways of thinking about memory are a kind of alternative conception (or misconception) of how memory actually works. In a similar way, our everyday ways of talking about communication are based on a kind of folk model that assumes that we can effortlessly represent our ideas in language, and that because we commonly share 'the same' language we can readily share ideas. A little thought will remind us that actually it not always easy to put our ideas into clear language, so perhaps sharing ideas is not so straightforward. We may take it for granted that we can share ideas so that two people have the same idea, as this is what TOM might suggest: other people have minds like mine, capable of having the same kinds of ideas, so if I write my ideas here, then my readers will experience the same idea.

It *is* reasonable to assume people do have similar minds and it may seem obvious that we all experience the world in much the same way—but just how similar our mental experiences are remains an open (and perhaps unanswerable) question. I suggest that folk psychology, the way we talk and think about minds, encourages those entering teaching to underestimate the task ahead of them. We talk as though minds can store information and that ideas can be readily communicated—but it does not take very much teaching experience to realise that our very clear explanations are not always understood as intended, and that students' minds are rather imperfect devices for storing and later retrieving the information we think we are imparting to them.

A Constructivist Perspective

Put simply, the constructivist perspective rejects the notion of the learner as a computer-like device with an input channel that allows a large amount of data to be fed in, and a memory store that can keep neatly catalogued and discrete inputs for future reference. Instead the apparatus of human cognition is understood quite differently (and indeed more in keeping what research in cognitive psychology and the learning sciences suggest is really going on). Learning is seen as being iterative, interpretive, and incremental.

Learning Is Incremental

Learning is incremental in the sense of occurring piecemeal or inchmeal. As suggested previously, working memory puts severe constraints on the amount of new material we can cope with at any one time. In effect learning occurs through a series of additions of small grain size. The 'learning quanta' that students can process are quite small, and there is no queuing system (like an email inbox) that allows students to keep other incoming information on hold until there is available processing capacity. If new information arrives faster than it can be processed then much of it will be lost from the system. Most of us have experienced this ourselves—we were following the lecture or documentary or film plot till we got to a bit where we had to carefully think through what we were hearing (or were distracted by something), and then we missed what came next.

This is not to say that there are not sometimes moments of intellectual epiphany, where something suddenly becomes clear, and the pieces start to fit into place—but this is largely about reorganisation of prior learning (see Chapter 9), perhaps triggered by the addition of some key 'missing piece of the jigsaw'. In terms of learning new material, teaching that presents ideas faster than students can properly consider them will not be effective.

A lesson or lecture that is organised around a few key new ideas, illustrated with a good many detailed examples, may be effective as long as our expectations and the structuring of the material fits with this aspect of human cognition. Our aspiration should be to communicate the key ideas, and see the detail as illustrating the key points. If students go away understanding and remembering the key points they can look to learn the detail later around that framework. Our teaching should be explicit, so that it is absolutely clear to the students what are the key points they are being asked to take on board, and what is just meant as supporting material. The lecturer who taught electrochemistry on my degree course demonstrated this principle well, although perhaps not quite hitting the most appropriate tone, when he advised us of the central importance of the Nernst equation: 'If you forget the rest of this bloody rubbish, just remember this one equation.' (At least, that is how I recall the recommendation being phrased.) His point was that much of the rest of the lecture content could be deduced or inferred from an understanding of that equation.

Learning Is Interpretive

Learning is interpretive in the sense that meanings are not *directly* communicated in our words, gestures, or other representations. Meaning making always takes place in the mind of the person being communicated to. The learner has to make sense of the words, hand-waving, diagrams, models, and so on presented in teaching. This making-sense process relies upon interpretive resources that the learner has already built up through their previous experiences.

If the teacher uses a technical term the learner does not know (or sometimes even if they just pronounce it differently), there is a good chance the learner will not construct the intended meaning for that word. If the teacher uses a word that has a range of meanings then the learner may not recognise which meaning to adopt (see Chapter 6). If the correct alternative meaning is obvious from the context then this is not a problem—but of course it must be obvious from the context *as far as the learner is concerned*, not just the teacher.

If what the teacher is explaining relies upon prior knowledge then the learner can only construct the intended meaning if they have undertaken the expected prior learning (and not if they were absent, or not paying attention, or misunderstood when that material was taught). Even if the learner has the prerequisite knowledge, this does not guarantee that the learner will realise this. Having available the appropriate interpretive resources does not always equate to accessing them at the expected times. As teachers we are well advised to be as explicit as possible when we are making an argument based upon what we hope is shared existing understanding.

A key interpretive resource is language: in particular verbal language, but also shared gestures, and in science a whole range of common representational formalisms. However, students may lack key vocabulary or have idiosyncratic meanings for some words (Watts & Gilbert, 1983), or may struggle to understand complex constructions—such as sentences with many clauses. Research has shown that just as some students in a class may not have learnt what we mean by a gamete, or a buffer, or a normal force, and so fail to understand sentences with key scientific terms, others may have trouble with knowing how to understand nontechnical vocabulary (Johnstone & Selepeng, 2001).

Our language problems may be idiosyncratic. The author once had a teaching colleague who, despite being obviously intelligent and having expertise in his teaching subject, and despite being a native English speaker, had some kind of block about the term 'notwithstanding'. Unfortunately this term appeared in some particular technical material he had to use in his work, leading to him seeking counsel whenever this conjunction was met. The author also taught a student in a college chemistry class who talked about 'electron shields' in atoms. It would appear this student had misheard (or perhaps originally been mistaught) the term 'electron shells'. He continued discussing electron shields in his college work apparently oblivious to how he was using an alternative term to the teachers and other students.

Symbolic formalisms that are very familiar to the teacher may be challenging to students even if they have been taught them. This may exacerbate the issue of the limited capacity of working memory, as students may need to commit some of their available working memory 'space' to thinking about the meanings of symbol systems that are considered by the teacher to be part of the language being used to communicate new ideas.

Learning Is Iterative

Our learning is iterative in the sense that we come into this world with limited interpretive resources to make sense of our experience. What we learn is not just the 'product' of cognitive processes, but also becomes part of our resource base for making sense of further experience. Textbox 3.1 presents some examples of students' suggestions of how scientific concepts are like everyday ideas and experiences. So as we go through life, we are constantly building up our interpretive resources for making sense of the world (both in formal learning contexts, and otherwise), and those resources become more powerful, and so we become more efficient at understanding the world. We may not always understand things in optimal ways, but we certainly get good at making sense of things—at least in ways that fit our existing understanding.

There is what might be considered dialectic at work in human learning. We interpret new information in terms of the ways we have available to understand the world, but if that was the whole story learning could only involve changes in how much we know and not reflect qualitative changes in our understanding and thinking. So although we rely on existing resources to make sense of the new, new experiences can still—if usually only slowly—bring about modification of those resources. This was the point made earlier about memory being reconstructive. From an evolutionary perspective it seems what we call memory has not evolved to offer us a high-fidelity record of past experience, but rather is a means of using past experience to inform our present behaviour to better help us survive into the future.

Textbox 3.1: Similarities between scientific concepts and everyday experience.

"An ionic bond is like love because it's all about two things being joined."

"Testosterone was like an agent because they both made things happen."

"A cell is like an ant . . . small things but when they work together."

"Condensing is like death [because] it's where you change from one state to another—from living to dead, from gas to liquid."

(13–14-year-old students)

Source: ECLIPSE project website; see www.educ.cam.ac.uk/research/projects/eclipse/.

Evolution seems not to have selected primarily for accurate recall, but rather to have selected for a very effective cognitive apparatus that is able to build up models of the world around us, and to modify them through experience. However, it also seems to have given us apparatus with a strong bias towards the status quo. Our perceptual systems are extremely good at recognising things in terms of the categories and concepts we already have available, and indeed will sometimes offer us false positives (such as those embarrassing moments when we greet a friend in a public place, only to realise he or she is a stranger startled by our familiarity; or when we think we have heard our own name called out in a waiting room, and get up only to discover that a somewhat different name was called). It seems that where there is not a definite match, the system offers a best-fit option. Presumably that has been selected for; perhaps it is better to recognise something and sometimes be wrong, than not to respond at all to the indications of a potential hazard or opportunity.

If we are very good at finding a match for a stimulus with something that is already part of our model of the world, we appear to be less ready to make changes in those models on the basis of things that do not fit very well. Human cognition seems to be set up to readily force what we are experiencing into the categories already available rather than to easily change the available categories. Such changes occur, but often only slowly and when much experience does not fit well into our existing ways of thinking. It has been suggested that this is perhaps just the result of natural selection (rather than some constraint on evolution of cognition). Perhaps in the kinds of environments where much of human evolution took place new experiences that could not be adequately dealt with by existing understanding and behavioural responses were rare: perhaps individuals who were too ready to change their ways of thinking tended to fare less well than those who tended to have a largely stable understanding of the world (Sweller, 2007).

If this idea is correct it explains the limited capacity of working memory for working with new information. For there seems to be a major asymmetry in how working memory works, such that whilst it can handle very few novel items at one time, it is able to chunk familiar material such that it can work with quite complex information as long as that has already been well integrated into existing patterns of thinking.

We might think of working memory as being like a haulage firm working for the construction industry that advertises its truck as having a capacity of seven items. If you want the company to move some bricks for you, it can only manage seven bricks at a time, as that is the capacity of its truck. However they could move a prefabricated house with no problem as that can be handled as one item, and so only takes up part of a truck's capacity. In a sense working memory does not offer a 'space' so much as a set of slots to which we can assign conceptual items. It is a bit like having a limited number of ports on a computer—sometimes we can attach a chain of devices to one port. The items can be large as long as we have already secured them into robust structures. We might also think of something like enzymes. The binding site that normally binds to some complex protein substrate can be completely occupied by a much smaller inhibitor molecule that happens to have the right configuration to bind at the site.

This is important for the teacher as it means that students can sometimes deal with quite complex conceptual material provided that most of it is already familiar and well established, and we only introduce a very limited novel component at any particular time. Learning is a process of slowly building up increasingly complex understandings of the world, and effective teaching takes into account this 'aufbau' principle of building up knowledge.

In Conclusion: Key Messages for Teaching

The constructivist perspective in learning is well established and supported by a good deal of research in the learning sciences—such as cognitive psychology. There is a lot more to learn about how the brain works, and hopefully brain research will in time help us refine our ideas of learning. There are different 'versions' of constructivist thinking, and there are debates among scholars about the flavour of constructivism—personal or social for example—that can best inform teaching. Discussion of constructivism is seen as now somewhat passé among some researchers with a range of other perspectives (sociocultural, activity theory) being mooted as more likely to move the field of science education forward.

Yet in terms of important messages for teachers and curriculum planners, the key ideas behind constructivism remain of central importance when planning teaching. Learning needs to be seen as a process of knowledge construction where the learner makes sense of a limited amount of new information at any time, always relying on existing knowledge and understanding to make sense of new learning. That is, learning is incremental, interpretive, and iterative.

The present book is ground on a personal constructivist perspective informed by cognitive models of learning, but that is not to the exclusion of other perspectives. Learning is a very complex set of processes, and may need to be considered from a range of perspectives to be well understood. In the following chapters a range of perspectives will be considered that can explain different aspects of learners' ideas in science, but it is argued that in practice (given the iterative nature of learning) learner thinking is often the outcome of the interaction of several of these factors. Being aware of these different potential contributions to learner thinking can support teachers as they develop their own mental models to make sense of how learners are interpreting teaching.

References

Bickhard, M. H. (1998). Constructivism and relativism: A shoppers guide. In M. R. Matthews (Ed.), *Constructivism in science education: A philosophical examination* (pp. 99–112). Dordrecht: Kluwer Academic.

Bodner, G. M., Klobuchar, M., & Geelan, D. (2001). The many forms of constructivism. *Journal of Chemical Education*, 78, 1107.

Claxton, G. (2005). *The wayward mind: An intimate history of the unconscious.* London: Little Brown.

Haglund, J. (2013). Collaborative and self-generated analogies in science education. *Studies in Science Education, 49*(1), 35–68. doi: 10.1080/03057267.2013.801119

Johnstone, A. H., & Selepeng, D. (2001). A language problem revisited. *Chemistry Education: Research & Practice in Europe, 2*(1), 19–29.

Matthews, M. R. (Ed.). (1998). *Constructivism in science education: A philosophical examination.* Dordrecht: Kluwer Academic.

Millar, R. (1989). Constructive criticisms. *International Journal of Science Education, 11*(special issue), 587–596.

Osborne, J. F. (1996). Beyond constructivism. *Science Education, 80*(1), 53–82. doi: 10.1002/(sici)1098-237x(199601)80:1<53::aid-sce4>3.0.co;2-1

Solomon, J. (2000). The changing perspectives of constructivism: Science wars and children's creativity. In D. C. Phillips (Ed.), *Constructivism in education: Opinions and second opinions on controversial issues* (pp. 283–307). Chicago, IL: National Society for the Study of Education.

Sweller, J. (2007). Evolutionary biology and educational psychology. In J. S. Carlson & J. R. Levin (Eds.), *Educating the evolved mind: Conceptual foundations for an evolutionary educational psychology* (pp. 165–175). Charlotte, NC: Information Age.

Taber, K. S. (2006). Beyond constructivism: The progressive research programme into learning science. *Studies in Science Education, 42*, 125–184.

Tobias, S., & Duffy, T. M. (Eds.). (2009). *Constructivist instruction: Success or failure?* New York, NY: Routledge.

Tobin, K. (Ed.). (1993). *The practice of constructivism in science education.* Hillsdale, NJ: Lawrence Erlbaum Associates.

Watts, M., & Gilbert, J. K. (1983). Enigmas in school science: Students' conceptions for scientifically associated words. *Research in Science and Technological Education, 1*(2), 161–171.

Wellman, H. M. (2011). Developing a theory of mind. In U. Goswami (Ed.), *The Wiley-Blackwell handbook of childhood cognitive development* (2nd ed., pp. 258–284). Chichester, West Sussex: Wiley-Blackwell.

SECTION 2
Making Sense of Student Thinking

4
INNATENESS AND DEVELOPMENT: COGNITIVE BIASES INFLUENCING LEARNERS' IDEAS

Introduction

Is it possible that learners' ideas are sometimes so difficult to shift because they are somehow encoded in the genes? At first sight this seems a very naive question. Genetics may have a lot to do with eye colour or blood type, but it seems somewhat fanciful to suggest that, say, students may consider insects are not animals because this idea is somehow represented in their genes. It is not suggested here that specific alternative conceptions that learners hold are *directly* coded in their DNA. However, this chapter does suggest that our genetic inheritance may *bias us* to thinking in certain ways—and there is considerable research suggesting the starting points for some aspects of human cognition are innate (Abrahams & Reiss, 2012; Elman et al., 1998). Learning is an interpretive and iterative process (see the previous chapter) so even if we do not have genes for specific conceptions, any initial biases built into our cognitive systems will channel our thinking in particular directions, and may be the starting point for developing ideas that can influence the learning of canonical scientific ideas.

Are There Innate Aspects to Human Cognition?

It is not always easy to know what should be considered to be under genetic control. Human development is certainly not preprogrammed in the sense that everything is determined at the moment of conception by the set of genes we are dealt. The environment always plays an important role, so, for example, many conceptions never lead to birth even where the zygote is perfectly viable. The genes in those individuals offer potential for developing into adult humans, but the potential is never realised. Similarly, a child born with genes predisposing them to be tall, but who is seriously malnourished throughout their childhood, will not develop into a tall adult.

Our genes can be considered as resources that offer certain possibilities for development, but might better be considered to be involved (metaphorically) in 'negotiating' or 'coaching' development rather than 'controlling' it. There are several levels involved in the expression of genes, with some genes in effect turning others on and off. The human genome has the potential for us to develop with several sets of arms and legs but when that happens (leading to a rare condition called polymelia) we consider there has been some kind of error in the development process.

Human Brains

Although we are all (even 'identical' twins) unique at some level of detail, we develop in similar enough ways for it to make sense to talk of 'the' human brain. Human brains develop in particular ways, and are significantly different from the brains of crocodiles, dogs, or elephants, for example. The human central nervous system (CNS) develops differently from the CNS of other species. Dogs, for example, have a much more acute sense of smell than humans. This is not just a question of their noses, but also relates to their brain structure. Dogs develop under the influence of their genetics to form a brain that commits a substantive amount of processing to signals from its smell receptors. Some nonhuman species, including some birds and insects, are tetrachromats, meaning that they have four sets of cones in their retinas, each type 'tuned' to a different frequency band. The brains of these creatures develop to interpret colour in terms of four primary colours, rather than the three primary colours that are the basis of human vision. Bats rely on sonar to find their prey in the dark, so their brains develop to process perceptions of what—to humans—is ultrasound and use these to inform a mental model of their world. It has been suggested that because of these differences there is a sense in which a human being could never really know what it is like, for example, to experience the world as a bat (Nagel, 1974). There are many other examples of how the brains of different creatures develop in particular ways that have been selected through evolution within the niches these animals occupy.

Human brains also have particular characteristics as a result of their normal development. For example, although research suggests some variation between individuals, it seems we all develop to have a working memory (see the previous chapter) with similar limited capacity.

Seeing Faces (and Following Mother)

One example of what is commonly considered an innate bias in cognition is the ability to recognise faces. It is believed that very soon after birth human children can recognise the general features of a face (Johnson, 2005). Whether it is reasonable to consider this as something that is 'in the genes' is perhaps not a helpful question. But the common human inheritance supports the development of the nervous system such that by the time of birth infants have the necessary apparatus to spot patterns in sensory input that have the features of faces. Children so young have had limited opportunity to learn to recognise the form of a face, and so this seems to be something that can be considered innate—in the same way that newly hatched ducklings have an innate predisposition to recognise the mother duck.

Such an innate cognitive ability can be considered pretty crude. Chicks will imprint on something other than mother if she is not around and something else fits the pattern they have been primed to seek out. Readers may have seen photographs of the ethologist Konrad Lorenz being followed around by geese that had imprinted on him, as though he was their mother. To say they thought he was their mother would be to anthropomorphise (see Chapter 6), and imagine that geese conceptualise the world as we do. However, the geese followed instinctive patterns of behavior that led to them following the large moving object in their perceptual field during the crucial period after hatching. Normally this object would be the mother bird, so we can understand why this instinct might have been selected even though it will sometimes have tragic consequences for some chicks.

Research into instinctive responses of this kind suggests that they are crude. Lorenz's boots look nothing like the mother bird to our eyes, but they apparently triggered the imprinting. Another example involving birds concerns the feeding of cuckoo chicks by host parent birds (who have likely lost their own offspring due to the presence of the cuckoo chicks). The cuckolded adult birds continue to feed the chicks even when they are not only much larger than their own offspring but actually a great deal larger than the adults doing the feeding. The adult bird is not equipped with the cognitive apparatus to question this situation, but follows innate instincts to feed any object that displays a very simple pattern common to chick mouths. These types of crude effects are also found in relation to mating behaviour, with, for example, some species of fish showing inappropriate responses to proxy objects presented by scientists. These objects can look quite unlike a potential mate for a fish to us, but have particular patches of colour that trigger courtship behaviour regardless. The apparent innate ability of humans to recognise faces is equally crude, as is demonstrated by the original typed version of the emoticon: :-)

The cost of having an inbuilt predisposition to recognise faces is that the pattern recognition process relies on very crude cues, and makes us susceptible to false positives—that is, seeing faces where there are no faces to be seen. We see faces in the shrubbery (perhaps explaining the common green man folklore), faces on craters on unoccupied cosmic bodies, faces in the butter melting on toast, in rock formations, in the clouds, and so on.

Innate predispositions of this kind are difficult to ignore, even if we think we know better. I have a photograph taken at the English coast where I can clearly see the face of an old man looking down from the clouds. I know this is just my brain overinterpreting the pattern of clouds—but that does not stop me seeing the 'man' when looking at the photograph. This is a well-recognised phenomenon in cognitive science—not all our knowledge is under our deliberate conscious control (Carey, 2009). What we know at a rational, deliberate level is complemented by 'knowledge' that is represented in our brains due to innate features that we are not always aware of, and cannot consciously control.

How Do Learners' Brains Develop?

Despite decades of research, there are some controversies about how human cognition develops. As will be clear from the previous account, it is not easy to separate out what is the 'natural' course of development, and what is down to a particular environmental condition. Indeed, the interactions between genes and environment are so complex it is often unproductive to even consider this question. A young child placed on a desert island soon after birth, and somehow provided with its survival needs, including excellent nutrition and scope for exploring its environment—but no contact with other people and human culture—would not develop into a normal human adult with what we consider adult intellectual capacities, despite having normal genes. Although it would be totally unethical to confirm this with a planned experiment, there have been cases where 'feral' children have developed over extended periods with no or virtually no contact with other humans, and 'normal' development is impaired. 'Normal' human development occurs in a social and cultural context (see Chapter 7).

This makes it difficult to know what a 'natural' course of development for human cognition is, but clearly the cognitive abilities of a typical adult are qualitatively different from those of a neonate. Young children lack patterns of thought we expect to find in normal adults.

Does Cognition Develop in Stages?

Probably the most famous and influential theory of cognitive development is that due to Jean Piaget who undertook extensive observation and interrogation of children at various ages to explore their patterns of thought. Piaget proposed a stage theory of development that suggested there were four main qualitatively different stages in intellectual development that all normal children passed through in sequence (Piaget, 1970/1972).

Piaget's model is widely used, although there has also been much argument about the details of his scheme. Piaget's model was a constructivist model (see the previous chapter) in the sense that Piaget considered that at each stage the youngster interacted with the world in ways supported (and constrained) by the available cognitive apparatus, and that this provided the experience for developing the cognitive apparatus needed for the next stage. The new born child experiences the world in a very direct way in terms of what they sense and how they can act on the objects around them by pushing, pulling, sucking, and so on. Yet by observing the effects of their actions on the objects of the world they start to develop a conceptual model of the world, and how it works, and how they can interact with it. This sensori motor stage gives rise what to what Piaget termed a preoperational stage, that then supports the development of concrete operations and finally what was termed formal operational thinking.

There are many technical and popular accounts of Piaget's scheme available (for example, Bliss, 1995), and here I will concentrate on general principles that are particularly important for thinking about learners' ideas in science. Of most interest to school and college science teachers is the distinction between the stages of concrete operations and formal operations, because if we accept the distinctions made by Piaget then science relies upon formal operational thinking which only normally develops during the secondary-education years.

Young children, even when they have acquired language, exhibit evidence of thinking which can seem irrational from an adult perspective. One type of test task used by Piaget concerned aspects of conservation—to see if children recognised conserved features of the world. Some of his tasks have been criticised as open to alternative explanations (Donaldson, 1978), although others are more difficult to explain away. So children may be shown two glasses with identical volumes of the same blue liquid and agree there is the same amount of liquid in both. If they then see the liquid from one glass poured into a taller, thinner glass, younger children (in the preoperational stage) will suggest that there is more liquid in the taller glass than in the untouched glass. To an adult this cannot be so as the amount of liquid (that is, volume) is not affected by being poured into a different container—so if there was the same amount of liquid in the two samples before the operation (of transferring to a different vessel) then there must logically be the same amount of liquid in both samples afterwards.

It has been argued that sometimes children's responses to these tasks are not as strange as they may seem; perhaps the child thinks—like us—that it is obvious that the amount of liquid does not change, and so assumes that the interviewer means something else by their strange question—the height of the liquid column perhaps? However similar results are found in a range of other conservation tasks. For example, if two rows of counters (perhaps buttons, or sweets) are arranged so that they are aligned and clearly each counter has a counter corresponding to it in the other row, then the preoperational child will agree that there is the same number in both rows. However, if the counters in one row are then shifted so their spacing is greater (see Figure 4.1), so there is no longer alignment between the rows, the child will suggest there are more counters in the row that stretches over the greater distance.

Thinking at this level is clearly going to limit the kinds of conceptual science learning that will be possible. For example, a child at this preoperational level is not ready to understand that a mole of gaseous carbon dioxide contains the same number of molecules as a mole of dry ice (solid carbon dioxide).

80 Making Sense of Student Thinking

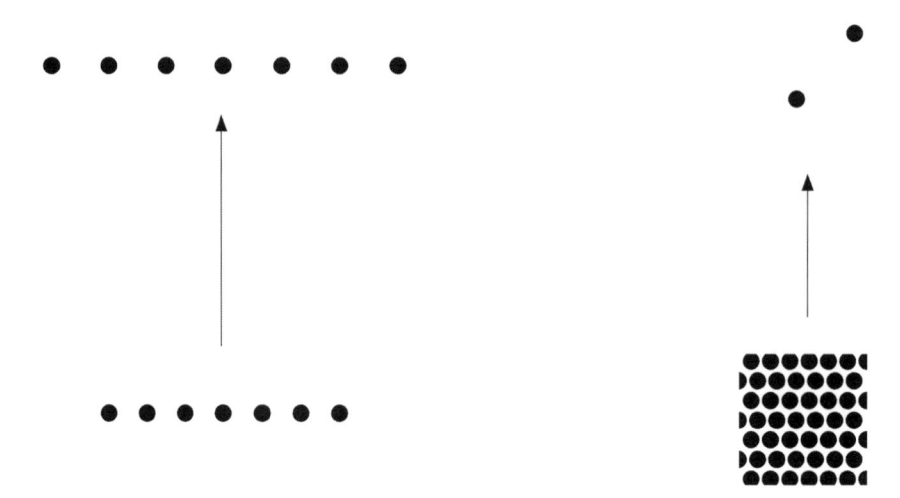

FIGURE 4.1 Young children who do not yet recognise conservation of number after a change in configuration are not ready to appreciate conservation of particles after phase change.

Young children may also make what seem illogical predictions about questions relating to mental phenomena (Goswami, 2008). So a child shown a scene where a puppet or doll hides an object, but then leaves the room before the object is moved, will expect the puppet or doll to know where the object now is. In a similar way if a child is shown an incongruous object in a familiar container, they may fail to appreciate that others will not expect it to be there. So a child might predict there will be cookies in the cookie jar, and admit to be surprised to be shown that instead there is a pencil. However, they will then suggest that if mummy (or a sibling, or a doll) is asked what is in the cookie jar, she will know that there is a pencil.

This relates to the development of a theory of mind (TOM as discussed in Chapter 3). At this point the child recognises that others have a mind such as their own, but cannot yet appreciate that others will not necessarily know the same things that they do. Indeed in another famous exercise young children shown models of mountain configurations make incorrect judgments regarding which model figures placed in various locations can see certain things, as if everyone sees from the same viewpoint as they themselves do. Children at this age are said to be egocentric as they cannot yet appreciate how anyone else could have a different perspective than themselves.

Formal Operational Thinking

In normal development children pass from preoperational thinking to concrete operational thinking at around seven years of age, so secondary-level teachers can assume their students will be able to understand such operations as the

> Textbox 4.1: A student expected mass to decrease as soil soaks up water.
>
> *Any idea how much [a pot of soil, mass 400 g, in which was planted a seed, 1 g, and which was then watered adding 49 g of water] would weigh now?*
>
> **[Four] hundred and fifty, no, because it will soak it up, wouldn't it, so just over four hundred.**
>
> *So we had four hundred grammes of soil plus pot, didn't we? . . . And we had one gramme of plant seed. . . . And forty nine grammes of water. But the water gets soaked up into the soil, does it? So when it's soaked up, you reckon it would be, what?*
>
> **Erm, four hundred and twenty.**
>
> *. . . If you poured the water in, quite quickly . . . if you could read what it said on the balance before it had a chance to soak up, do you think it would say four hundred and twenty grammes straight away?*
>
> **No, it would probably be just under, erm, four hundred and fifty.**
>
> *And it would gradually drop down to about four twenty say, would it?*
>
> **Yeah.**
>
> *Might be four hundred and fifteen? Could it be four hundred and twenty-five?*
>
> **Yeah.**
>
> **(Sophia, c. 11 years old)**
>
> Source: ECLIPSE project website; see www.educ.cam.ac.uk/research/projects/eclipse/.

conservation tasks described previously. At the concrete operational level students are able to think about concrete events, but are said to have less success in operating on a theoretical level.

Textbox 4.1 presents a secondary student apparently unable to conserve mass in a hypothetical situation—a thought experiment rather than something actually handled and observed. It has been widely observed that younger students have difficulty conserving mass in reactions involving gases as reactants or products (Andersson, 1990), but here Sophia seems unable to appreciate that mass is conserved when a plant is watered. Sophia seems to appreciate that initially the weight registered would be that of the pot, soil, seed, and water—but she seems to think that as the water soaks into the soil it will cease to be registered.

This is a conception that seems irrational to the science teacher, and we might not expect a secondary-age student to think this way—but as with some of the other examples in this book, actually asking students what they think can be surprising and quite revealing. Sophia's comments reflect student responses to a probe exploring student ideas about what happens to the mass of a solute as it dissolves (see Figure 4.2). Students were asked about three examples (sugar, salt, and copper

82 Making Sense of Student Thinking

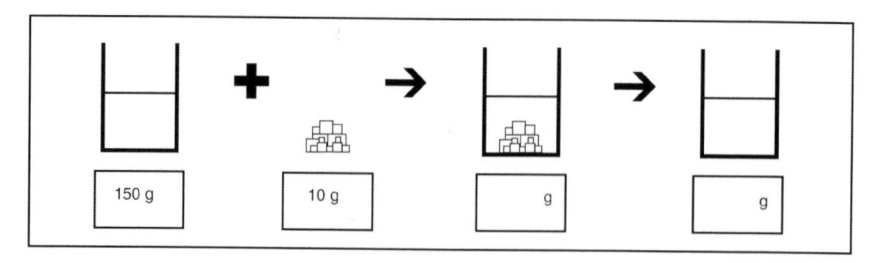

FIGURE 4.2 What will be the mass of the solution? (adapted from Taber, 2002, p. 19).

sulphate), and had to suggest the mass reading on a balance when the solute was first added to water, and then after it could no longer be seen (Taber, 2002). Only about half the students in two lower secondary classes (11–13-year-olds) were able to demonstrate they conserved mass. However, on being asked what had happened to the solute, students who did not recognise that its mass would still register as part of the solution often responded in ways that made it clear they knew the material was still present (for example, 'The sugar dissolved into the water which made it look like the sugar has disappeared').

Young people are said to normally attain formal operational thought at around 11–12 years of age, which coincides with the start of secondary education in many countries. However, this may not be an immediate transition, and for many learners it may continue over much of their secondary schooling. Formal operations is necessary for full scientific thinking as it allows us to form a mental representation of something, and then treat that representation as an object that we can mentipulate—that we can operate on as a mental object. That is, we can use concepts iteratively without needing concrete referents to support our thinking. Clearly much scientific thought is of this kind—and without this ability much that is taught in school science will challenge learners (Shayer & Adey, 1981).

Criticism of Piaget's Model

Piaget's theory remains highly influential today, many decades after his research was first published. Inevitably, and quite rightly, such influential work has been subject to extensive criticism relating to limitations of methodology and, in particular, the interpretations Piaget brought to bear (Sugarman, 1987; Sutherland, 1992).

One major area of concern is the extent to which it is sensible to conceptualise student thinking in terms of general cognitive skills that are applied across all domains of thought. There is considerable evidence that human thinking does not arise from a level playing field, but rather some areas of cognition are given a 'head start' because we have evolved innate ways of thinking (see Chapter 5). Piaget had to adjust his theory to explain why cognitive development often seemed to be uneven, and some commentators consider this to be due to an overemphasis in his model on general domain-independent cognitive skills (ways of thinking that can be applied to any topic) and a neglect of domain-specific features of human cognition.

Related to this is the way Piaget's model inevitably leads to a focus on what not to expect—what learners of a particular age would not be expected to be able to do. As educators we should be very wary of negative expectations about learners. Even if Piaget's model is fundamentally right, students develop at different rates, and an actual 11-year-old (a real individual) need not reflect the typical 11-year-old 'epistemic subject' (the nominal learner). Moreover, researchers have argued that the restrictions revealed by Piaget's data did not always imply the lack of the underlying cognitive processing skills, but might relate to limitations in working memory or attentional control (Carey, 2009).

The science teacher is unlikely to have the time to explore the extensive research into these areas, and the debate around how to interpret such research, in any detail. However as good scientists we should be aware that there is a substantial base of data supporting Piaget's general findings about the normal limitations on the kinds of cognitive work learners of different ages are able to carry out, even if we consider Piaget's theory as just that: describing one particular model of what goes on during cognitive development.

Post-formal Operations?

Recent research suggests that brain development continues 'well into early adulthood' (Oliver, 2011) and so long after the end of compulsory schooling. Although Piaget's model put formal operations at the pinnacle of development, some have argued that formal operation with its focus on logic is not sufficient for some purposes. Often we have to make decisions where logic alone is not enough to support us—there may be insufficient or inconsistent evidence, and we may have to take into account value judgments that draw on personal systems of values. One educational theorist has linked this with the acquisition of wisdom, which tends to develop through life (Sternberg, 2009).

Certainly, science curricula increasingly not only ask learners to understand abstract scientific concepts, but also to consider socioscientific issues where there are no 'right' answers as judgements have to be informed *both* by scientific knowledge and understanding and by extrascientific considerations and value judgments (Sadler, 2011): Are nuclear power plants acceptable given safety concerns? Should we reject wind farms where local people object to their appearance? Should material from aborted fetuses be used in medical research? Should people with serious inheritable conditions be counselled to adopt instead of reproducing? Should governments pressure parents to have children vaccinated against life-threatening infectious illnesses? And so on.

Teaching science for scientific literacy also involves students developing a nuanced understanding of the nature of science, where all knowledge is considered provisional (in the sense of being open to reexamination given new evidence) and students are asked to understand how scientific ideas are advocated and provisionally accepted despite the absence of absolute proof.

A number of lines of research suggest that many secondary-age students may find this challenging, and that learners generally go through a series of stages in their understanding of knowledge and evidence (Kuhn, 1999). Originally, knowledge is considered to be absolute and certain (and authorities such as teachers and textbooks may be considered infallible). Later the learners will come to appreciate that things are seldom that simple. In the humanities, learners will find teachers refer them to authors with opposing arguments, without then suggesting there is a clear preferred view. In the sciences it will be found that all experiments underdetermine theories (there is always another possible theory which would also match the data), that experiments do not ultimately refute theory as any experiment relies on auxiliary theories which can be sacrificed to save the phenomenon, and that often scientists working in particular fields are fully aware of anomalies which potentially bring into question revered theories, but which are 'quarantined' (that is, put aside for later consideration) rather than taken as refutations. Even science is not decided simply by applying straightforward logical rules.

The common student response to finding that there is no absolute standard of truth and no certain knowledge tends to be a shift towards relativism: the idea that if we cannot decide for sure that is true, then it is just a matter of personal choice or opinion, and there are no grounds for making objective judgments in such matters. Only later do learners reach a stage where they have developed a coherent set of personal values that they can apply when faced with complex issues to take up a committed stance despite the lack of clear evidence in favour of any particular position. Some researchers have suggested that this form of development often continues well in to the college years or beyond (Perry, 1970).

Should Teachers Assume Learners Cannot Cope With Abstraction and Complexity?

The potential message for teachers from research into cognitive and intellectual development is both an important and a dangerous one. At one level this kind of research can be very helpful. It suggests that it is inappropriate to expect most pre-secondary level students to be able to engage in certain types of logical thinking, and warns that even during the secondary years most learners are often only slowly mastering the ability to undertake the kind of mentipulation of concepts that is characteristic of the way scientists think about their theories and models. It suggests that even at the undergraduate level students may respond to complex situations and questions that cannot be definitely characterised and answered by a retreat into relativism; if we cannot know for sure, or cannot definitely decide what is best, we may as well consider all options as equally preferable.

Matching Demand to Level of Development

These are important findings if we do not wish to confuse, frustrate, and demoralise our students. We need to know the kinds of thinking that our students are likely to be capable of, and not present material or set up tasks that are likely to clearly require cognitive abilities learners do not yet have. However, it is also clear that this approach can encourage a defeatist attitude—making teachers too cautious. It is a common complaint of learners who are more 'gifted' in science (perhaps those further along in their intellectual development) that school science lacks real challenge for them (Taber, 2007).

Making Demands That Support Development

It is also very important to appreciate that although development may be seen as an unfolding of natural potential, it does not occur in a vacuum, but relies upon the right environmental conditions. One research project (CASE, Cognitive Acceleration through Science Education) has reported having been able to support learners' cognitive development through a curriculum of scaffolded tasks that ask children at the start of secondary school to regularly engage with activities linking to formal operational thinking (Adey & Shayer, 1994). The suggestion is that careful use of this curriculum (for example, one session per fortnight over the first few years of secondary education, at the age when most learners are ready to develop 'formal operational thinking') leads to gains at the end of the secondary years—not only in science, but also in other curriculum subjects. That is, CASE-type activities do not simply help learners to conceptualise the particular scientific contexts of the tasks (such as the principle of moments) but actually aid the development of the general thinking skills involved in higher-level abstract thinking (Adey, 1999).

A key feature of this kind of work is that it is scaffolded. That is, students are not simply set a task that is beyond their current level of development, and left to struggle, but rather the task is contextualised such that there is suitable support available to help the learner make progress (see Chapter 6). For the scaffolding to work well it has to provide sufficient structure to reduce the demand on students to a series of modest steps that they can realistically engage with, with the scaffolding gradually 'faded' as the learner is able to increasingly manage larger steps in the process unaided.

Are There Mental 'Modules'?

One longstanding debate about the nature of human cognition involves the question of whether the brain should be seen as a general purpose processing apparatus, or whether it has innate modules supporting particular domains of thought (Hirschfeld & Gelman, 1994). That is, does our genetic inheritance prepare us for particular cognitive challenges we are likely to face, or do we simply inherit a highly flexible general-purpose 'thinking machine' that can be applied to whatever we might meet in life.

As readers might suspect this is not the kind of question that has a straightforward answer (so luckily I am expecting my readers to have developed an ability for post-formal thinking which can cope with something more nuanced than an either/or answer!). A more useful question might be to ask *to what extent* the human brain will develop innate modules suitable for specific cognitive tasks, and *to what extent* it provides a general purpose thinking apparatus.

The Piagetian model discussed previously largely concerns general-purpose thinking skills. So a student who has attained the stage of formal operational thinking should be capable of demonstrating this across the curriculum. That said, this will often depend upon their familiarity with the topic area; when learners are faced with an unfamiliar topic they may not initially be able to demonstrate their highest level of thinking. Yet a student able to undertake complex mentipulation of abstract ideas in science, should also be capable of the same kind of thinking in, for example, history as well.

For many purposes this model of general cognitive abilities works well. No one is born with an innate ability to play chess, but all normally developing people will have the ability to learn to play the game at some level. Those who commit considerable time to the game over many years will come to represent an enormous amount of detailed information about chess positions in their brains—but those who never play chess do not have an 'unused' area of their brain which was reserved for chess positions!

Is There a Mental Language-Acquisition Device?

On the other hand there is evidence that we may have evolved innate predispositions for certain types of learning. Language is a core faculty for humans and it does seem that language learning is not simply a matter of the brain acting as a general-purpose thinking machine. The ability of quite young children to develop reasonably competent use of spoken language in a few years, despite being exposed to only a modest range of the vast (potentially infinite) number of possible constructions allowed in their local language, and usually having limited deliberate instruction, seems incredible unless the brain has some degree of 'pre programming' preparing it to specifically learn language. Although there are many quite different human languages, they seem to follow similar basic rules suggesting that in some sense our brains are predisposed to learn a certain kind of language—the kind that human societies have developed. Normal human brains develop to include apparatus that is predisposed to learn human language—although equally suitable for learning English or any of the other different languages human cultures adopt.

There seems to be a sensitive period in development when this 'language-acquisition device' tends to activate, after which the ability to effectively learn a language diminishes. So young children generally tend to incidentally learn their home language, much more effectively than older students learn a second language supported by qualified teachers. Language learning is perhaps the most well-known area where it is suggested that an innate specialised learning apparatus forms as part of normal development. But there are claims that other common areas of human experience have also given rise to predispositions to certain kinds of learning.

A Domain of Naive Psychology

We have already met one of these domains in terms of the theory of mind (TOM). The development of TOM is considered a normal part of human development. Children develop beyond the stage when they cannot distinguish what others might know from what they themselves know, to be able to form inferences about the feelings, thoughts, and motives of others. Indeed we come to make assumptions about what others might think about our own feelings and motives, and take those into account in our own behaviour. It is commonly thought this is supported by an innate tendency that has been selected in evolution because of the value of being able to model the minds of others.

A Domain of Folk Biology

This may lead us to ask if other areas of human experience are important enough that genes have been selected because they predispose us to particular patterns of thought. One area where this seems likely is in our interactions with other components of the biota. Throughout human evolution other animals and plants have been key to survival—the ability to find food, and avoid becoming food, and find shelter have relied upon making sense of the living world, and developing discriminations between tasty and toxic, and between the animal that is the predator and the animal that is productive to domesticate. We should not be surprised therefore that we may have an inherent capacity for natural history.

This links to our perception of what are sometimes called 'natural kinds', in that we do seem to 'naturally' recognise certain categories of organism. People generally readily adopt categories such as birds or fish which relate to categories also used in biology—although people may not readily recognise a seahorse as a fish. Similarly, many people consider mushrooms as plants, even though in scientific terms they are distinct in quite fundamental ways. For many people the term 'animals' both excludes humans, and tends to be limited to other chordates. So for many children, insects, for example, do not count as animals. Probably only biologists, science teachers, and pedants consider signs warning that no animals are allowed in premises to be incongruous in places where people are clearly welcome—such as shops and restaurants. For everyone else, it is pretty clear what an animal is in everyday discourse—and it is obvious that when we are told 'no animals', this usually means that dogs are not permitted, humans are welcome, and spiders will generally be tolerated.

The Species Problem

A predisposition to compartmentalise individual organisms as instances of discrete types fits well with the general species principle in biology, even if the particular categorisations people naturally tend to form are sometimes not aligned with the scientific categories. However, this innate ability to recognise natural kinds may actually be a major problem when teaching modern biology because of how we naturally think of different natural kinds as having their own essences.

A tiger is a tiger, and is inherently different from a lion. Children readily recognise that although a dog is a four-legged animal, a dog that has lost a leg is still a dog, albeit a three-legged dog. Children also tend to realise that although a zebra is a horse-like animal with stripes, simply painting a horse to look like a zebra does not change it into a zebra (Keil, 1992). This all seems promising, and modern biology would explain the essence of a particular kind of animal as based upon its genotype. Although individual animals (or plants or fungi, etc.) have their own individual sets of genes, members of the same species have very similar sets of genes, whereas members of closely related species—whilst still sharing a good deal of genetic similarly—show more pronounced differences.

This scientific understanding relates to an evolutionary perspective where we understand that rather different species have common ancestors if we go back far enough in time, and that the different genetic lines have separated only very slowly. Today a tiger is distinct from a lion, but once there was a common ancestor species that was neither. Zebras are distinct from horses because we are considering 'gene pools' that have separated and slowly become more distinct.

Species are not absolute, and certainly not eternal. At any moment of time we can assign the vast majority of individual organisms as instances of one species or another, but only because we are working with a 'freeze-frame' of the evolutionary movie. If we go back ten thousand years, ten million years, a hundred million years, and so forth we will increasingly find more of our current species categorisations redundant, and a greater and greater proportion of the biota failing to fit into the species 'boxes' we use today.

So in terms of making sense of the biota experienced by any one human being within a lifespan measured in decades, an innate tendency to see natural kinds as some kind of ontological absolute—as *the kinds of* living things that exist—is very helpful, giving human children a 'head start' in making sense of the world around them. Yet this predisposition to assume species are immutable can act as a major obstacle in coming to understand the modern scientific account of the origins of species—as part of an ongoing series of slow shifts in the kinds of organisms in the world. Accounts of the origins of the world which posit the special creation of different types of living things, which then can each only give rise to more of their own type (see Chapter 7), are at odds with science but may fit very well with innate tendencies we have inherited. Ironically, evolution may have equipped us to tend to reject the idea of evolution.

A Domain of Folk Mechanics

Another area of human experience that is important for our survival, where it has been suggested that we may inherit predispositions for certain kinds of thinking, is mechanics. Our lives depend upon us being able to manipulate objects in the environment, and build and use tools to extend the capability of our anatomy. Making spears and boomerangs, starting fires, building shelters, and so forth has always been a key part of human experience even if the scale and sophistication has increased in the past few thousand years.

There is certainly evidence that even very young children seem to have expectations about object permanence. Studies are undertaken with babies that suggest that they are very surprised when an object is placed behind some obstruction, and has then (due to the researcher's trickery) disappeared when the obstruction has been removed (Carey, 2009). So we may have innate expectations about the ontology of the world—we may be predisposed to perceive objects and expect them not to just disappear. Such predispositions would seem helpful as that is how the world generally is. We can appreciate the survival value in assuming that your enemy or potential lunch is still there when it disappears out of view behind a bush.

However, by the same token, we may also have predispositions about the way the world is that are unhelpful in learning the canonical scientific accounts of the world. Perhaps we have a predisposition to expect moving objects to come to a stop unless acted upon by some agency—a predisposition to develop an impetus-like conception that when an object is pushed, pulled, or thrown it is given a certain amount of motive force that is used up as it moves and limits how far it goes. A predisposition to form such a conception may well be very useful in the everyday world, but can act as an impediment to learning Newtonian mechanics where the key notion is inertia, not impetus. This idea is developed in the next chapter.

References

Abrahams, I., & Reiss, M. (2012). Evolution. In P. Jarvis & M. Watts (Eds.), *The Routledge international handbook of learning* (pp. 411–418). Abingdon: Routledge.

Adey, P. (1999). *The science of thinking, and science for thinking: A description of Cognitive Acceleration through Science Education (CASE)*. Geneva: International Bureau of Education (UNESCO).

Adey, P., & Shayer, M. (1994). *Really raising standards: Cognitive intervention and academic achievement*. London: Routledge.

Andersson, B. (1990). Pupils' conceptions of matter and its transformations (age 12–16). *Studies in Science Education, 18*, 53–85. doi: 10.1080/03057269008559981

Bliss, J. (1995). Piaget and after: The case of learning science. *Studies in Science Education, 25*, 139–172.
Carey, S. (2009). *The origin of concepts.* Oxford: Oxford University Press.
Donaldson, M. (1978). *Children's minds.* London: Fontana.
Elman, J., Bates, E. A., Johnson, M. H., Karmiloff-Smith, A., Parisi, D., & Plunkett, K. (1998). *Rethinking innateness: A connectionist perspective on development.* Cambridge, MA: MIT Press.
Goswami, U. (2008). *Cognitive development: The learning brain.* Hove, East Sussex: Psychology Press.
Hirschfeld, L., & Gelman, S. A. (Eds.). (1994). *Mapping the mind: Domain specificity in cognition and culture.* Cambridge: Cambridge University Press.
Johnson, M. H. (2005). Subcortical face processing. *Nature Reviews Neuroscience, 6*(10), 766–774.
Keil, F. C. (1992). *Concepts, kinds and cognitive development.* Cambridge, MA: MIT Press.
Kuhn, D. (1999). A developmental model of critical thinking. *Educational Researcher, 28*(2), 16–46.
Nagel, T. (1974). What is it like to be a bat? *Philosophical Review, 83*(4), 435–450.
Oliver, M. (2011). Towards an understanding of neuroscience for science educators. *Studies in Science Education, 47*(2), 211–235. doi: 10.1080/03057267.2011.604478
Perry, W. G. (1970). *Forms of intellectual and ethical development in the college years: A scheme.* New York, NY: Holt, Rinehart & Winston.
Piaget, J. (1970/1972). *The principles of genetic epistemology* (W. Mays, Trans.). London: Routledge & Kegan Paul.
Sadler, T. D. (Ed.). (2011). *Socio-scientific issues in the classroom: Teaching, learning and research* (Vol. 39). Dordrecht: Springer.
Shayer, M., & Adey, P. (1981). *Towards a science of science teaching: Cognitive development and curriculum demand.* Oxford: Heinemann Educational Books.
Sternberg, R. J. (2009). WICS: A model of positive educational leadership comprising wisdom, intelligence, and creativity synthesised. In J. C. Kauffman & E. L. Grigorenko (Eds.), *The essential Sternberg: Essays on intelligence, psychology and education* (pp. 377–431). New York, NY: Springer.
Sugarman, S. (1987). *Piaget's construction of the child's reality.* Cambridge: Cambridge University Press.
Sutherland, P. (1992). *Cognitive development today: Piaget and his critics.* London: Paul Chapman.
Taber, K. S. (2002). *Chemical misconceptions—prevention, diagnosis and cure: Classroom resources* (Vol. 2). London: Royal Society of Chemistry.
Taber, K. S. (Ed.). (2007). *Science education for gifted learners.* London: Routledge.

5
DEVELOPING INTUITIONS ABOUT THE WORLD

Introduction

In principle we can make a distinction between instinct and intuition. Instinct suggests that which is bred in, that is part of the genetic inheritance. Examples of this include chicks imprinting on their mothers, and parent birds responding to gaping chick mouths by providing food. We might think of reflexes, such as blinking when something comes too close to our eye, as being instinctive. We do not learn these behaviours from specific experience, but rather they develop 'automatically'.

Intuition is in principle something quite different—it is the outcome of learning from experiences, albeit at a preconscious level such that the knowledge we have is not open to conscious inspection and deliberate reflection. In everyday life we often use our intuition to make decisions—going with a 'gut feeling'. Such decisions cannot be justified logically as we do not have an explicit basis for making them. Despite this, we rely on intuition to support us, especially when faced with having to make quick decisions. If we consider the myriad decisions a teacher makes in a single class—constantly judging what to say, to whom; what to ask, to whom; when to intervene, and when to just observe; and so forth—it seems clear that teaching would become impossible if we had to stop and logically justify each of those decisions.

If we are making decisions in this way, but not relying on weighing up evidence, applying conceptual frameworks, and developing a logical argument, then we might wonder how our intuitions work. It is probably fair to concede we do not know for sure, but the way in which our brains are wired as neural nets provides some insight. Research with artificial neural nets, electrical circuits made of interconnected units with variable connection strengths between them (akin to the way synaptic connections can change over time), has shown that such arrangements allow a kind of tuning process. So, for example, such a system can be 'trained' to discriminate sonar reflections from submarines and shoals of fish by adjusting the network connections iteratively from some random starting point.

It seems likely that something similar is going on in our brains. The artificial neural nets are not designed on the basis of some algorithm (for example, that tells us how a sonar reflection from a sub is different to that from fish) but come to do the job by trial and error—given sufficient 'experiences' and suitable feedback on performances. If parts of our own cognition are like this then this means we acquire a form of knowledge (intuition) that cannot be formally represented as an algorithm or set of rules, but rather is the outcome of pattern recognition systems we have developed on the basis of past experience. The reason why we do not trust X may not be one specific thing like his close-set eyes, or his choice of aftershave, but rather the outcome of how our perceptions of him are filtered through a neural net that has adjusted its connectivity in the light of previous experience with people we trust or found we should not trust.

In principle then we can distinguish between instinct (which is innate) and intuition (which is based on experience); in practice it may not be so easy to know which is operating at particular times as both seem to lead to us behaving without deliberation and in ways we can only rationally justify (if at all) after the event.

F-v Thinking—Operating With an 'Intuitive Theory'?

So it was suggested in Chapter 2 that learners very commonly come to school with an existing way of thinking about force and motion. This is sometimes called F-v thinking because it associates force with the state of motion of a body (velocity), rather than with a change in the state of motion of a body (acceleration). In school and college physics the Newtonian theory is taught which uses a concept of inertia and associates force with acceleration. So in canonical physics the inertia of a body is a measure of its tendency to remain in the same state of motion (whether that is stationary or moving) and an applied force brings about a change in the state of motion (acceleration) which is greater the greater the force, but also depends upon the body's inertia. This physics works pretty well, and—despite the Newtonian framework being known (due to the work of Einstein) to have limitations—gives a pretty accurate account of this aspect of the world under most circumstances. As forces are vectors, it is always the net force that needs to be considered, and this leads to learning difficulties as often some forces are more salient than others. So children are aware of the forces they apply, but less aware of the effects of friction, air resistance, and normal reaction forces (such as the upwards force acting on an object on a table).

The way force and motion is conceived by most children reflects the pre-Newtonian idea of impetus as a kind of absorbed motive force imparted by a push but which becomes exhausted unless further forces are applied. Thus sometimes this conception is called an impetus alternative framework. The impetus idea is somewhat akin to momentum in canonical physics.

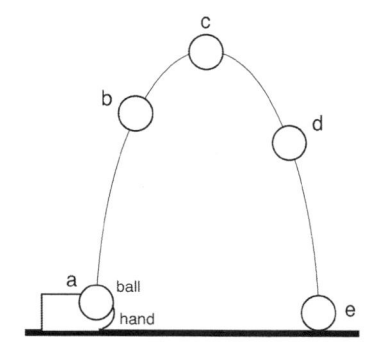

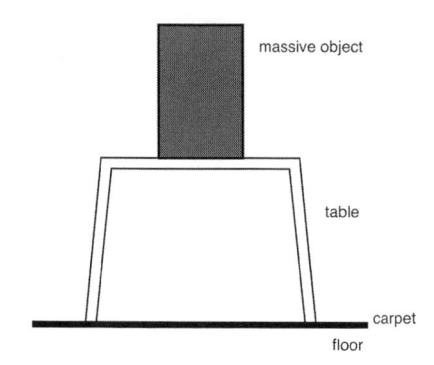

FIGURE 5.1 What forces are acting?

For example, I interviewed a 16-year-old student about his understanding of forces acting in several situations (Taber, 1997)—two of which are shown in Figure 5.1. In the case of the ball thrown in the air, Kabul thought that at positions (b) and (c) the ball would be subject to a force from the hand, but that by point (d) 'probably it has used up all its force in accelerating'. He believed that this force would be at a maximum the instant before the object was thrown, would be slightly less at (b), and less still by (c). Kabul conceded some of the force might remain by (d), but not enough to overcome gravity. The object was stationary at (e), and therefore Kabul did not think any forces were acting.

In the previous chapter it was suggested that perhaps there was a predisposition to adopt F-v thinking that is part of our genetic inheritance, as this way of thinking provides a sound-enough way of thinking about much everyday experience of moving objects. In general, inanimate objects stop moving pretty soon after any applied forces acting to make them move cease. However, this conception could also be explained in terms of the operation of a more generalised pattern recognition apparatus in our cognition—in effect, developing expectations based on abstraction from previous experiences.

This is not the only aspect of the scientific way of thinking about forces that seems counterintuitive to students. Many students fail to appreciate the need for normal forces—such as those that prevent us falling through the ground due to our weight. When asked about the massive object placed on a table (see Figure 5.1) Kabul thought that the force of gravity would act on both the object and the table. This was, according to Kabul, the only force acting on the massive object, but the table was also subjected to a force from the massive object, also acting toward the floor. So according to Kabul's analysis, neither the table nor the massive object were moving, although both were subjected only to downward forces. When he was asked why the massive object did not fall downwards Kabul replied that is was 'being supported by the table', although it would seem he did not consider *this support* as an instance of a force.

This reflects one of the p-prims (phenomenological primitives; see Chapter 2) proposed by Andrea diSessa: 'supporting'. According to diSessa (1993, p. 220) people recognise 'supporting' when what is perceived as a 'strong' or 'stable underlying object keeps [an] overlaying and touching object in place'. As the stability of the supported object is seen to be due to the underlying support, people do not recognise any need for further explanation (such as a normal force balancing the gravitational force acting).

Building Intuition From Common Patterns in Our Sensory Experience

A newborn child certainly does not have to learn to make sense of sensory experiences entirely from scratch. The neural connections that develop to allow the processing of visual information, for example, develop in highly complicated ways apparently largely as a result of the unfolding of genetic instructions. We are hardwired to be able to readily spot edges and movement in the visual field. However, it also seems that our brains are set up to recognise common patterns in sensory information, and to then in effect 'hardwire' themselves to subsequently expect and notice those patterns. This is the type of process considered to lead to the development of the implicit knowledge elements sometimes called p-prims.

An example of this effect occurs in learning a language. The human vocal apparatus can produce a wide range of sounds, and only a selection of these is used in any particular language. One of the reasons learning a foreign language is sometimes so difficult is because of the need to hear and produce sounds quite unlike those familiar from ones native language. So the sounds used in a particular language are a bit like an archipelago of islands rising above the sea, if the sea is considered to represent the range of sounds that could be used in spoken languages. Different languages offer different patterns of islands.

Now when children are born they do not know in advance which language they will hear and learn—they have no map of the sea to show them where the local islands are. That would not matter if people were precise in speech production and all members of the same language community clearly produced precisely the same sounds. In practice people have different voices and sometimes only approximate the 'right' sounds when they speak. In effect, some of the sounds produced by people are not on the islands at all, but are like swimmers or even boats that are some distance from shore. Incredibly, as the young child hears his or her local language he or she comes to recognise similarities in the sounds used, and his or her brain in effect produces a map of where the islands are—the locations of sounds most commonly used as clumps on the map of the 'sound sea'. Once the map is developed the brain no longer treats each sound heard as being like a map grid reference, but assigns it to the relevant island. Those sounds which occur offshore (so to speak) are also assigned to the closest island and considered to be located there.

This process means that the person's perception of vocal sounds changes so that he or she in effect only hears the sounds expected in their language community, even when speech production is not perfect. To shift metaphors, the effect is like having an automatic spell-checker on your email inbox. People might send you misspelt messages, and occasionally you may be sent email written in a different language to your own, but (due to the spell-checker) when you open your emails you always find everything is perfectly spelt. Of course, a spell-checker only makes best guesses, so sometimes sentences do not make sense when the wrong spelling is selected automatically, or a word not in the spell-checker's dictionary is replaced, or entire swathes of another language are rendered into a nonsense string of local words.

This effect has been demonstrated using sound synthesisers that can produce fine variations in sound. These can be set up to produce a whole sequence of sounds that gradually shift between two sounds that are used in local spoken language—say a 'p' sound and a 'b' sound. The synthesiser starts with a canonical 'p', say, and then shifts slowly to a canonical 'b' in a similar way to software that morphs between different images. However *what is perceived* is not a gradual morphing. Although an oscilloscope display will show a gradual change in the waveform being produced, the person will hear a string that sounds like p-p-p-p-p-p-p-p-p-p-p-b-b-b-b-b-b-b-b-b-b-b-b-b. The person's brain first recognises the sounds as being closest to the 'p' island, until a point when it 'decides' they are closer to the 'b' island. Of course this 'decision' is made completely preconsciously—the person is conscious of repeats of one letter that suddenly shifts to being a different letter (even though there is actually no sudden shift in the sounds, but just a very gradual variation across a spectrum between the two endpoints). We are all familiar with the person with the speech defect or the person with a strong accent who is difficult to understand, but generally our brains present to us speech as if people are producing the same canonical sounds, filtering out much of the variation due to age, gender, and so on. Figure 5.2 offers a visual analogy of this phenomenon.

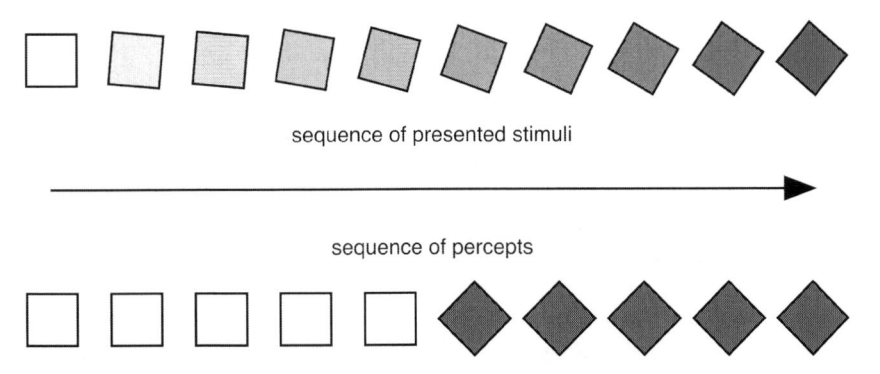

FIGURE 5.2 A visual analogy for how our brains process speech sounds: when a sequence of sounds shifting between two familiar speech sounds are presented (top row) our brains assign each to what is judged the closest recognisable speech sound (bottom row).

The Role of Implicit Knowledge in Cognition

Effects such as this warn us that perception is not simply 'sensing' the world about us. Perception is an interpretive process—our ears detect complex patterns of sound, but these are neatly categorised into familiar types. It is as if people are poor players of fretless string instruments, but our brains manage to make (nearly) everyone sound like they are playing a carefully tuned fretted instrument. Similarly, our retinas detect patches of light, but we *see* faces, people, buses, test tubes, and moons around Jupiter, organelles through a microscope, and feathers imprinted in a fossil of a reptilian wing. And some people may see ghosts, moving statues, and angels, or hear satanic messages in recordings by rock artists. What we perceive is not necessarily what there is.

The ability of our nervous systems to in effect have knowledge of the world that allows brains to expect certain types of patterns and recognise them is essential to us. We could not possibly function if we had to consciously interpret all incoming sensory information, so most of this is done automatically for us. Not only are there predispositions we already have at birth (such as recognising faces; see Chapter 4), but the human cognitive system is set up to recognise common patterns and set up automatic systems to look out for and spot these (as when listening to speech) so that we learn from common experiences to be able to automate more and more of the process of interpreting sensory information.

In general, this ability is highly adaptive and enables us to quickly deal with extremely complex information, and only to have to consciously focus on things that are 'flagged' in the system as especially important, or which cannot be fitted into the available expected patterns—we tend to notice what seems incongruent. But what we gain in speed through automation leaves us open to errors that we cannot readily spot.

Applying Implicit Knowledge in Learning Science

The implicit knowledge elements that operate to automate perception by interpreting sensory information in terms of common patterns previously experienced in the environment are general-purpose features of cognition. This means they are not especially tied to learning about science, but they are activated in science learning just as in all other aspects of life. Collectively, these implicit knowledge elements are resources for making sense of our experiences and as such they complement the concepts we have formed and which are consciously available to us. When we are consciously attempting to make sense of the world, we apply the various conceptual frameworks that we can access and can think about how these might or might not be relevant to a particular situation or problem. Our implicit knowledge does not work in this deliberate way, but rather is automatically applied *before* we become conscious of our perceptions. Unlike the conceptual frameworks we deliberately apply, we cannot inspect or access this implicit knowledge, and it is not in a form we could directly mentipulate (for example, it is not a verbal formulation or an image, or a scene we can imagine, as consciously available knowledge often is).

So when students are learning science (or any other subject) in class, they will often perceive what they are told and shown in terms of implicit knowledge elements—let's call them implicit conceptions—that they are not even aware are being activated. Sometimes the implicit conceptions that are activated are able to fit quite well with the scientific accounts presented in class—but sometimes not. One of the reasons that learners' ideas are so important to learning is because when the learner makes sense of teaching in terms of their existing understanding of the world they may assume they have understood as the teacher intended, and this is by no means always the case.

Consider the extract in Textbox 5.1 from a conversation with an 11-year-old student who was recalling what she had learnt about space in primary-school science lessons. She told me there were nine planets (which was the commonly accepted number of planets in the solar system at the time), but when she tried to remember them she included the sun and moon, and we ended up with a list of eleven bodies.

The dialogue in Textbox 5.1 concerned Sophia trying to explain the difference between a planet and a star—something she did not seem to have explicitly considered before. She knew that stars only appeared tiny because of their great

---

Textbox 5.1: A student's differentiation between planets and stars.

"Do you know what a planet is?

It's like a sphere in space, kind of. Though we don't know if animals live there or not . . . [A body found in space might be a planet] if it was round, if it was a bit lumpy, a bit—if it was quite big, not like a little star, well there's no stars that little . . .

Why do they look so little?

Because they are a long way away.

What's the difference between a star and a planet then?

A star's made up of different things, but planets—can't—cause you don't really see a planet, so you just see stars quite a lot.

So how can you see the stars and not the planets, do you think?

I think the stars, some stars, are closer, maybe, than planets."

(Sophia, c. 11 years old)

Source: ECLIPSE project website; see www.educ.cam.ac.uk/research/projects/eclipse/.

distance (something she appeared to have learnt) but then tried to explain why stars may sometimes be more visible than planets in terms of them being closer. This seemed to be an intuitive response drawing on a general and quite reasonable notion that things that are nearer tend to be easier to see. However, this contradicted what she had learnt about stars being 'a long way away'.

Applying Intuitive Rules

Stavy and Tirosh (2000) have described how people seem to develop intuitive rules that they automatically apply to certain situations, and which Stavy and Tirosh consider 'are expressions of the natural tendency of our cognitive systems to extrapolate' (p. 87). They suggest we develop intuitive rules such as 'more A-more B', 'same A-same B', and 'everything can be divided'. These rules seems to relate to commonly observed patterns that can then be assumed to apply in other situations—and so have a similar nature to the p-prims proposed by diSessa from studying the ideas of physics students. He proposed what he called 'Ohm's p-prim' (from its relevance to the example of electrical resistance) where 'an agent that is the locus of an impetus . . . acts against a resistance to produce some sort of result' (diSessa, 1993, p. 126).

Some of Stavy and Tirosh's proposed rules seem to relate to ideas of symmetry (for example, more of this gives more of that), and this may link with some strongly held ideas in chemistry. For example, later in the chapter there is an example of a common alternative conception that in an atom the nucleus produces a certain amount of force that is somehow *shared out* between different electrons (see Textbox 5.6). A very common alternative conception related to symmetry is the alternative conceptions that atoms or ions are inherently more stable when they have 'full' electron shells, regardless of the net charge this might require (see Textbox 9.1 in Chapter 9). Secondary-age students have been found to commonly rate ions such as Na^{7-} and C^{4+} (and even Cl^{11-}) as more stable than neutral atoms. Whilst there is some chemical sense in seeing species with full electron shells as more inert ('all other things being equal') as the nuclear charge is well shielded from all directions, this does not allow a highly charged ion to be stable given the repulsions between similar charges.

Another student conception that may derive from this kind of intuition about symmetry in the world is the idea that plants will respire less (or not at all) during the day. Where scientists see respiration and photosynthesis as having quite different roles, students may tend to understand them as simply alternative ways for a plant to source energy. For example, one 14-year-old explained to me that plants mostly respire at night 'because' they were photosynthesising during the day (see Textbox 5.2).

This is an interesting, and odd, idea when considered from the scientific perspective. Respiration is needed to support all the plant's activities, so if the plant is photosynthesising during the day then, all other things being equal, we might

Developing Intuitions About the World 99

> Textbox 5.2: Respiration is night work for plants.
>
> *"[Respiration is when] we use oxygen to, and glucose to release energy. . . . you are respiring all the time . . . 'cause you're making energy and you need energy to do everything.*
>
> *[Plants] mainly do it at night. 'Cause they're photosynthesising during the day, 'cause they need the light . . . They respire more at night, because—they do it then instead of in the day because they do photosynthesis during the day, but they still respire a little bit."*
>
> *(Mandy, c. 14 years old)*
>
> Source: ECLIPSE project website; see www.educ.cam.ac.uk/research/projects/eclipse/.

expect it to respire more in the day. Of course there may be other considerations: one of these might be lower temperature at night such that metabolism would run at a slower rate (which should lead to a *lower* respiration rate at night). Another 14-year-old, Ralph, talking to me about the same topic, explained how he understood the plant to be busy during the day collecting the resources it needed to make energy, which it then processed into energy during the night (see Textbox 5.3).

> Textbox 5.3: A student conception of the plant collecting resources during the day to make energy at night.
>
> *"Plants actually haven't got muscles, so they can't move by themselves so they have to, erm, absorb light through, erm, they have to do kind of passive energy things, so they have to kind of absorb things, so they absorb water from the soil, and nutrients, and they absorb sunlight, and they create energy from that . . . I'm not sure, a hundred percent, they gather the kind of resources in the day, and then at night they kind of make, I don't know, they have, they do reactions or something where, er—I'm, not a hundred percent sure . . . because there is no sun at night, so they don't need to absorb any light then so they can close off the, erm, parts of the leaf that let in light, and they can just focus on making energy . . . [during the day] they absorb, er, they just kind of the pores, the holes are open, they let the light in and the, they absorb, the plant absorbs it and uses it, and stores it, along with the water and nutrients that it keeps in the roots. It keeps doing that all day, and then it makes it into energy at night. It might make a bit of energy during the day, I'm not sure, but it will be mostly focused on gathering more nutrients in the sunlight."*
>
> *(Ralph, c. 14 years old)*
>
> Source: ECLIPSE project website; see www.educ.cam.ac.uk/research/projects/eclipse/.

Ralph's explanation invoked a kind of logic, even if it required resources like light to be somehow captured and kept for use later. Ralph did not seem to be thinking in terms of cellular respiration, and indeed if it had been possible for plants to store up sunlight in this way, it might seem to make good sense to collect resources when they were available, and to process them later. However, Mandy's response is in some ways more intriguing.

Mandy recognised, at least in the case of herself, that respiration needed to be continuous, Indeed, she also explained that the rate varied with her level of activity: more 'when you are doing exercise. Running around a lot', and less 'when you're sleeping or just sitting watching tele[vision]'. However, she did not transfer this logic to the case of plants, and she was not able to offer any explicit argument for why the plant would respire 'mainly' at night. Rather, Mandy seemed to implicitly link this to when the plant was not photosynthesising. Her intuition was that the plant would respire more when it was not able to photosynthesise—but she could not suggest any reason why this should be so, and simply implied this was an alternative activity as though the plant would share out its activities.

Things That Are 'Just Natural'

As intuitive knowledge is not open to reflective analysis, it does not take the form of, or support, argued explanations for how things are, but simply consists of expectations based on past patterns. When things happen in the world that do not fit our well-established expectations, we may be surprised, and experience an uncomfortable state sometimes called cognitive dissonance. We tend to be uneasy until we have found an explanation that satisfies us. However, when what we perceive can be readily fitted with our expectations we tend to pay little attention, and do not seek to explain things—rather simply take for granted that 'that is the way the world is'.

We might think of this as the 'natural attitude' as opposed to the scientific attitude which requires us to analyse events and look for theoretical explanations regardless of whether something fits our expectations or not. In some of my own research I asked students a series of 'why?' questions (like a rather inquisitive child testing its parent's patience). Often students would soon get to the point where they had no explicit explanation to offer, and would revert to saying that was just how things were—that it was just natural for things to be that way (Watts & Taber, 1996).

This in itself is not so surprising. Science itself cannot do any better in principle. Any explanatory chain ultimately stops with 'because that's just the way the universe seem to be'. In science, however, we seek to reduce the number of such fundamental principles to a minimum. Students however are often content to terminate explanatory chains long before reaching anything resembling a fundamental scientific principle. So whereas science seeks to develop explanatory schemes for the natural world, in everyday life people often tend to just to take for granted what is seen as natural—and then justify as just natural what they take for granted!

> Textbox 5.4: One secondary student talks about two phenomena she explains as natural: reflexes, and minerals in food.
>
> *"Well say if you're in like danger, or something's going to hurt you, you move away from it, it's kind of a natural thing. I don't know, I don't really know how, but . . ."*
>
> *"It's only very tiny amounts . . . I don't know, 'cause it's natural, so . . . it's kind of what's in it, in the food already, so you just need to, eat enough of each food . . . well it's kind of just, I don't know, it's just in it, it's already there, you don't need to put it in."*
>
> *(Mandy, c. 15 years old)*
>
> Source: ECLIPSE project website; see www.educ.cam.ac.uk/research/projects/eclipse/.

So, for example, when I interviewed Mandy when she was about 15 she had not given much thought to how reflex actions occur, or how there could be minerals in food—these were just things that were natural (see Textbox 5.4).

A General-Purpose Explanation or Schema for Action

An example of the kind of pattern that people commonly learn to abstract from experience and then expect to see in the world concerns how actions occur. This has been given the technical name of 'the experiential gestalt of causation'. A gestalt is a pattern that is perceived as a whole rather than as just an accidental coincidence of different elements. A cartoonist's caricature of a public figure will actually take the form of a limited number of lines but we recognise it as being the intended victim. We do not perceive a pattern of lines, but a drawing of a familiar person's face—indeed the production of any line drawing relies on the person viewing the image perceiving the objects represented and not just a pattern of lines. When the drawing is done well we do not look at the lines and try and work out what is represented, we immediately see a girl in a boat with a dog (or whatever). Similarly we may immediately 'see' that a snowman has a face rather than observe a carrot and some stones on a pile of snow.

The gestalt of causation is a pattern with three components: an object (sometimes called the patient) that is acted upon, and an agent that acts, and an instrument that is used to act (see Figure 5.3). Many common experiences fit such a pattern—the footballer kicks the ball with her foot, the pool player strikes the pool ball with a cue, the cat knocks the ornament with its tail, and so forth. It has been suggested that this pattern fits so many situations that it becomes part of most people's intuitions about how the word actually is. As this is *implicit* knowledge, this does not mean that students and others are labelling the roles of agent and patient, and certainly not that they think, 'Ah, another example of the experiential

102 Making Sense of Student Thinking

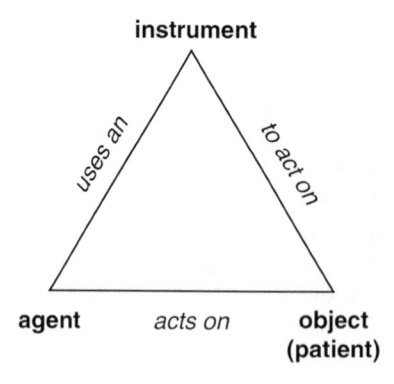

```
         instrument
            △
           ╱ ╲
     uses ╱   ╲ to
      an ╱     ╲ act
        ╱       ╲ on
       ╱─────────╲
  agent   acts on   object
                    (patient)
```

FIGURE 5.3 The 'experiential gestalt of causation'.

gestalt of causation at work'; quite the opposite—they just take for granted that the world works this way and do not question or problematise the cause of action.

The notion of an agent is something (someone) with agency. One implication of this implicit conception is a tendency to animism or anthropomorphism (discussed further in Chapter 6). That is, young children in particular tend to consider inanimate objects as being alive (animism), and perhaps even as having deliberate intentions to carry out acts in the way people do (anthropomorphism). So if the wind blows down the washing line this may be seen as the deliberate action of some agent.

Older children and adults are less likely to actually accept that the wind (for example) can act deliberately—however, the gestalt of causation has become well established and may insidiously influence our thinking without us noticing. So, for example, high school students or college students often seem quite happy to talk about atoms as being active agents that bring about effects to meet their own needs. This seems ridiculous—17-year-olds talking about the desires of individual atoms of matter—but it seems to be very common (see Chapter 6). We might feel this is just metaphoric language, as clearly teenagers do not really see atoms as living things—but once such language becomes well established it may come to be used as if a satisfactory explanation, and so negate the need for the scientific account that might be taught in high school or college.

The experiential gestalt of causation may explain why students find it difficult to adopt Newton's third law that sees forces as mutual interactions between two bodies (see Figure 5.4). So, for example, from the scientific perspective there is a force acting *between* the earth and the moon (the force attracting the moon to the earth is equal in magnitude to the force attracting the earth to the moon) or between the earth and the sun (the force attracting the earth to the sun is equal to the force attracting the sun to the earth), but students seem to implicitly consider the larger object as the agent and the smaller object as the patient that is acted upon, and so see the force as one way, or at least see the force acting on the moon as greater than that acting on the earth (for example, see Textbox 5.5).

```
           gravity
             /\
         /      \
     uses its   to act on
       /          \
      /_____\
   Sun   attracts   Earth
```

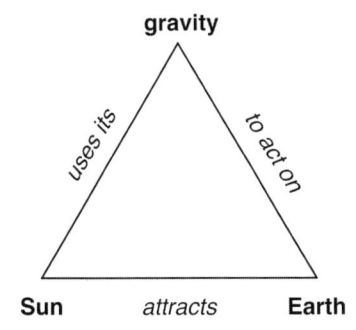

FIGURE 5.4 The orbit of the earth seen as due to a one-way interaction.

Textbox 5.5: Student perception of an asymmetrical force between the earth and the sun.

"We did all about orbits of things like the Earth orbiting the Sun . . . if there's an object with a small amount of mass then it's not going to give off as much pull as something ten times bigger as it. So . . . the Sun would pull more on the Earth."

(Bert, c. 15 years old)

Source: ECLIPSE project website; see www.educ.cam.ac.uk/research/projects/eclipse/.

This way of thinking about forces also often dominates student thinking at the much smaller scale of atoms, where students often readily recognise force acting on electrons due to the nucleus, but are less likely to consider that electrons can attract the nucleus as much, if at all. Seeing the force as being 'of' or 'from' the nucleus, rather than being *between* the nucleus and an electron can lead to students considering the force available from the nucleus being conserved and shared between electrons. That is (from this alternative perspective), a nucleus has a certain charge, which produces a certain force, which can be shared among the electrons it is attracting (see Textbox 5.6). This seems a perfectly intuitive pattern, but unfortunately is inconsistent with the scientific account (Taber, 1998).

It is possible to see the influence of this way of thinking—in terms of active agents and instruments—in many different contexts. For example in chemistry learners often see chemical reactions in terms of one reagent being active and acting upon another which is seen as the passive patient, and spontaneous processes such as dissolving may be considered to only occur where there is an 'instrument' such as stirring or heating applied (Taber & García Franco, 2010).

Indeed there a strong similarity between this gestalt, said to be acting at a preconscious level in our cognition, and the explicit representation at the

104 Making Sense of Student Thinking

> Textbox 5.6: An advanced-level chemistry student explains patterns in successive ionisation energies in terms of a conserved amount of nuclear force being distributed among electrons.
>
> *"As once each previous electron is removed there is greater attraction by the nuclear charge on the remaining electrons, so the same nuclear charge is pulling on less number of electrons so there is a higher energy needed."*
>
> *"because once the first electron is removed there is increased pull from the nucleus on the second electron as it is the only one in that shell"*
>
> *"You need more energy each time you remove an additional electron... 'cause there's the same nuclear charge pulling on less electrons so there's a greater electrostatic force ... each time."*
>
> *"They'll be attracted more, because the same positive charge pulling on less electrons, so, it's more on each electron [as] the amount of energy that that nuclear charge used in pulling that outer electron which is one plus, is like distributed across the other remaining electrons, that same energy."*
>
> *(Umar, c. 17 years old)*
>
> Source: ECLIPSE project website; see www.educ.cam.ac.uk/research/projects/eclipse/.

heart of a key area of thinking about learning from a sociocultural perspective. Activity theory (the 'first generation activity theory model'; see Figure 5.5) is an influential perspective where social situations are analysed in terms of the role of tools (such as machines, speech, gestures, music, etc.) in mediating action (Daniels, 2001). Claims about the influence of implicit knowledge structures such as the experiential gestalt of causation are often considered primarily in relation to students, but are equally relevant to the ways all of us perceive and think about experience.

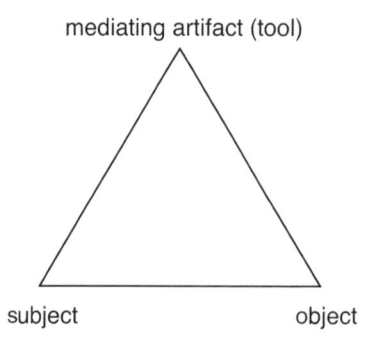

FIGURE 5.5 The basic elements of activity theory (adapted from Daniels, 2001, p. 86).

References

Daniels, H. (2001). *Vygotsky and pedagogy*. London: Routledge Falmer.
diSessa, A. A. (1993). Towards an epistemology of physics. *Cognition and Instruction, 10*(2/3), 105–225.
Stavy, R., & Tirosh, D. (2000). *How students (mis)understand science and mathematics: Intuitive rules*. New York, NY: Teachers College Press.
Taber, K. S. (1997). *Understanding chemical bonding: The development of A level students' understanding of the concept of chemical bonding* (Doctoral thesis, Guildford, University of Surrey).
Taber, K. S. (1998). The sharing-out of nuclear attraction: Or 'I can't think about physics in chemistry'. *International Journal of Science Education, 20*(8), 1001–1014.
Taber, K. S., & García Franco, A. (2010). Learning processes in chemistry: Drawing upon cognitive resources to learn about the particulate structure of matter. *Journal of the Learning Sciences, 19*(1), 99–142.
Watts, M., & Taber, K. S. (1996). An explanatory gestalt of essence: Students' conceptions of the 'natural' in physical phenomena. *International Journal of Science Education, 18*(8), 939–954.

6
THE ROLE OF LANGUAGE IN LEARNING SCIENCE

Language is central to human culture, and is widely recognised as a key tool in learning. Teaching relies heavily on the use of language (Edwards & Mercer, 1987). Analysis of science teaching shows how skilled teachers use language as a nuanced tool to persuade students of the viability of the scientific accounts (Lemke, 1990; Ogborn, Kress, Martins, & McGillicuddy, 1996). Much of this language is spoken (or written), but verbal communication is just one part of a broader range of symbolic language (gestures, formulae, etc.) used in science teaching (Kress, Jewitt, Ogborn, & Tsatsarelis, 2001).

The Development of Explicit Knowledge

The previous chapter emphasised how much of the 'knowledge' we use to support our thinking is implicit in nature. It does not comprise explicit concepts that we can reflect on and discuss, but rather is the result of the brain learning to recognise and expect familiar patterns in experience that make up our tacit models of how the world is—how it works. Such implicit knowledge is highly influential in directing student thinking but operates out of sight. The things we come to take for granted may be harder to question than those views we come to through a process of careful reflection.

However, clearly not all of our knowledge is of this implicit form—the very existence of books such as this is evidence of that. We do develop a great deal of knowledge that is explicit to us. We also have the faculty to be aware not only of our environment and our selves, but *of that awareness*. We can reflect on our knowledge, and on ourselves as knowers and learners (this is considered further in Chapter 8).

The ability to consciously form conceptions of the world that are open to reflection offers the possibility of more flexibility in our behaviour—rather than just responding to our intuitions we can pause, consider, and deliberate on a course of action. So although we do not have direct access to the operation of our implicit knowledge, we do have the ability to form a different kind of representation of (at least some of) that knowledge in a form open to conscious inspection. Some of this explicit knowledge takes the form of images (Cheng, 2011; Karmiloff-Smith, 1996), but much is linked to our use of language. We form declarative knowledge that we can represent to ourselves and others in terms of verbal propositions. This book contains many examples of verbalisations of learners' knowledge and thinking that reflects their declarative knowledge.

Sometimes when we ask students questions, their responses are verbalised reflections of the activation of their implicit knowledge. We may ask them about some matter they have had no reason to previously reflect on, and so their response—although presented in language—*reflects* their intuitive knowledge. However, we not only have the ability to form explicit representations of our implicit knowledge, but also to form permanent mental representations of what we have made explicit, that then become available for reflection, revision, and application (a theme developed in Chapter 9).

Teachers and educational researchers should then be aware that learners' answers to our questions may (a) sometimes be the in situ creation of a way to verbalise something that up to that point had not been explicit to the learner, but (b) at other times can be based on consciously accessible declarative knowledge that has already become well established as explicit verbal constructions.

Language, Culture, and Vicarious Learning

One of the main affordances of language is that as well as providing a way to describe our ideas to ourselves, it also makes it possible to represent our ideas to one another. This allows us to learn indirectly from the experiences and reflections of others.

The activation of intuitive knowledge is experienced subjectively as a feeling, as a sense of what is going on, or what to do in a particular situation. We cannot directly share our intuitive knowledge with others. However, being able to form explicit conceptualisations of the resulting intuitions that we can represent in language (verbal language, or gestural language, or symbolic imagery of some kind) allows us to represent our ideas in a form that others can interpret in terms of their own explicit conceptions that they have abstracted from their own intuitive knowledge (Taber, 2013b). This allows the development of human culture, and offers almost infinite possibilities for learning that is not directly based on one's own direct experiences. The computer I am writing this text on is connected to millions of other computers allowing me to access representations of millions of different people's own ideas about a wealth of different things. I have never seen the Egyptian pyramids, visited the Galapagos Islands, won a major sporting championship, formed compounds of noble gases, been subject to Lysenko's scientific censorship, or been separated from a hypothetical twin to go on a near-light-speed galactic cruise. Yet I can know something about all these (and myriads more) topics from my interpretations of the inscriptions made by others as public representations of their own ideas. Language makes this possible.

Forming Melded Concepts

The Soviet psychologist Lev Vygotsky (1934/1986) discussed the importance of language as a key tool to mediate the reproduction of culture. He talked about how scientific concepts (taught concepts) had to be linked to the individual's spontaneous conceptions of the world as part of the process of conceptual development. This idea has two important consequences when we think about learning in science.

Learners equipped with language are able to learn verbal information, such as, for example, when reciting poetry or learning the lines for a play. This can, however, be rote learning. By contrast, meaningful learning occurs when new learning is related to what is already known and understood. Ultimately, however, this understanding has to be ground in the conceptions of the world the learner has constructed from his or her own direct experiences—based on his or her own intuitions.

So our direct experiences of the world lead to us developing implicit knowledge, which supports the development of explicit conceptions. We then interpret new learning acquired using the symbolic tools of culture (language) through the conceptions of the world we have developed (see Figure 6.1)—and can form melded conceptions that have a dual origin: interpreting the representations of other people's ideas in terms of our own spontaneous conceptions (Taber, 2013b).

This process is iterative. We acquire new conceptions from our academic and informal learning, and these then become additional resources for interpreting other inscriptions (or verbalisations, etc.) for further new learning. Yet ultimately all our learning is ground, directly or indirectly, on the conceptions we have developed from reflecting upon intuitive knowledge deriving from our own experiences in the world. This can become a highly convoluted process, so it may not be immediately obvious how our own direct experience of the natural world enables us to learn about pyramids along the Nile or the electronic structure of xenon tetrafluoride.

It has been argued that all our concepts are ultimately based on direct experience of the world, which then act as the basis for understanding more abstract ideas analogically or metaphorically (Lakoff & Johnson, 1980). So when we claim to be 'down' on our luck or 'under' the weather we make metaphorical use of basic spatial relationships. Teachers who are 'soft' on poor behaviour or as 'hard' as nails have the same material properties—but we usually understand what is meant by such metaphorical language. (However, some learners on the autistic spectrum may have difficulty with understanding what is intended by this kind of language.)

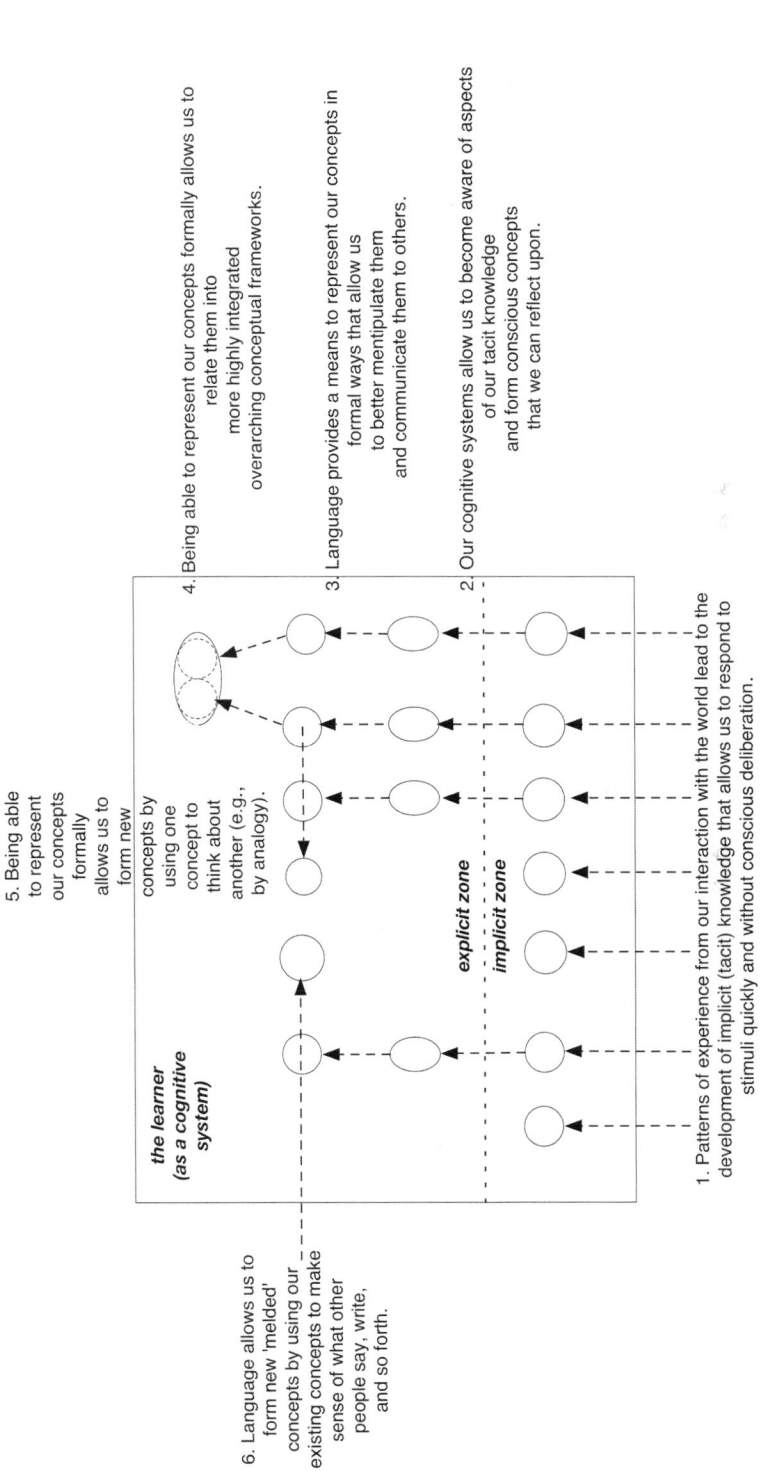

FIGURE 6.1 A schematic of human cognition: language allows us to form concepts that are not directly based on what we have experienced.

Teaching as Making the Unfamiliar Familiar

A good deal of human thinking is based on metaphor, and we inevitably use metaphor in teaching and general human communication. Teaching is a process of making the unfamiliar familiar, and as learning is an interpretive, iterative process this often relies on making comparisons with what is familiar. The teacher explains something new in terms the students can make sense of—by seeking referents in what the learners already understand. We sometimes refer to 'anchoring' new learning to existing conceptual frameworks—and that is of course itself a metaphor!

Part of the job of the teacher is to talk into existence for learners entities that they cannot directly experience (Ogborn et al., 1996), and so the science teacher is involved in a rhetorical programme of creating in learners' minds conceptions of electrons, food webs, mitochondria, oxidising agents, magnetic fields, spiral galaxies, transpiration, and the like. Through this process learners can form their own conceptions of things that are tiny, very far away, in the distant past, or completely abstract.

Part of this work can involve student practical activity or demonstrations. Microscopes can allow students to see organelles in cells (if not electrons or quarks). Magnetic fields cannot be seen, but there are simple demonstrations to help learners visualise them (such as the Perspex box containing iron filings in a viscous fluid, with a tunnel into which a magnet can be inserted).

However a good deal of this work depends upon the teacher using language of various forms to make links between the unfamiliar ideas and the conceptual resources already available to learners. This in large part involves verbal language, but increasingly it is recognised how such communication is more effective when it is multimodal—involving gesture and various kinds of graphical representations such as flow charts, diagrams, and so on (Kress et al., 2001).

Learning as Participation in a Discourse Community

The key role of language in learning is recognised in approaches to learning that emphasise the cultural and social context of learning. One particular perspective considers learning in terms of participation in the 'discourse practices' of a particular cultural group. Coming to science lessons involves being immersed in, and coming to adopt, particular ways of thinking and behaving—and in particular, communicating—that are considered appropriate in science. These would differ *in some ways* from those operating in the mathematics classroom, or the humanities classroom.

This idea links well to the account of the scientific community developed by the physicist and historian of science T.S. Kuhn. Kuhn's account of how scientific revolutions occurred, and perhaps just as significant why they did not occur more often, was highly influential and led to the wide-scale adoption of the notion of 'paradigms' and 'paradigm shifts' into discussions of academic fields and cultural trends.

Kuhn saw those working in a particular scientific field at any time as operating within what he termed the 'disciplinary matrix'. This can be considered to be a multifaceted set of norms, standards, expectations, and so forth that relate to such matters as accepted methodology, common terminology, key theoretical principles, accepted forms of evidence, interpretations, and so forth. Kuhn did not think that new scientists were formally taught all of these things, but rather that through a kind of apprenticeship the research student and early postdoctoral researcher came to adopt them. Working in a lab or research group, reading the rated journals in the field, and attending the specialist conferences contributed to a kind of learning by immersion. Over time the research student moved from what has been termed legitimate peripheral participation (Lave & Wenger, 1991) to being accepted as a fully participating member of the research community in the field.

School science, or college biology for example, is somewhat different to training within a research group in at least four important ways:

- It usually involves formal teaching according to some kind of established curriculum, whereas the novice scientist is usually working on an assigned problem, and takes on various formal and informal learning on a 'as-and-when-needed' basis to help them in their work.
- The curriculum is also broad enough to encompass the wider discipline rather than focusing on the norms in one specialist area.
- The school science group usually consists of a very broad pyramid of experience—one experienced professional (the teacher) perhaps assisted by teaching assistants or auxiliaries with limited specialist subject knowledge, and a group of 20 or more novices. By comparison, the novice scientist is nearly always working in a group context where there are several senior professionals (faculty) and various journeymen scientists (postdocs) to turn to for advice, as well as students at different stages of their research.
- In school settings, and to some extent in college settings, the science learner appears for an hour or two, and then disappears to become a modern languages learner or perhaps a social studies learner, and likely has to move through several more disciplinary contexts before returning to the community of the science classroom—perhaps some days later. The novice scientist, by contrast, tends to live, eat, and sleep his or her research—and if not, at least spends most of his or her working week immersed in the lab or research group.

So school science learning will not equate to the scientific induction available to a graduate research student. Yet this does not negate the notion of school science taking on some features of this process. It certainly makes sense to consider the science classroom as more than just a room where the teacher talks about science (as opposed to history or some other subject), and to instead see it as the context for sharing in the practices of science. Having students undertake front-line scientific research is, whilst not entirely unknown, often unrealistic. However, expecting students to adopt scientific values and scientific modes of interrogating evidence and argumentation, and to undertake genuine enquiries (where the answer is not already available in the textbook) can certainly give an authentic impression of science.

The Challenge of Border-Crossing Into the Discourses of Science

The notion of learning science as participating in a discourse community suggests that authentic science teaching should not just be teaching about science, but should seek to offer learners the chance to engage in the discourse practices of science—the way scientists use language to communicate an attitude to the world and a way of thinking about it.

By definition, such a way of talking—and of thinking—is somewhat alien to many learners in terms of the ways of talking and thinking they engage in outside of the classroom. Indeed entering the science classroom (and this would also apply to other academic disciplines) has been described as a border-crossing (Aikenhead, 1996) because for many learners it means leaving the security of comfortable and familiar ways of thinking, and entering a strange culture where things are done differently.

That is not a bad thing, as education should offer people a chance to become aware of and experience different ways of thinking and of being—young people should be introduced to the different aspects of human culture whether these be the arts, sports, humanities, or sciences. However, it may be challenging for many learners, and sometimes alien enough to be uncomfortable. In the next chapter this theme will be considered in terms of how what is presented as knowledge in the science curriculum may sometimes clash with beliefs brought from the home or local community. However, border-crossing may also operate at the more functional level of how talk is used, and that is considered here.

The 'Natural Attitude' and the Use of Language in Understanding Nature

Argumentation is central to science. The 'life-blood' (in a metaphorical sense, of course) of modern science is the journal article. A scientific paper is in effect a knowledge claim, and its supporting argument. Indeed science writing is a genre in its own right, that generally eschews a narrative account of research (telling the story of the discovery) and focuses instead on justification (Medawar, 1963/1990). To be accepted for publication a scientific paper has to make a novel claim (so that it can be considered to add incrementally to the body of scientific knowledge) and to present a clear, logical case for that claim based upon the presentation and analysis of what is judged by others to be sufficient evidence and logical argument.

Scientists and science teachers probably take this for granted, but it is a form that few people meet outside of academic writing. Whilst there is clearly a rhetorical aspect to scientific papers (Gross, 1996), this is only tolerated within the norms of the genre, and attention-grabbing, hyperbole, and so forth are not accepted. However, it has been argued that most students do not come to appreciate this readily, because they are familiar with using language rather differently in everyday discourse. Joan Solomon studied how groups of learners discussed energy (Solomon, 1992), and concluding that the key imperatives that drive such discourse are social rather than epistemological. That is, learners tend to seek to use talk to maintain social cohesion rather than using it as a tool of logical analysis and intellectual debate! Solomon considered this way of talking—and thinking—as part of 'the natural attitude'.

That is not to suggest that students are necessarily incapable of undertaking meaningful debate and argumentation in the classroom, but rather they need to be inducted into the norms of academic dialogue, as it is often alien to how they habitually use language. Students need to learn how to use dialogue in the science classroom, and to practice these skills before they can apply them effectively (for example, without having to commit much working memory space to focusing on the rules of effective dialogue). Approaches to teaching children to use language more effectively as a tool for learning have been developed, and shown to be effective (Mercer, Dawes, Wegerif, & Sams, 2004).

Creating New Entities Through Language

Part of the job of the science teacher is to help students look at the familiar (and perhaps taken-for-granted) as phenomena to be understood in scientific terms. However, equally important is the job of persuading learners to accept totally new entities that are not familiar and to consider them as 'real'—or at least as reasonable constructions of reality (Ogborn et al., 1996). (This is an important distinction, but a problematic one. We are often dealing with theoretical categories and models which technically have a conjectural status, but students may not always be ready to appreciate such a distinction, as is discussed in Chapters 1 and 4). Science teachers, however, have often come to consider genes, electrons, retroviruses, quarks, black holes, and canonical forms of the benzene molecule as real as tables and chairs (and perhaps somewhat more real than the national debt or gross domestic product).

Where teachers can show learners an amphibian or a cactus, or the reaction between potassium and water, or the way a spring extends under increasing load, it is not so straightforward to show a class the Krebs cycle, the oxygen-oxygen double bond, or the transverse oscillations of electromagnetic radiation. Such theoretical notions have to be constructed with arguments, indirect demonstrations, models, metaphors, and analogies that connect with what is already familiar. This process is often most effective when it is multimodal and draws upon multiple representations, but usually depends critically on the teacher's verbal language.

So for example, the transverse nature of electromagnetic radiation might be demonstrated using a microwave kit where the polarised signal is blocked by a filter composed of parallel metal strands—but depending how the filter is aligned with the polarisation of the radiation. (Those readers not familiar with this high school physics demonstration will probably be appreciating the limitations of verbal language alone in reading that brief description.) However, the demonstration—which involves seeing how the reading on an electrical meter connected to the microwave receiver changes with the orientation of the filter—clearly does not by itself allow the learners to form an effective mental model such that the notion of transverse waves becomes real to them. Rather the demonstration is one tactic employed as part of a more extended strategy that will probably include a range of demonstrations and activities (students using Polaroid filters in different alignments), and various diagrammatic—and perhaps graphical—as well as gestural representations. These different tactics will all be coordinated through the teacher's verbal narrative.

Language as the Hidden Persuader

Chemical educator Hans-Jürgen Schmidt wrote about how language can provide labels that act as hidden persuaders (Schmidt, 1991). One example concerned the term 'neutralisation', which is used to refer to an acid-base reaction going to completion. In chemistry we can 'neutralise' a sample of an acid with the right amount of a base, and it is common to ask students to undertake calculations involving mole ratios, solution volumes, and concentrations. We also use the term 'neutral' to describe a solution that is considered to be neither an acid nor a base.

The implication seems to be that acids and bases are some kind of chemical opposites (a notion that seems to link well with many students' intuitive notions of how the world is, cf. Chapter 5), and anything neutral is something between that has the properties of neither acid nor base. (This does not fit the scientific account, as water, despite being neutral, is able to act as either an acid or a base depending upon the conditions.) Many students learning about neutralisation in chemistry infer (reasonably) that *the product of a neutralisation reaction is neutral*—that is, that *to neutralise means to make neutral*. However this leads to an alternative conception that the product of a neutralisation process is always neutral. This is only the case when the acid and base have the same strength, not when a weak acid is neutralised by a strong alkali or vise versa. So salts formed by neutralisation may give acidic or basic solutions. When we use the term *neutral* for something which is nether acidic nor basic, *and* we label a reaction between an acid and a base that goes to completion as a *neutralisation*, we should not be too surprised if learners take their cue from how language normally works, and assume that the neutralisation process produces something neutral.

There are other examples of the labels we use in science acting in this way. An object that spins has angular momentum, and some subatomic particles also have inherent angular momentum. So scientists refer to electrons, for example, as having spin, by analogy with familiar objects with angular momentum like spinning tops. The spin of electrons (assigned values of ±½ in quantum theory) is commonly referred to as being 'spin up' or 'spin down', often indicated by arrows drawn as ↑ or ↓. Such language reinforces learners' tendency to understand subatomic particles as being just like small grains or specks of matter. Yet the image we may form of electrons as somehow spinning like tops is not appropriate—electrons do not spin in that sense (Beiser, 1973).

Even the word 'particle' suggests that atoms, molecules, and electrons are just like the matter we are familiar with, but on a much smaller scale. This is problematic in chemistry where the experienced properties of matter are considered to be emergent properties of entities which in themselves do not behave like familiar particles of matter. So molecules, ions, and atoms are not like hard billiard balls with their clear edges, but rather are fuzzy entities that fade away with no clear boundaries. Whereas at the scale of a billiard ball it is very easy to decide where the ball's surface is, an atom, molecule, or ion does not have a definite surface. When we draw atomic structures we have to find alternative ways to represent them, such as an arbitrary cut-off that shows where we would detect the electrons 'in' that atom 95% of the time. The use of the familiar word 'particle' may persuade learners they are being taught about something that is just an extremely small version of something like a marble or a grain of sand, rather than something that is quite unfamiliar from everyday experience. Teaching as 'making the unfamiliar familiar' can go wrong if learners latch on to unhelpful familiarities.

Anthropomorphic Language

Anthropomorphic language describes objects, or nonhuman organisms, as if they are like people—as if they have human emotions and can act in the world in the way humans can. We saw in Chapter 3 that as part of normal development people acquire a 'theory of mind' (TOM) that enables them to consider what other people are thinking, and sometimes we talk as though inanimate objects have minds.

Anthropomorphic Language in Popular Accounts of Science

It is not unusual for popular accounts of science written by scientists themselves, or by science journalists, to use anthropomorphic language. Developmental biologist Lewis Wolpert referred to cells in the developing embryo which 'make the decision to become a humerus' (Wolpert, 1992, p. 137) and cites Robert Boyle referring to two slabs of marble falling apart in a vacuum 'wanting that pressure of air, that had formerly held them together' and Robert Millikan talking of an oil

> **Textbox 6.1: Communicating using anthropomorphic language—why would an insect 'attack' a plant?**
>
> *"These little beasts [caterpillars] are some of the most voracious crop feeders which attack [sic] cotton, soyabean, cabbage, peppers, tomatoes and alfalfa . . ."*
>
> Source: Emsley, 2010, p. 9.

drop with an electron 'sitting on its back' (pp. 95–96). In a 'popular science' book with the title of *Taming the Atom* (itself potentially implying atoms are the kind of entities which are wild but can be tamed) the author refers to 'the intimate act of molecular mating' (von Baeyer, 1993, p. 121).

Textbox 6.1 presents a more recent example from a book arguing for the role of chemistry in a sustainable future. The choice of the term 'attack' seems to deliberately conjure up a context of a war between crops and those organisms that eat them for sustenance. Not all such organisms of course: we (human organisms) would not attack them, and indeed we seek to nurture and protect them. We will 'harvest' the crops for the good of mankind, whereas the 'beasts' engage in an 'attack'. It is reasonable to suggest we seek to *protect* the crops as this is a deliberate act; presumably a caterpillar has no deliberate intention in relation to harming a crop plant, but just an instinct to feed. At the very least this is an *anthropocentric* framing, deliberately used by a skillful writer as a rhetorical device. Arguably, from the perspective of the plant itself (were it able to adopt a perspective), being nibbled by 'beasts' and being scythed by a combine harvester might both be considered something of an attack.

Cells do not make decisions in the sense in which people make decisions, and crop-eating beasts do not set out to be pests. Such language is used metaphorically, and when metaphor is used skillfully it frames an event or situation from a particular perspective to suggest things to the reader that go beyond cold objective facts. Teachers, like writers, use such devices to build a narrative in class, and this can be a very powerful tool to engage learners. However, as teachers we do need to be aware of the way that such ways of talking may influence student thinking about the science. We have seen (in Chapter 3) that acquiring a TOM that posits purpose in others (and may be overgeneralised beyond people) is part of normal human development, and we also saw in Chapter 5 that one very common implicit knowledge element (the experiential gestalt of causation) leads us to identify 'agents' which bring about changes we perceive in the environment. We should not then be surprised when our students offer anthropomorphic explanations (such as the examples given later in the chapter) if we use metaphorical expressions in our teaching, without clearly indicating the extent to which such language is acceptable in formal writing (such as in assessments).

Teleological Language

Another common narrative form that is not usually admissible in scientific explanation is teleology. A teleological explanation is one that uses the end point as the explanation. Teleological explanations may have some validity when they concern sentient agents that are able to have a purpose in mind, which they work towards bringing about—although even then we might seek a complementary mechanical explanation that tells us how the end point was achieved. Whilst writing this text I am making a cup of coffee. One level of explanation for the appearance of this cup of coffee in the universe is my desire to drink it, but we could also seek levels of explanation related to the actions involved in making the coffee, in the physiology concerned with water regulation in the human body, the origins of flavonoids and stimulants found in plants, and so forth.

As with anthropomorphic language, there might well be a useful role for teleology in learning abstract ideas, as it can offer a narrative that makes sense to learners, and therefore acts as a starting point for learning about a topic. However we would, as with anthropomorphic language, hope that once this narrative allows the student to become familiar with the general topic area or issue concerned, they will then seek more scientific forms of explanation. A difficulty again is that human language tends to commonly be 'poetic' and rich with metaphor, and such language is both engaging and seductive. The use of teleological language in biology—for example, in considering changes brought about through natural selection (Ruse, 1986/1993)—has been the focus of academic debate (Tamir & Zohar, 1991; Zohar & Ginossar, 1998).

Argumentation and Learners' Explanations in Science

In recent years there has been a substantive emphasis in some research on the role of argumentation in science education, reflecting how argumentation is so important in science itself (Erduran, Simon, & Osborne, 2004). The scientific literature is less a set of accounts of research than a set of arguments for particular knowledge claims (Medawar, 1963/1990). That is, in writing a scientific paper, the scientist's job is not to provide a comprehensive account of some particular research, but rather to claim something that was not known before, and to present a case for that claim through an argument from evidence. This requires the organisation of material such that to the reader there is a clear line of argument—from the rationale for the research, through the choice of methodology, to the findings, and then the conclusions that can reasonably be drawn.

We might tend to associate argumentation with disputes, but all scientific work is based on developing and presenting arguments, and understanding scientific explanations involves understanding the argument being made. For example, Figure 6.2 presents the form of the 'logical chain' of an argument that advanced secondary-level students will be expected to understand, and to reproduce, in chemistry classes.

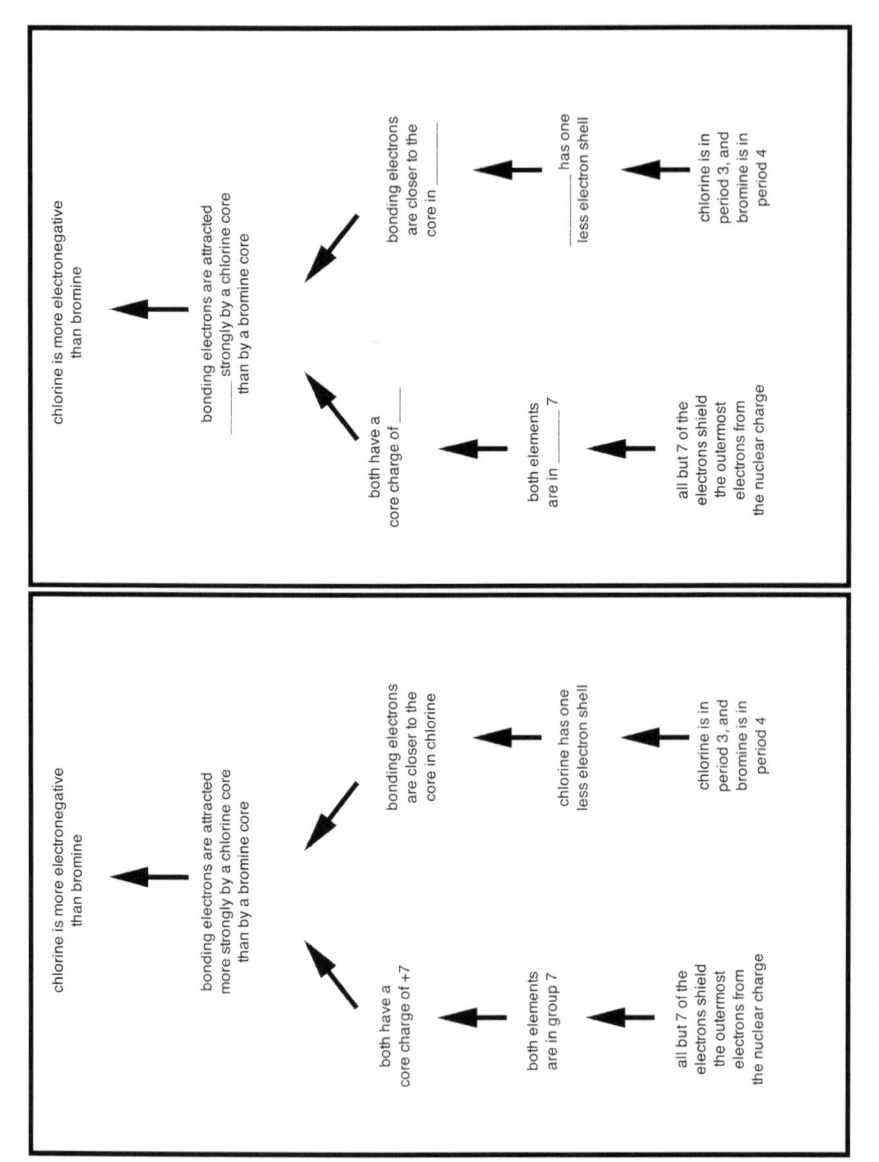

FIGURE 6.2 Scaffolding learning about high-school chemistry explanations (adapted from Taber, 2002, pp. 175, 192).

Figure 6.2 represents an explanation for a difference in electronegativity between two elements. Here a comparison is made between two elements in the same group, and so with the same core charge (left-hand branch) but in different periods so the outermost electrons are at different distances from the nucleus (right-hand branch). Advanced chemistry students will be expected to understand and produce explanations relating to two elements in the same group of the periodic table (as here), or comparing two elements in the same period. They will also be expected to work with similar kinds of explanations related to other comparisons: covalent radius, ionisation energies, acid-base behavior, boiling temperature of hydrides, and so forth. Given that in most of these situations the student could be asked about a range of examples, and often in alternative forms (the example in Figure 6.2 could have been worded in terms of bromine being *less* electronegative), this is an area where rote learning is of limited value and students need to understand the principles involved and be able to work out what factors are relevant and in what sense.

Yet, as Figure 6.2 suggests, even these apparently simple comparisons are formally quite complex, and the task may easily overload the working memory (see Chapter 3) of the novice learner. Figure 6.2 includes two versions of the argument forming the explanation; the second has some key terms removed, and is intended as the basis of a learning activity where students are 'scaffolded' in their learning to build up such explanations by being asked to work through incomplete examples. The missing terms in the right-hand version of the scheme can all be deduced from the information provided (for someone who has a basic understanding of the prerequisite concepts). This figure was included in classroom materials that can be used to diagnose students' current ability to construct explanations of this kind or to scaffold learning (Taber, 2002).

Scaffolding involves offering learners temporary structured support in completing tasks that would otherwise currently be too challenging whilst they develop skills or knowledge (this is discussed further in later chapters). The partially incomplete scheme in Figure 6.2 provides a scaffold for someone who already has the necessary understanding of the basic ideas (atomic structure, core charge, relationship of atomic structure to period table position, meaning of electronegativity, significance of core charge and atomic size) but may not yet be able to select the relevant ideas and organise them into a coherent argument. It would be useful as a scaffold if by using this (and similar examples) a learner developed the capacity to construct suitable explanations with progressively diminishing support of this type (that is, what is known as 'fading' the scaffolding).

Much of the research on argumentation in science education has drawn upon the philosopher Stephen Toulmin's analysis of argumentation (Erduran, Simon, & Osborne, 2004), which uses a particular terminology (for example, warrants, backing, qualifiers) and a particular form of representation to support the analysis of valid (or otherwise) arguments (Toulmin, 1958/2003). This formal system represents the logic of arguments, and may seem fairly straightforward to most scientists and science teachers. This kind of logical analysis of argument has in the past probably been implicit in much science teaching, but not made a focus of explicit attention. Examining learners' own explanations in science may provide us with grounds for thinking (a) that it would be valuable if students can be given tools (such as a vocabulary for talking about components of arguments) to support their developing use of, and ability to critique, formal arguments, but (b) that the formal analysis of argument is likely to be challenging for many students.

Features of Learners' Explanations

This chapter draws in part on explanations offered by 13–14-year-old students as part of a sequence of lesson activities to develop their thinking about the nature of a scientific explanation (Taber, 2007). A warm-up activity asked students (mostly working in pairs) to offer explanations for a range of phenomena. The phenomena were selected to be beyond what they would likely have already been taught about in school. This had only been intended as a way of getting students to start thinking about the nature of explanations. In the event the students seemed to really enjoy the challenge, and a wide range of sometimes quite ingenious suggestions were offered.

Simplistically, we might consider that an explanation is a response to a 'why' question—although sometimes the question may only be in the mind of the person offering the explanation. (Not all requests for explanation will include the word 'why', but I think it is reasonable to suggest that such requests *can* generally be phrased as why questions.) Table 6.1 offers four crude categories of types of response that may be given when a 'why' (or equivalent) question is asked. These can be illustrated with a hypothetical example, such as the question 'why does the earth move round the sun?' (see Table 6.2).

It is useful to look at this hypothetical example before considering some actual examples of student explanations, to illustrate both the main types of responses a request for an explanation can elicit, but also to acknowledge how judging responses is not always straightforward. The first category of response in Table 6.2 does not have the surface features of an explanation, as it does not address the question asked. The other three examples all have the general form of an explanation—they provide a response that seems to offer a reason.

TABLE 6.1 Types of responses to invitations to offer an explanation (adapted from Taber & Watts, 2000).

Surface structure (form) of explanation ('because' response to 'why' question)	Logically sound/ coherent	Scientifically correct	Status
no	not applicable	not applicable	not an explanation
yes	no	not applicable	pseudo-explanation
yes	yes	no	alternative explanation
yes	yes	yes	canonical explanation

TABLE 6.2 Examples of the main categories of response to requests for explanation.

Response to 'why does the earth move round the sun?'	Comment	Class of response
People used to think the sun went round the earth.	Does not address the question posed	Not an explanation
Because the earth is in orbit about the sun.	Has the form of an explanation, but simply rephrases information given in the question	Pseudo-explanation
Circular motion is a natural form of motion, as anything moving in a circle has angular momentum which is conserved.	Has the form of an explanation, but uses ideas contrary to accepted science	Alternative explanation
The gravitational force between the sun and earth provides the centripetal force to constantly change the earth's direction of travel.	Has the form of an explanation, and uses accepted scientific ideas	Canonical explanation

The second example has been classed as a pseudo-explanation, as usually we would not consider a simple rephrasing of a question as a genuine explanation. However, there may be occasions where this response would be acceptable—perhaps a teacher is testing the adoption of new vocabulary, perhaps the notion of orbits, and in that particular context the class teacher considers this a suitable level of explanation. Usually, however, we would not consider this a suitable explanation in response to this question. This kind of rephrasing is one common form of pseudo-explanation, and others are discussed below.

The third and fourth examples do take the form of genuine scientific explanations—they draw on general theoretical ideas to fit the explanandum (what is to be explained) within an explanatory scheme. We might expand the third argument slightly to show the logical structure:

- Anything moving in a circle has angular momentum.
- Angular momentum is conserved.
- Something moving in a circle will continue to do so (unless a force acts to change its angular momentum).
- So circular motion is a natural form of motion that needs no further explanation.
- Therefore, as the earth is moving in a circle, it will continue to do so.

This is the kind of logical explanation that the science teacher seeks from students, and which requires students to have developed 'formal operational thinking' (see Chapter 4). However, this explanation is not scientifically acceptable: it has commendable logic, but includes poor science.

The final example can also be expanded:

- The earth moves around the sun, as it is constantly accelerated by a centripetal force that changes the earth's direction of motion.
- The centripetal force provides just the amount of centripetal acceleration needed for the earth to orbit the sun.
- The centripetal force is provided by the gravitational attraction between the earth and the sun.

This response is similar to the previous explanation in terms of providing an answer that fits the specific question (about the earth and sun) into a wider theoretical scheme (about conservation of angular momentum, or about forces acting to produce centripetal acceleration). However, this latter example uses ideas that better fit canonical scientific principles.

The expansion of these two examples also illustrates the incompleteness of many explanations met in science classrooms. A simple response will often only offer an implicit sense of the full logic of the argument, and moreover will usually omit, and perhaps assume, certain aspects (cf. Figure 6.2). Even the expanded form of the canonical explanation is only a partial explanation. If this was a question asked in a science lesson, then the level and detail of the response sought could vary considerably. Does the person seeking an explanation wish for the response to include reference to the elliptical form of the earth's orbit? Should a full explanation clarify that the focus of the earth's orbit is actually the centre of mass of the sun-earth system? And so on.

A 'full' explanation would also include something about how the earth came to be orbiting in the first place—something about the formation of the solar system. We can imagine that one teacher asking 'why does the earth move round the sun?' might be looking for an explanation of why the massive earth changes its direction of motion in space (that is, seeking an answer about centripetal force and gravity), whilst another was looking to ask why the planets are moving in the first place (that is, seeking an answer about the formation of the solar system from a collapsing, rotating gas cloud).

Judging an explanation then is a contextual matter—whether an explanation is considered satisfactory can only be judged in terms of the intentions of the person seeking an explanation, what is considered can be taken for granted as not needing explanation in this particular context (for example, can we take for granted the earth is moving to start with?), and what level of detail is expected (for example, do we need to consider the noncircular nature of the orbit?).

Learners' Pseudo-Explanations

Pseudo-explanations have been described as '*because-type-responses* to *why-type-questions* which do *not* logically fit the phenomenon to be explained into a wider conceptual scheme' (Taber & Watts, 2000, p. 348). A range of types of

TABLE 6.3 Types of pseudo-arguments: students can offer a wide range of 'explanations' that do not meet the criteria of a scientific explanation (adapted from Taber & Watts, 2000).

Category of pseudo-explanation	Description
Tautology	Using what is to be explained (often rephrased) as the explanation; circular argument
Teleology	Explaining in terms of a perceived purpose (when there is no sentient agent to bring about deliberate changes)
Anthropomorphism	Explanation that assumes that nonhuman agents share human feelings, values, beliefs, and so forth
Explanation by labelling	Giving a technical term for what is to be explained as if naming it explains it
Explanation by description	Describing the thing to be explained in more detail, without offering any causes, mechanism, and so forth
Confusing cause and effect	Giving an effect of some phenomenon as its cause
Confusing correlation and causality	Taking something that occurs alongside the explanandum (perhaps due to the same underlying cause) as the cause of the explanandum
Faulty logic	Basing the argument on deductions that are not valid, and do not logically follow
Substituting knowledge justification for explanation	Offering the reasons for thinking that something is the case as being the reason for it being that way

pseudo-explanations were identified from examining advanced-level chemistry students' questions in interviews, and these are listed in Table 6.3.

Some of these types of explanations will be illustrated with examples from some of my own conversations with secondary-age science learners.

Tautology: Talking in Circles

So in Textbox 6.2, 11-year-old Morag in effect justifies her claim that everything is made of particles, in terms of her belief that everything is made of particles. Whilst her 'faith' in the idea (and her teacher's authority) is impressive, her rationale falls short of scientific justification.

A slightly less obvious example is presented in Textbox 6.3, where Ralph might be said to 'explain by synonym'. He was not sure why a transplanted stomach might reject a host body (itself an interesting reversal of the usual perspective) but offered a couple of tentative suggestions. One of these was that the body would be rejected because it was not accepted!

> Textbox 6.2: A student justifies believing in the particle model of matter.
>
> *"Particles are little, little-little-little things that make up every solid, liquid or gas . . . in a screw, you know one of them really little screws? There would be—millions and millions and millions of them . . .*
>
> Who told you that?
>
> *My science teacher.*
>
> And you believe your science teacher?
>
> *Yeah.*
>
> How does your science teacher know that, because I can't see any particles.
>
> *Well, I don't know.*
>
> But you think it is probably true?
>
> *Yeah, 'cause everything is made out of particles."*
>
> *(Morag, c. 11 years old)*
>
> Source: ECLIPSE project website; see www.educ.cam.ac.uk/research/projects/eclipse/.

> Textbox 6.3: A student's notion of a transplant rejecting a body.
>
> *"So if you didn't have the stomach, then the whole thing just wouldn't work, and the you'd probably die eventually, well would die unless you had a replacement stomach . . . if someone else who died had donated their stomach, which is a rather unusual thing to donate, it probably wouldn't work, but it might. . . . it's just how if the stomach would heal together with the body it's been placed in, or if it would reject the body, and just wouldn't work. [Why do they reject sometimes?] Erm, different blood types, or just the fact they don't accept it, I'm not quite sure."*
>
> *(Ralph, c. 14 years old)*
>
> Source: ECLIPSE project website; see www.educ.cam.ac.uk/research/projects/eclipse/.

Of course, examples such as these may be a kind of 'rhetorical tautology' where the respondent is perfectly aware they do not have a strong reason, and so offer some relevant-sounding words to fill up the space where the explanation belongs as a means to take their 'turn' in the conversation. However, there are times when tautological explanations appear to be used unintentionally. A key area here is in explaining the properties of materials in terms of particle models.

> Textbox 6.4: Particles are often considered to have the properties of the substances they make up.
>
> *"But a sponge, the particles are like, the particles are more kind of like, they're still the same, but it's just spread out more, so it can absorb more water."*
>
> *(Morag, c. 11 years old)*
>
> *"Well in the plant, there is particles . . . the particles, plants are soft, some plants are soft, and you, when you squeeze them they're, they feel soft and, erm, but the table is hard so I think that the particles would be slightly different, but they would have, because they hold this different shape, and they would, they would be . . . they would be softer as well."*
>
> *(Bill, c. 11 years old)*
>
> Source: ECLIPSE project website; see www.educ.cam.ac.uk/research/projects/eclipse/.

It is well recognised that the abstract and theoretical nature of concepts such as particle theory present a challenge to learners (see Chapter 1). The scientific perspective is that the observed properties of materials at the phenomenological level can be explained as emergent properties, due to the way the particles—which have quite different properties—behave en masse (Taber, 2012). The particle models are not only posited at a submicroscopic scale, but are conjectured entities in the domain of theoretical ideas, not actual objects that students can observe and manipulate (Taber, 2013a). A common error among learners is to explain the properties of the bulk materials in terms of particles assumed to have the properties to be explained (Brook, Briggs, & Driver, 1984), as in the examples in Textbox 6.4.

Teleology: Seeing Nature as Purposeful

Textbox 6.5 offers examples of student comments that could be considered teleological. It is possible that the explanation of the moon's lack of atmosphere was intended to be flippant (although, perhaps not), but the first example is quite typical of ways of talking about biological adaptations as being purposeful. We might say that birds have wings *to enable them* to fly, but of course the scientific account does not imply there is any sense of purpose, rather that some variations were selected as they gave those individuals slight advantages over their conspecifics. Having a proto-wing allowed individuals to survive better and reproduce because they could jump further or glide—not because there was any sense of them deliberately working towards flight. The final quote in Textbox 6.5 seems to imply that everything is here for a purpose—even when we do not know yet what it is.

> Textbox 6.5: Students' teleological explanations of natural phenomena in terms of purposes.
>
> **Apples fall from trees because** *"it is the intension [intention] of the tree that the pips have their own source of nutrients as they start to grow, and the apple is eaten or rots."*
>
> **The moon does not have an atmosphere because** *"no one lives there so there[']s no point."*
>
> *"The nucleus is kind of like the sun in our universe, it's like the thing everything orbits around, I'm not quite sure what it does though . . . Chances are [it does something], cause otherwise it wouldn't be there, but I'm not quite sure yet what it does."*
>
> *(Students, c. 14 years old)*
>
> Source: ECLIPSE project website; see www.educ.cam.ac.uk/research/projects/eclipse/.

Learners' Anthropomorphic Language

Children's language often demonstrates anthropomorphism when they explain their ideas about scientific topics. So in the example in Textbox 6.6, a 14-year-old rationalises why nonhuman parents sometimes eat their young according to a 'cruel to be kind' rationale that would require the parents to both (a) have made a deliberate decision to kill and eat their offspring, and (b) to mean well in doing so!

Anthropomorphic language is often used by learners when talking about the behaviour (a term that could be seen as anthropomorphic) of submicroscopic particles such as molecules, atoms, and electrons. Some examples of this kind of talk is provided in Textbox 6.7.

One way of describing the way Derek and Bill are talking about particles is to consider that they are using language to describe something abstract and unfamiliar (the nature of matter at submicroscopic scale) in terms that make sense to them—considering that particles are behaving as self-conscious agents that like to spread out and get their

> Textbox 6.6: Cruel to be kind? A student makes sense of infanticide as an act of compassion.
>
> **Some animals sometimes eat their own young because** *"they feel thretand [threatened] or hungry and feel that there [their] young are not capable of handaling [handling] the style of life and don't want to make them suffer."*
>
> *(Student, c. 14 years old)*
>
> Source: ECLIPSE project website; see www.educ.cam.ac.uk/research/projects/eclipse/.

> Textbox 6.7: Two lower-secondary-age students describe the behaviour of gas particles in anthropomorphic terms.
>
> "... you get a gas, which the particles can move a lot more than solid and liquid, they can move wherever they like ... As far away from each other as possible ... 'cause they like to have a lot of space, so they can expand ... they like be as well away from each other as possible."
>
> (Derek, c. 11 years old)
>
> "Gases, they try and fill whole room, they don't, like liquids, they stay at the bottom of the container, but gases go fill, go everywhere and fill, try and fill the whole thing ... It tries to get out of everywhere, so if you put it in the bottle, it would be trying to get out ... liquids the particles move quite a lot because ... they have energy to move, so they try and move away, but their particles are quite close together ... The gases, their particles try to stay as far away from each other as possible ... because they are trying to spread out into the whole room ... they're far apart and they try and expand."
>
> (Bill, c. 11 years old)
>
> Source: ECLIPSE project website; see www.educ.cam.ac.uk/research/projects/eclipse/.

own space. Given that learning involves making sense of the unfamiliar, and people can only make sense of something new in terms of things that they are already familiar with, it seems these kinds of narratives, molecular 'just-so' stories, could have a useful function in helping learners come to make sense of abstract ideas in science.

However, there is clearly a significant and important difference between the kind of narrative reflected in Textbox 6.7 and what would be considered an acceptable scientific explanation. Such narratives may be useful staging posts in progression in learning, but will not suffice as final destinations. We might expect that the kinds of language used here will decrease as students become more familiar with the molecular world, and so adopt a more scientific way of thinking and talking through their immersion in the discourse of the scientific learning community (the science classroom). However, such language is still found with learners much later in their scientific learning career. Indeed one researcher who interviewed undergraduate chemistry majors 'noted throughout the course of the interviews and analysis that students ascribed sentience to atoms and molecules' (Nicoll, 2001, p. 715).

Textbox 6.8 gives an example of an advanced secondary student who refers to what an atom will want to do, but then is able to offer an alternative narrative based on forces. This student, Lovesh, seems to have been using language poetically here, and has little difficulty shifting to a different genre of explanation.

However, even at this level it is not always clear that students are aware that anthropomorphic language (and the explanations it supports) are not admissible in science. Some comments of one of Lovesh's classmates, Jagdish, are given in

128   Making Sense of Student Thinking

> Textbox 6.8: A student uses anthropomorphic language to talk about a sodium atom, but then offers an alternative account in terms of attraction.
>
> *"[A sodium atom] hasn't got a, a full outer electron shell, [the] outer electron shell hasn't got eight electrons in . . . It will want to donate the electron to another atom . . . Well because that outer electron is less attracted to the nucleus, it can easily be transferred, attracted by another atom."*
>
> (Lovesh, c. 17 years old)
>
> Source: ECLIPSE project website; see www.educ.cam.ac.uk/research/projects/eclipse/.

> Textbox 6.9: A student uses anthropomorphic language to talk about a sodium atom in terms of desires, feelings, and awareness.
>
> *"If [this sodium atom] was on its own and anything else was like an . . . infinite distance away, yeah, it would be [stable] because there's nothing to, interact with it, and, I mean even if it wanted to form a lower energy level, a more stable compound, it would have no means of doing it . . . If you had a, another force in contact with it, and that force could have a significant effect on it, then I think this atom would want to lose an electron and become an ion, but on its own, no, I think it's just happy on its own . . . At the moment because it's on its own, I don't think it knows that it wants to form a compound, but if there was another chlorine atom, in, like quite near it, and the distance was small enough for the atoms to have an effect on each other, I think the sodium atom would realise that it could form a more stable configuration by giving one of the electrons to the chlorine and forming a bond, and so it would be at lower energy level . . . I think it feels [the presence of the chlorine atom]."*
>
> (Jagdish, c. 16 years old)
>
> Source: ECLIPSE project website; see www.educ.cam.ac.uk/research/projects/eclipse/.

Textbox 6.9. Jagdish's explanation relies on an atom that realises what is going on around it and knows what will make it happy. Jagdish was clearly aware of the possibility of forces acting, but unlike in Lovesh's case, her explanation depended upon the atom as a sentient being.

Worryingly, research suggests that a fair proportion of secondary-age students seriously entertain the notion that atoms and molecules are alive. One Canadian study with 16–18-year-olds suggested half the students thought atoms were alive (Griffiths & Preston, 1992). There seems to be a link with being alive, and having inherent motion. Perhaps the 'experiential gestalt of causation' (see Chapter 5,

Figure 5.3) is at work here; where no external agent seems to be the cause of motion, then it may be assumed that there is a sentience at work bringing about movement through willpower.

Limited Explanations

Knowing the name for something is clearly not the same as understanding it. However, student 'explanations' sometimes amount to little more than providing a different label for the phenomenon they are asked to consider. See, for example, the 'explanations' in Textbox 6.10. We might say that we classify glass as transparent because light passes through it, but *not* that the reason glass is transparent is because light passes through it.

Textbox 6.11 presents an account offered by one student in the final year of compulsory school science (in England) explaining about how he had been set a home-study task to find out about how animals have adaptations to fit them for particular habitats. Bert talked about changes that come about, initially as a response to environmental stimuli, and then inherited over time.

Bert offers some features of a scientific explanation—for example, negative feedback mechanisms to respond to environmental conditions in the short term. However the longer-term effects—both for the individual animal and the succeeding generations—seem to be 'explained' in hand-waving terms that are little more than a redescription of what is to be explained: 'they just learn to do that . . . after a while it just adapted . . . they'd just learn it's just naturally there now'. The word 'just' does a lot of rhetorical work in student explanations such as these—implying that's just the way it is, so there is no point in asking me to explain further.

Students will sometimes also recognise an association that leads to them ascribing causation in ways inconsistent with scientific notions of cause and effect. Consider the extract of dialogue in Textbox 6.12: that fish can survive with cold blood might suggest they do not need insulation, but being ectothermic does not explain *why* fish can survive without keeping warm.

Textbox 6.10: Pseudo-explanation—explanation by definition or naming: students' suggested explanations of optical properties.

Light reflects from mirrors because "of reflection. As light travels in straight lines and it bounces off."

Glass is transparent because "the light moves through it rather than bouncing off of it, like it does on opaque objects."

(Students, c. 14 years old)

Source: ECLIPSE project website; see www.educ.cam.ac.uk/research/projects/eclipse/.

> Textbox 6.11: From response to environmental stimulus, to inherited adaptation.
>
> "*Our homework we did about adapting, like how polar bears adapt to their environments . . . things like it has white fur for camouflage so the prey don't see it coming up. Large feet to spread out its weight when it's going over like ice. Yeah, thick fur to keep the body heat insulated.*
>
> So how does adaption take place?
>
> *I don't know. It may have something to do with negative feedback. Like you have like, you always get feedback like in the body to release less insulin and stuff like that. So in time people like or whatever, organisms, learn to adapt to that. Because if it happens a lot that makes a feedback then it comes, yeah, then they just learn to do that. Okay, like the polar bear, like I don't know, it may have started off just like every other bear, but because it was put in that environment, like all the time the body was telling it to grow more fur and things like that, because it was so cold. So after a while it just adapted to, you know, always having fur instead of, you know, like dogs shed hair in the summer and stuff . . . I'm not sure, it just . . . I don't know. Like, erm, like the body senses that it's cold, it goes to the brain, and the brain thinks, well how is it going to go against that, you know, make the body warmer.*
>
> And then over a period of time, what happens then?
>
> *Erm, I guess it just it doesn't really need that impulse of being cold, it's just naturally there now, to tell it to do it more. I would probably think many generations later.*"
>
> **(Bert, c. 15 years old)**
>
> Source: ECLIPSE project website; see www.educ.cam.ac.uk/research/projects/eclipse/.

> Textbox 6.12: Having cold blood as an explanation for not needing to be warm.
>
> "*Why have fur or hair?*
>
> **'Cause it keeps us warm.**
>
> *Okay. So why don't birds have fur or hair, it might keep them warm as well?*
>
> **'Cause they've got feathers.**
>
> *Okay, what about fish then, don't they need to keep warm?*
>
> **They've got cold blood, so they don't need to.**"
>
> **(Sandra, c. 11 years old)**
>
> Source: ECLIPSE project website; see www.educ.cam.ac.uk/research/projects/eclipse/.

> Textbox 6.13: An alternative notion of 'cause'.
>
> "And we could say therefore, that the reason that some people go towards the Liverpool [football] ground, is because they're wearing red, and the reason some people go towards the Everton ground [another football ground in Liverpool], is because they're wearing blue. Now would that be a fair description?
>
> **Yeah.**
>
> And do you agree with the sense of cause and effect there—that people go to watch Liverpool because they're wearing red hats and red scarves? And people go to look at Everton because they're wearing blue hats and blue scarves?
>
> **Yes.**
>
> . . .
>
> If you go to the swimming pool, and watch people swimming . . . is it fair to say that it's caused by what [type of swimming costume] they are wearing, that determines which room they go and get changed in?
>
> **Yes.**
>
> It is?
>
> **Yes.**
>
> That's the cause of it?
>
> **Yeah. It's also conventional as well."**
>
> **(Annie, c. 18 years old)**
>
> Source: ECLIPSE project website; see www.educ.cam.ac.uk/research/projects/eclipse/.

It is quite possible to consider this example reflects poor expression rather than necessarily flawed thinking. However, the exchange presented in Textbox 6.13 leaves less room for ambiguity. Eighteen-year-old Annie seemed to have an alternative conception of the very notion of 'cause'. I noticed the way she was using 'because' in her talk, and tested out whether she would agree with a fallacious argument using 'because' in the same way.

An example of flawed logic is presented in Textbox 6.14. Students were asked to suggest why pigs have curly tails. This response draws upon a sound line of argument from evolutionary thinking. Perhaps the pig evolved from an earlier type of animal that had good use for a tail, but for modern pigs the tail is no longer adaptive, in which case the energy cost of producing a tail would lead to there being a selective advantage to those animals with genes for shorter tails. This would have been a good response had the question asked why pig tails were short (at least if it referred to wild pigs not subject to artificial selection). However there is no logical reason offered by the student for why a curly tail costs the pig less energy to produce than a straight tail.

132 Making Sense of Student Thinking

Textbox 6.14: An example of a pseudo-explanation? A student's suggestion for why pigs have curly tails.

Pigs have curly tails because "they have developed from an animal with a long tail and have evolved to the stage where they need no tail, but it is still there and is taking a curly form to save energy."

(Student, c. 14 years old)

Source: ECLIPSE project website; see www.educ.cam.ac.uk/research/projects/eclipse/.

The examples offered in this chapter could be multiplied many times, and the alert teacher who is sensitive to their own students' explanations could soon build up their own store of examples. Student explanations may be inadequate because they do not understand the science involved. However, even when learners do have a good understanding of relevant concepts, they need to recognise them as relevant and applicable to the situation they have been asked to explain. Even then, they will only be able to offer an adequate explanation if they understand the structure of scientific explanations and have the literacy skills to express themselves clearly (see Figure 6.3). As always, language both affords and constrains what teachers and students can communicate in science classes.

understanding of scientific concepts

identifying relevance of scientific concepts

understanding of logical structure of explanation

proficiency in expressing ideas

→ **student explanation**

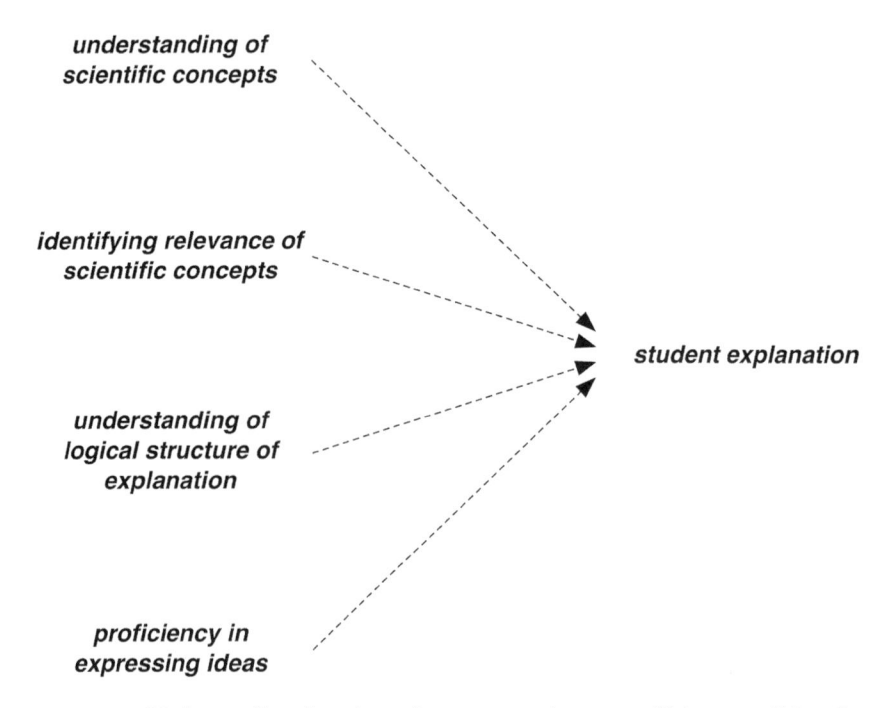

FIGURE 6.3 Understanding the science is a necessary, but not sufficient, condition for offering a scientific explanation.

References

Aikenhead, G. S. (1996). Science education: Border crossing into the sub-culture of science. *Studies in Science Education, 27*(1), 1–52.

Beiser, A. (1973). *Concepts of modern physics* (2nd ed., international student ed.). Tokyo: McGraw-Hill Kogakusha.

Brook, A., Briggs, H., & Driver, R. (1984). *Aspects of secondary students' understanding of the particulate nature of matter.* Leeds: Centre for Studies in Science and Mathematics Education, University of Leeds.

Cheng, M. M. W. (2011). *Students' visualization of scientific ideas: Case studies of a physical science and a biological science topic* (Doctoral thesis, King's College, University of London, London).

Edwards, D., & Mercer, N. (1987). *Common knowledge: The development of understanding in the classroom.* London: Routledge.

Emsley, J. (2010). *A healthy, wealthy, sustainable world.* Cambridge: RSC.

Erduran, S., Simon, S., & Osborne, J. (2004). TAPping into argumentation: Developments in the application of Toulmin's argument pattern for studying science discourse. *Science Education, 88*(6), 915–933.

Griffiths, A. K., & Preston, K. R. (1992). Grade-12 students' misconceptions relating to fundamental characteristics of atoms and molecules. *Journal of Research in Science Teaching, 29*(6), 611–628.

Gross, A. G. (1996). *The rhetoric of science.* Cambridge, MA: Harvard University Press.

Karmiloff-Smith, A. (1996). *Beyond modularity: A developmental perspective on cognitive science.* Cambridge, MA: MIT Press.

Kress, G., Jewitt, C., Ogborn, J., & Tsatsarelis, C. (2001). *Mulitmodal teaching and learning: The rhetorics of the science classroom.* London: Continuum.

Lakoff, G., & Johnson, M. (1980). The metaphorical structure of the human conceptual system. *Cognitive Science, 4*(2), 195–208.

Lave, J., & Wenger, E. (1991). *Situated cognition: Legitimate peripheral participation.* Cambridge: Cambridge University Press.

Lemke, J. L. (1990). *Talking science: Language, learning, and values.* Norwood, NJ: Ablex.

Medawar, P. B. (1963/1990). Is the scientific paper a fraud? In P. B. Medawar (Ed.), *The threat and the glory* (pp. 228–233). New York, NY: Harper Collins. (Reprinted from *Listener, 70,* September 12, 1963, 377–378).

Mercer, N., Dawes, L., Wegerif, R., & Sams, C. (2004). Reasoning as a scientist: Ways of helping children to use language to learn science. *British Educational Research Journal, 30*(3), 359–377. doi: 10.1080/01411920410001689689

Nicoll, G. (2001). A report of undergraduates' bonding misconceptions. *International Journal of Science Education, 23*(7), 707–730.

Ogborn, J., Kress, G., Martins, I., & McGillicuddy, K. (1996). *Explaining science in the classroom.* Buckingham: Open University Press.

Ruse, M. (1986/1993). Teleology and the biological sciences. In M. Ruse (Ed.), *The Darwinian paradigm: Essays on its history, philosophy and religious implications* (pp. 146–154). London: Routledge.

Schmidt, H.-J. (1991). A label as a hidden persuader: Chemists' neutralization concept. *International Journal of Science Education, 13*(4), 459–471.

Solomon, J. (1992). *Getting to know about energy—in school and society.* London: Falmer Press.

Taber, K. S. (2002). *Chemical misconceptions—prevention, diagnosis and cure: Classroom resources* (Vol. 2). London: Royal Society of Chemistry.

Taber, K. S. (2007). Choice for the gifted: Lessons from teaching about scientific explanations. In K. S. Taber (Ed.), *Science education for gifted learners* (pp. 158–171). London: Routledge.

Taber, K. S. (2012). Key concepts in chemistry. In K. S. Taber (Ed.), *Teaching secondary chemistry* (2nd ed., pp. 1–47). London: Hodder Education.

Taber, K. S. (2013a). Revisiting the chemistry triplet: Drawing upon the nature of chemical knowledge and the psychology of learning to inform chemistry education. *Chemistry Education Research and Practice, 14*(2), 156–168. doi: 10.1039/C3RP00012E

Taber, K. S. (2013b). *Modelling learners and learning in science education: Developing representations of concepts, conceptual structure and conceptual change to inform teaching and research.* Dordrecht: Springer.

Taber, K. S., & Watts, M. (2000). Learners' explanations for chemical phenomena. *Chemistry Education: Research and Practice in Europe, 1*(3), 329–353.

Tamir, P., & Zohar, A. (1991). Anthropomorphism and teleology in reasoning about biological phenomena. *Science Education, 75*(1), 57–67. doi: 10.1002/sce.3730750106

Toulmin, S. (1958/2003). *The uses of argument* (updated ed.). Cambridge: Cambridge University Press.

von Baeyer, H. C. (1993). *Taming the atom: The emergence of the visible microworld.* London: Viking.

Vygotsky, L. S. (1934/1986). *Thought and language.* London: MIT Press.

Wolpert, L. (1992). *The unnatural nature of science.* London: Faber & Faber.

Zohar, A., & Ginossar, S. (1998). Lifting the taboo regarding teleology and anthropomorphism in biology education: Heretical suggestions. *Science Education, 82*(6), 679–697. doi: 10.1002/(sici)1098-237x(199811)82:6<679::aid-sce3>3.0.co;2-e

7

THE INFLUENCE OF EVERYDAY BELIEFS

In the previous chapter, the notion of learning science as participating in a discourse community was considered. It was suggested that sometimes the culture of the science classroom with its particular norms is quite alien to many students, and that entering the science classroom has been compared to a border-crossing into a foreign country with a dissimilar language and customs (Aikenhead, 1996).

This operates at a number of levels, and in the previous chapter, there was a focus on aspects of language use in science, and the kinds of scientific thinking that language is used to support and communicate. In this chapter, two other aspects of this cultural shift between science and everyday life are considered. One aspect is what might be called folklore or folk science: things that are widely believed, but which are at odds with scientific accounts of the world. At a more fundamental level, students may hold fundamental beliefs about the nature of the world or how one comes to know about it, which are either inconsistent with, or unsupportive of, the scientific perspective.

The Influence of Folk Science on Learning Science

In Chapter 5, common alternative conceptions about force and notion were considered. In particular, learners tend to expect that a moving object will come to rest simply because this is the natural course of events (rather than because some force is acting upon it). It is easy to see how such alternative conceptions develop based on direct experience of the world.

Some other common alternative conceptions are less easy to explain in this way, and seem to have their origins at least partially in cultural influences. Chapter 6 discussed how the acquisition of human language allows us to somewhat shortcut direct experience as the source of our knowledge of the world. Although everything we know has to ultimately build upon what we have abstracted from our direct experiences of the world, we are able to learn vastly more than is possible from direct experience by interpreting other people's accounts of their knowledge. However, this channel for learning can be just as effective (or ineffective) when we are told things that are in disagreement with canonical science, as when we are taught scientific accounts of the world. If a respected teacher has an alternative conception of some science concept, then he or she may be as skilled at teaching this 'wrong knowledge' as those other concepts, where his or her knowledge better reflects canonical science.

Beyond the classroom, there are many ideas in wide circulation which are inconsistent with scientific accounts, and which an individual will be exposed to in the discourse of family members, peers, the media, and the general populace. This kind of information is sometimes labelled as folk knowledge. Sometimes there are ideas that are widely expressed by some parts of a society whilst being treated more critically in other quarters—what the more sceptical might refer to as 'old wives' tales' (a term that simultaneously manages to demonstrate prejudice based on age, gender, and marital status all at once!).

Sometimes ideas of this kind may be considered as little more than superstitions, but widely adopted superstitions can have real effects in the world. So builders have been known to leave out the number 13 when numbering houses down a road. Perhaps the builders thought that number 13 was unlucky. However, more likely, the builders considered that enough people think 13 is 'an unlucky number' to make it harder to sell house number 13.

Textbox 7.1 presents one student's explanation of aging, based on an everyday notion that bodies wear out just like artifacts—'nothing lasts forever'. Textbox 7.2 reports a futile attempt to have a student engage with what happens to the material in a fuel when it burns—the everyday notion that the fuel has been 'used up' offered a sufficient explanation for Sophia, and she did not appreciate the basis of my question motivated by a scientific perspective on matter and chemical change. The problem I tried to pose (what happens to the material that was the fuel) was interpreted as a practical problem that could be solved by refilling the fuel burner.

Textbox 7.1: An explanation of ageing based on folk science.

People age because "they get worn out. Eventually the vital parts of the body become unrepairable and the limbs slowly become more useless. Cells diminish over the years and eyes become over-used. Nothing lasts forever. As the brain is used it cannot be repaired, limbs are worn and bones become weak."

(Student, c. 14 years old)

Source: ECLIPSE project website; see www.educ.cam.ac.uk/research/projects/eclipse/.

> Textbox 7.2: Being 'used up' is a sufficient explanation when a fuel burns.
>
> "So what happens to paraffin when it burns then?
>
> **It keeps on burning . . .**
>
> I see, but otherwise it just carried on burning, did it? Did it carry on burning for ever . . . ?
>
> **No, 'cause it would run out.**
>
> So where does the paraffin go then?
>
> [There was a pause, of about 4 seconds. Sophia laughs, but does not offer an answer.]
>
> And what happens to the level of the paraffin in the burner?
>
> **It gets lower and lower.**
>
> So why's that, what's happened to it?
>
> **'Cause you are using all of it up, when it's burning.**
>
> So it gets all used up does, it—so what happens when it's all used up?
>
> **You have to refill it."**
>
> (Sophia, c. 11 years old)
>
> Source: ECLIPSE project website; see www.educ.cam.ac.uk/research/projects/eclipse/.

Sometimes such 'everyday' ideas tend to be specific to particular cultures. For example, a number of folk beliefs related to pregnancy are found in the West Indies. Pregnant women are advised to eat lots of slippery cooked ochroes (to make delivery easier) and to drink lots of milk if they want a baby with a lighter skin tone, and they are considered to be able pass on their fertility to plants they have contact with (George & Glasgow, 1988). These examples reflect aspects of systems of magic—where properties can be transferred by association (Rosengren, Johnson, & Harris, 2000).

Folklore includes various isolated ideas that have developed credence over time, but there can also be more extended and widely held systems of beliefs, or fundamental ways of thinking, that underpin the way people view their worlds—these are sometimes termed worldview.

The Influence of Worldview on Learning Science

Worldview goes beyond isolated ideas, and refers to a relatively coherent view of the nature of the world, and the things in it, that informs a person's thinking. Worldview often concerns reliable ways of knowing about the world, as well as that knowledge itself, and may be linked to moral judgements. That is, worldview can encompass ontology (what kinds of things exist in the world), epistemology (how we come to know), and axiology (how we should act).

Because science has an epistemological component, it is sometimes suggested that there is a 'scientific worldview', although there are good reasons to suggest that this is a simplification. People of quite different fundamental views about the world can do science, and it seems more sensible to suggest that science presupposes a particular set of values that are consistent with a range of—but not all—worldviews (Taber, 2013).

Traditional Ecological Knowledge

One issue where worldview has been recognised as important is in teaching science to learners from cultures such as those of aboriginal peoples (such as the First Nations in Canada) who have a traditional and sustainable way of life informed by a well-established way of thinking about and relating to their natural environment. Whilst all such cultures are somewhat unique, it is reported that often scientific (that is, modern, so-called Western, scientific) ways of thinking are inconsistent with key features of the worldview adopted by these people (Inglis, 1993).

In particular, distinctions between technical scientific knowledge and practical knowledge (for example, distinctions between theory and practice) are considered unhelpful, and the way knowledge is understood and communicated through example and narratives often does not distinguish a *scientific* way of knowing from what others might consider a *spiritual* way of knowing. Ways of thinking about living in the environment in relation to other species have developed which may seem to outsiders as a mixture of folklore, superstition, and trial and error, mixed with deep insight into ecological relationships.

It is possible to overromanticise the extent to which such groups have found ways to 'live in harmony with the land' or indeed the quality of life provided by such cultures (which can often be harsh). Yet such cultures have often developed what we might consider philosophies to underpin their lifestyles and support sustainability. For example, the Native American Hopi culture has a strong emphasis on respect for all livings things that informed the development of villages based on agriculture.

The previous chapter introduced the notion of border-crossing as a metaphor for how the science classroom may appear an alien culture to some learners. That is not an entirely negative thing of course—education is about helping people become open to new aspects of human culture and different ways of thinking. However, it has been suggested that border-crossing into traditional science classrooms may be especially challenging to learners from traditional cultures. So, as one example, the practice of keeping animals in cages in science classroom to allow them to be observed (or worse!) by students is seen as totally inappropriate in some traditional cultures—as something that offends moral sensitivities (Allen & Crawley, 1998).

Religious Beliefs and Science

A particular area of potential inconsistency between a learner's worldview and science teaching may occur in relation to religious beliefs. This is a complex area as there are diverse views on whether science can be consistent with religion, and of course religious faiths are themselves very diverse in nature.

Some scientists have argued that science requires the adoption of a worldview that excludes the possibility of the supernatural, and that science and religion are therefore intrinsically inconsistent. Whilst this view has been strongly argued, it is certainly not the general view of scientists, and indeed a great many active and successful scientists hold various religious faiths (Berry, 2009). It is certainly clear that being religious is not an impediment to doing useful science, as copious examples such as Galileo, Newton, Hooke, Faraday, and many others illustrate. Galileo and Newton are particularly interesting cases.

Galileo Galilei is famous for having clashed with the Roman Catholic Church. There has been much scholarship on this episode, and the extent to which the dispute was as much about church politics or church authority, rather than just about the substantive issue of how the relationship between the heavenly bodies were to be understood. There was an existing tradition in the Christian churches that when empirical evidence clearly contradicted accepted interpretation of scripture, then the *interpretation of* scripture could need to be reexamined. In retrospect, it is very clear the church came to the wrong judgement in terms of whether Galileo's arguments justified a reinterpretation of scripture—but it seems generally accepted that Galileo was a devout Christian who wanted to correct church teaching rather than question fundamental issues of doctrine.

Similarly, Newton was a very devout man who undertook his science in something like the 'natural theology' tradition—that is, seeing the work of (what we now call) scientists in terms of understanding the works of the Creator rather than questioning the existence of a creator. It seems from modern scholarship that Newton—for many people a kind of prototype of a modern scientific thinker—allowed his scientific work to be influenced by a range of ideas that we might consider 'metaphysical', some religious and others that we might now dismiss as superstitions (that is, a kind of numerology that we might think of as a more sophisticated take on thinking number 13 was unlucky). Newton, unlike Galileo, is now considered to have held ideas that would have put him seriously at odds with the doctrine of his church. If, as now thought, Newton was a Unitarian, someone who did not accept the traditional Christian notion of the Holy Trinity (the distinction between, yet unity of, God the Father, the Son, and the Holy Spirit), then his ideas could have led to his losing his academic post at least. (At that time all academics at Cambridge had to accept the articles of faith of the Anglican Church—a key element of which was the divinity of Christ as both fully man and fully God.) As with Galileo though, Newton was a highly religious person, and his scientific work was at least in part driven by his religious convictions.

What is clear is that Newton's thought, whilst leading to highly influential and canonical scientific work, was influenced by extrascientific factors that would generally now be seen as very suspect (Topper, 1990). All of us—students, teachers, working scientists, and even those lauded as the 'scientific greats'—are influenced by the worldviews we have adopted, and which inform what we tend to take for granted, and so do not even think to question in our own thinking.

The Scientific Attitude and Worldviews

Given that there is no consensus among the scientific community about the relationship, if any, between science and religion, it is not possible to present a 'scientific view' on the issue. That has not prevented some high-profile scientists from arguing that science excludes the possibility of the supernatural (for example, a creator god who can work outside of the purview of science). These scientists present the view that science is atheistic, and often approach a 'scientistic' materialist perspective that science provides the only basis for reliable knowledge, and that everything that exists is part of the material world and so is open to scientific explanation. These ideas can make up a coherent set of beliefs about the nature of things that perhaps amounts to a worldview.

There is absolutely nothing wrong in principle with this position as long as it is recognised as being a *prescription* of how some people would like science to be, and is not taken as a *description* of what science is like. Scientists such as the Oxford biologist Richard Dawkins and Oxford chemist Peter Atkins are quite within their rights to advocate for this kind of science.

However, this position is certainly not an accurate account of how science is today, nor how it has been in the past. Scientists generally agree that it is inappropriate to admit supernatural explanations into science (it is like this because that is how God did it!), but they do not all think this implies there is no supernatural realm. Similarly scientists do not generally agree with the idea that scientific knowledge excludes the possibility of other kinds of knowing that might be useful to and valued by people.

A good many scientists find a personal religious faith quite consistent with scientific work, and the vast majority of these scientists adopt a view somewhat like that shown by Galileo—that is, that scientific work offers the most reliable accounts of the way the world is, whilst other aspects of human culture, such as religion, offer complementary insights into such matters as whether there can be said to be any ultimate purposes to our lives. Religious scientists adopt worldviews that encompass the supernatural—belief in a creator God for example—without this preventing them adopting the scientific attitude in their work: being sceptical, seeking evidence, looking for alternative interpretations, testing ideas, and so forth. There are also other scientists who adopt a view that Thomas Huxley suggested was actually the most appropriate for scientists: agnosticism. An agnostic takes a principled view that we can have no certain knowledge of the existence—or nonexistence—of God.

Scriptural Literacy and Rejection of Science

There is clearly a range of quite different worldviews consistent with scientific work—but that does not mean *all* worldviews can be accommodated (Taber, 2013). Whereas Galileo favoured the Christian tradition that the interpretation of scripture should be consistent with empirical evidence, there are some religious groups who adhere to particular interpretations of religious texts despite these being highly inconsistent with the accounts developed through scientific work based on the collection and interpretation of evidence. Probably the most high-profile and significant case is those religious groups who consider the traditional creation accounts of their faith to be intended as accurate technical accounts, rather than as narratives offering spiritual and moral insights.

This is certainly an issue among some Muslim groups, for instance, but here I will use fundamentalist, young earth creationist, Christian groups as an example. For some of these Christian groups, the two accounts of the creation in the early chapters of Genesis are considered to be accurate technical accounts. Such groups may believe that God created the world in six days; that all human beings are the offspring of one original pair; that all animals were vegetarian before man sinned and invited evil into the world; that the creation occurred a few thousand years ago; that God sent a worldwide flood to kill virtually the entire human creation, apart from one family of eight people who repopulated the earth; and that the main types of organisms on earth were created in much their present form, having only undergone minor variations since the creation. This worldview may also encompass a moral belief that man is distinct from and superior to other species, and that the rest of the biota is here for man's convenience.

It is certainly easy to see how these conclusions can be drawn from the decision to read Christian scriptures in a particular way. Indeed it seems likely many students from nonfundamentalist backgrounds also assume that Christians should take the Genesis accounts as technical reports (Taber, Billingsley, Riga, & Newdick, 2011). However, these beliefs are completely incompatible with a vast amount of evidence that has been collected over many decades by many thousands of scientists—working in a whole range of fields such as geology, astrophysics, paleontology, genetics, and so forth. Accepting the young earth creationist worldview seems to involve belief in a God that went to an incredible effort to mislead his people by giving his world every appearance of being created through processes quite different to the actual events.

Student Rejection of Evolution on Religious Grounds

We have seen earlier in the book (in Chapter 1) that understanding natural selection requires the coordination of a complex set of ideas. It was also argued in Chapter 4 that the notion of evolution may be at odds with our intuitive understanding of the biota as composed of discrete natural kinds—something that reflects our own experiences of living in the world for such a tiny portion of its immense history. We might expect that on first meeting evolution in science classes, many learners might find it an odd and counterintuitive idea.

So for example when one student told me he had been learning about enzymes in digestion and in plants, he commented that these have been 'specially designed' (see Textbox 7.3). This might be considered teleological language (see Chapter 6), but Rory considered God to have designed enzymes for use in the special creation of different species.

Science lessons, however, can present some of the fossil and other evidence that supports the scientific account of evolution by natural selection. Given the sheer overwhelming mass of evidence for evolution, it may be difficult for the science teacher to understand how anyone could rationally reject the fact of evolution, even if they were less readily convinced by natural selection as an explanation.

Yet whilst some students may have conceptual difficulties with the concept that can be addressed by good teaching using the usual strategies of examples, analogies, models, and so forth, many other students are simply not open to considering the possibility of evolution. It is not that these students cannot understand the arguments or the evidence, but simply that they will not engage with the possibility. They may be as bemused or affronted as the science teacher would be if a student claimed that

---

Textbox 7.3: A religious worldview as a lens for understanding the specificity of enzymes.

"We just basically talked about the general structure of the enzyme. I mean you've got enzymes in like the stomach . . . something that's made to break something down into smaller molecules, without being used up itself. And it's yeah, it's like specially designed to do that job.

Specially designed?

Yeah.

. . . Who designed them?

God.

. . . When did He do that?

When He first created the world.

Seriously?

Yeah.

So this was all done in one go, was it?

Well I guess so."

(Rory, c. 15 years old)

Source: ECLIPSE project website; see www.educ.cam.ac.uk/research/projects/eclipse/.

they had had a perpetual motion machine, or an alien spacecraft, in their bag: how many science teachers would be happy to consider the argument and evidence the student might offer with a truly open mind? I imagine for many students who reject evolution, they give the idea as much credence as I gave to the claims of a history teacher at my own secondary school who would tell pupils that she had been a king's mistress in a previous life. I now suspect this may have been a pedagogic tactic to engage student interest—at the time I just dismissed the idea as ridiculous nonsense.

Long (2011) has written a fascinating account of his interviews with some students (and indeed teachers) in the United States who reject evolution. This makes it clear that at least in some cases the choice is not between the scientific account and the religious account per se, but between rejecting something taught in school that has little direct relevance in their lives or rejecting the values and beliefs of their families, their communities, their church leaders—and perhaps in their own minds their God and their chance for securing eternal life. When so much seems to be at stake, it is not so strange that the vast corpus of scientific evidence counts for little.

Moreover, in some communities, it is not as if the scientific evidence and arguments are simply being contrasted with religious beliefs. Rather, students will be presented with arguments and evidence said to show that the case for evolution is actually very weak, that there are alternative interpretations of the evidence that do fit the scriptural accounts, and indeed counterevidence showing that 'macro'-evolution (that is, evolution of whole new groups of organisms from quite different precursor groups) cannot have occurred. Rory, who had talked of the special design of enzymes, suggested in a later interview that species did undergo adaptations if their habitat changed, although he felt the mechanism for this was beyond human understanding (see Textbox 7.4). The notion that 'God moves in mysterious ways' is not consistent with scientific values (that suggest all aspects of the natural world are at least in principle open to scientific investigation) and is quite at odds with the natural theology of many early modern scientists of strong religious faith.

Textbox 7.4: A student's belief about limitations on human knowledge.

"God created [fish] . . . to be suited for the environment they were in, but if the environment slowly changed, their bodies would slightly adjust.

How did He do that?

We shouldn't, humans don't have the power to understand that.

So we don't know?

No."

(Rory, c. 15 years old)

Source: ECLIPSE project website; see www.educ.cam.ac.uk/research/projects/eclipse/.

Authoritative voices with teaching positions in respected institutions and scientific qualifications write books and give talks claiming that there is no scientific evidence for evolution on earth or in the heavens, and that belief in evolution can be shown to contribute to broken marriages, communism, Nazism, sexual perversion, and so forth (Morris, 2000). In many cases, students will be exposed to more hours of antievolution propaganda outside school than formal teaching about evolution—especially in parts of the world (such as parts of the United States) where teachers are aware that many parents are against the teaching of evolution. It may be unreasonable to expect schoolchildren to recognise the merits of the scientific account when their learning about evolution takes place in such contexts. That is not to suggest that science teachers should abandon teaching such an important scientific idea. However, we need to understand our learners as well as our science, and so be prepared to (a) appreciate the depth of some students' objections and (b) treat their strongly committed views with respect (Reiss, 2008)—even when they seem indefensible from a scientific perspective.

References

Aikenhead, G. S. (1996). Science education: Border crossing into the sub-culture of science. *Studies in Science Education, 27*(1), 1–52.

Allen, N. J., & Crawley, F. E. (1998). Voices from the bridge: Worldview conflicts of Kickapoo students of science. *Journal of Research in Science Teaching, 35*(2), 111–132. doi: 10.1002/(SICI)1098-2736(199802)35:2<111::AID-TEA3>3.0.CO;2-V

Berry, R. J. (Ed.). (2009). *Real scientists real faith.* Oxford: Monarch Books.

George, J., & Glasgow, J. (1988). Street science and conventional science in the West Indies. *Studies in Science Education, 15,* 109–118. doi: 10.1080/03057268808559951

Inglis, J. T. (1993). *Traditional ecological knowledge concepts and cases.* Ottawa: International Program on Traditional Ecological Knowledge International Development Research Centre.

Long, D. E. (2011). *Evolution and religion in American education: An ethnography.* Dordrecht: Springer.

Morris, H. M. (2000). *The long war against God: The history and impact of the creation/evolution conflict.* Green Forest, AR: Master Books.

Reiss, M. J. (2008). Should science educators deal with the science/religion issue? *Studies in Science Education, 44*(2), 157–186. doi: 10.1080/03057260802264214

Rosengren, K. S., Johnson, C. R., & Harris, P. L. (Eds.). (2000). *Imagining the impossible: Magical, scientific and religious thinking in children.* Cambridge: Cambridge University Press.

Taber, K. S. (2013). Conceptual frameworks, metaphysical commitments and worldviews: The challenge of reflecting the relationships between science and religion in science education. In N. Mansour & R. Wegerif (Eds.), *Science education for diversity: Theory and practice* (pp. 151–177). Dordrecht: Springer.

Taber, K. S., Billingsley, B., Riga, F., & Newdick, H. (2011). Secondary students' responses to perceptions of the relationship between science and religion: Stances identified from an interview study. *Science Education, 95*(6), 1000–1025. doi: 10.1002/sce.20459

Topper, D. (1990). Newton on the number of colours in the spectrum. *Studies in History and Philosophy of Science Part A, 21*(2), 269–279. doi: 10.1016/0039-3681(90)90026-5

8
THINKING ABOUT KNOWING AND LEARNING: METACOGNITIVE AND EPISTEMOLOGICAL LIMITATIONS ON SCIENCE LEARNING

In earlier chapters it was suggested that one faculty that is fundamental to human intellect is the ability to be aware of, and reflect upon, our own mental activity. Whilst this is certainly not comprehensive (as suggested in Chapter 5, much of our knowledge is tacit, and operates without our conscious control or awareness), it is nonetheless vital to our ability to develop critical patterns of thought. This chapter considers the role of students' thinking about their own thinking in their science learning.

Spontaneous Learning and Not-So-Spontaneous Learning

Humans are naturally learners. As earlier chapters have suggested, our cognitive apparatus has evolved to both interpret experience for us, and to modify itself in response to that experience—to learn from experience so it can do a better job of making sense of the world in the future. Our ability to learn spontaneously seems especially effective in terms of implicit learning—developing the kind of tacit knowledge that we are not directly aware of. So learning a mother tongue whilst still an infant is largely automatic. Parents may actively seek to correct errors, but it seems that we learn the local language to which we are exposed as children without deliberate tuition from others or particular efforts on our own part.

We learn to crawl, and walk, by a simple process of trial and error. This learning is purposeful in the sense that we learn these skills to achieve objectives (such as claiming objects out of reach) but without conscious awareness of how we are using feedback from the environment to modify the way we coordinate our muscles. We know when we reach our goal, or when we fall over trying, but the means by which we make progress is outside of conscious control. At an inaccessible level in our central nervous system we are building up models of how to control and coordinate our limbs that can then be drawn upon at will without any direct access to those implicit knowledge structures.

Much the same is true when we abstract models of how the world works from the patterns perceived in perceptual data. By the time children start school they have developed implicit knowledge relating to the movement of objects and how to bring about changes in those movements. These implicit models of object motion and how to influence it are then generally found to appear at odds with the formal descriptions of physics when learners try to make sense of the scientific description of force, velocity, momentum, acceleration, and so forth in terms of their intuitive understanding (see Chapter 5). The formal scientific concepts do not usually map well onto the intuitive understanding, so formal teaching tends to lead to students developing alternative conceptions as they attempt to make sense of the new terminology and concepts in terms of their existing understanding.

Spontaneous learning is automatic, although it may involve many exposures to, and feedback from, stimuli (children do not get up and walk at the first attempt). However 'academic' learning is, typically, different. For one thing it usually involves communication through some form of symbolic language (for example, spoken or written language, but also charts, diagrams, etc.), and it requires the learner to make sense of communication that *represents* something else (an idea, an experience) rather than directly making sense of his or her own experiences as in spontaneous learning.

Spontaneous Learning in the Laboratory and the Field

To some extent the same types of processes that support spontaneous learning *can* work in formal educational contexts. Science is a practical as well as a theoretical subject, and involves laboratory and fieldwork. These are contexts where manipulation of apparatus and materials and observational skills become very important. Careful use of a volumetric pipette and staining samples for microscopic examination (or even focusing a microscope on the slide) are skills that are largely learned through trial and error, using feedback from the effects of our actions. Such experience leads to the development of tacit knowledge that is very important in scientific work (Polanyi, 1962/1969).

Even here there is an important role for formal tuition. Guidance from a skilled teacher, supporting the learner in carefully conceptualising his or her actions and effects, can considerably accelerate a raw trial-and-error process which might not only be slow, but also expensive in terms of materials used and, potentially, equipment damaged. But ultimately a certain amount of experience is needed to get a feel for using the apparatus and carrying out the techniques. Indeed, laboratory scientists sometimes develop a feel for this particular laser or that specific electron microscope which they cannot readily make explicit and explain to others (Collins, 2010).

A similar point can be made about the work of naturalists who can learn to readily distinguish members of similar species—something that depends upon a tutor (or a well-illustrated field guide) to offer guidance, but then relies on direct experience with specimens themselves. In an extreme case, the Nobel laureate Barbara McClintock worked so closely with her maize plants that she came to develop what might be commonly called 'a sixth sense' about what was going on in the plant genetics that preceded formal conceptual understanding—'a feeling' for the organism (Keller, 1983). That is, McClintock was a scientist who recognised and valued the way she developed intuitive knowledge about her work, even though this was not available to conscious inspection.

As with manipulation, so with observation. Many aspects of practical work in science depend upon observational skills, and these draw upon the body's automatic pattern-recognition abilities, albeit again informed by conceptual knowledge. When the former president of the United Kingdom's Institute of Physics, Jocelyn Bell Burnell, was a doctoral student she discovered pulsars when she recognised a pattern in data obtained from a radio telescope as something significant deserving further attention.

Experienced paleontologists and anthropologists are often able to spot small fossils or bone fragments in a field or on a beach that are not noticed by most people. The rich visual field is full of small objects of different shapes and shades and the novice needs to carefully pay attention to each item and consider whether it might be something of interest. The expert is often able to readily pick out potential specimens from the complex field of material without seeming to need to examine the individual objects. Similarly, experienced archaeologists can often interpret subtle patterns in the landscape that suggest where there may be sites of former human habitation beneath—whereas the novice may not distinguish these signs from the natural irregularity of the landscape.

This ability links to the movement known as gestalt psychology (Koffka, 1967), which had a particular focus on how perceptual discriminations are made. In the visual field for example, we see objects and people, rather than just shapes and patches of colour. Indeed, we recognise a friend or family member's face in different lighting conditions and from different angles, and at different distances—that is, different patterns of activation of the retina relating to different shapes, colours, movements, and so forth are all recognised as the same face. We *see* the face—showing that a good deal of processing of raw sensory information occurs in the brain before the highly processed signal triggers conscious awareness of the perception.

The gestalt psychologists were very interested in how during perception very complex sensory fields were divided into 'figure' and 'ground'—how we pick out an object against the background. Popular accounts of this work often focus on optical illusions and ambiguous figures (Is it a duck or a rabbit? Is that a vase or two faces?). The Necker cube is a two-dimensional representation of the outline of a cube which is ambiguous as it is drawn without perspective so that it is not clear which is the nearest face (see Figure 8.1).

Geologist and crystallographer Louis Albert Necker reported in 1832 how he often experienced 'a sudden and involuntary change in the apparent position of a

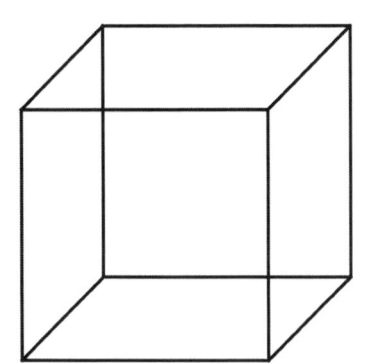

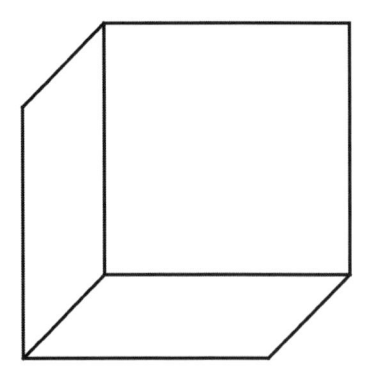

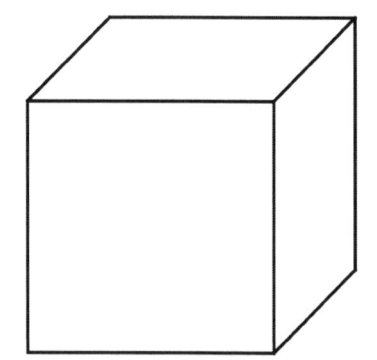

FIGURE 8.1 The Necker cube (top): which face of the ambiguous figure is nearest the viewer?

crystal or solid represented in an engraved figure . . . while examining figures and engraved plates of crystalline forms'. The automatic pattern recognition abilities of human perception will present one face as being nearest the viewer—but by an act of will you can decide that is the furthest face, and so see the image differently. Indeed one can repeat this 'gestalt-shift' at will, and, as Necker suggested, 'see the solid in which position [you] chose, and to make this position vary at pleasure' (p. 337).

When Galileo first observed moons around another planet, he found it hard to persuade others of his discovery. Some refused to look considering what he was suggesting as heretical. Others looked but did not see what Galileo did—a combination of their prior beliefs and the limitations of the instrument meant that they did not see anything they interpreted as bodies around Jupiter. Similarly, the planet Uranus had been spotted but considered just another star many times before it was recognised as being within the solar system.

Similarly in the laboratory, we have to learn to observe through experience—for example, when identifying structures seen through a microscope. Another example is flame tests. We may be told that calcium salts give a brick-red flame and potassium salts a lilac flame, but it is through experience of seeing the flames that we learn how to recognise the actual colours these labels represent. Learning the colour of a flame from a calcium salt depends upon spontaneous learning processes, whereas learning the label 'brick red' may require more deliberate effort.

Thinking and Learning From Laboratory Work

Laboratory work has long been recognised as a core feature of science education, and in some national contexts has traditionally been assigned a good deal of class time. There are different kinds of 'practicals', and indeed practical work can have very different aims—including learning specific techniques, carrying out enquiry work, or reinforcing theoretical ideas. Different 'practicals' may be meant to develop manipulative skills or to support learning about the nature of science or to support the learning of specific science concepts. It is common for students (and sometimes teachers) to inappropriately label *any* science practical work as 'an experiment'—an example of everyday language.

Practical work intended to support conceptual learning has particular challenges. If students are undertaking the practical to reinforce theory that has already been taught then they should know what is to happen in advance, and may feel they are learning little. Teacher demonstration may sometimes be a better option here, although learners do often enjoy doing the manipulations themselves.

However, setting the same student practical work before teaching the theory, although offering a more authentic experience of discovery, is also problematic, as students will often fail to notice, or even misinterpret, the phenomenon that is meant to be of interest (perhaps finding less-significant features as more salient). In either sequence, students may be too focused on the manipulation to really engage with the intended phenomenon, and may lack the expertise to realise when a handling error gives an entirely different outcome to that intended—or as can often happen in electrical circuit work, results are influenced by faulty lamps, old cells with high internal resistance, intermittent connections due to leads with broken wires beneath the insulation, and switches with corroded contacts! This is problematic if students are expected discover scientific ideas for themselves from the practical work (Driver, 1983)—which will seldom happen unless the teacher expertly scaffolds the laboratory work.

Abrahams and Millar (2008) have distinguished between hands-on and minds-on practical work, the former leading to very busy and often highly engaged students who may have little idea after the event what they were actually expected to learn from the lesson. When learners are handling materials and following instructions to carry out unfamiliar processes, then their working memory is likely to be occupied in just 'doing the practical', leaving limited capacity to reflect on its significance.

> Textbox 8.1: A student describes carrying out 'some sort of experiment thing'.
>
> *"I really don't get what it was, erm, you had some sort of, erm, sodium alginate solution or something, and some sort of, I don't know, calcium chloride thing, and you had to make these little, erm, I think sort of like little sodium alginate beads and sort of—pour milk over them or something [laughing] and then collect the milk and then test it, for something . . . I don't know, they just said it would change colour"*
>
> (Amy, 16 years old)
>
> Source: ECLIPSE project website; see www.educ.cam.ac.uk/research/projects/eclipse/.

Abrahams interviewed many secondary students in England about their experience and memories of practical work in science. He found many students claimed to enjoy practical work in science, but most could recall only a few specific practicals and even for those seldom had a good appreciation of what they were meant to learn from them (Abrahams, 2011).

Even when students choose to continue with sciences as elective subjects, they still may not fully benefit from practical work. Textbox 8.1 presents the account of one such student who had selected to continue with biology (and chemistry) as she recalled an experiment she had just completed in her advanced-level biology class. Amy reported that the class had been told the purpose of the 'experiment thing' would become clear in a later lesson but observed that 'I don't really get why we had to do it first'.

Metacognition, Self-Regulated Learning, and Study Skills

A common term used to describe aspects of the human ability to be aware of and control aspects of cognition is '*meta*cognition'. In teaching there are a range of related ideas such as 'learning-to-learn', 'study skills', and 'self-regulated learning' which are used to discuss the developing ability of learners to take more responsibility for their own learning, rather than relying on close supervision and constant appraisal from a teacher.

In formal educational contexts we can tend to think of students as taking a more passive role in learning, with the teacher being responsible for directing learning—interpreting the curriculum (see Chapter 10), devising learning activities, and assessing student progress. Whilst the teacher is more experienced and knowledgeable, and is charged with a professional role, classroom teaching relies on a partnership between students and teachers. If the students decide to be awkward and to only follow teachers' instructions to the letter and to refuse to cooperate in the management of learning, then the teacher's job becomes almost impossible and little learning occurs.

Normally we rely on most students wanting to learn and cooperate (hopefully for more positive reasons that just avoiding sanctions) and using their own common-sense and privileged knowledge of their own learning to follow the spirit as well as the letter of the teacher's direction. Indeed 'direction' is a useful analogy here, for the well-run class is not an 'authoritocracy' relying on the teacher's status, but more like a dramatic or musical production where the teacher inspires and leads, but each player needs to commit to using their own skills and efforts to create something new (in this case personal knowledge). This is certainly recognised in the formative assessment movement (sometimes called 'assessment *for* learning', to contrast with 'assessment *of* learning') where the teacher is encouraged to offer feedback that students can use to improve their own learning (Black & Wiliam, 1998).

Active Learning and Metacognitively Informed Learning

It has long been recognised that learners need to actively process material for effective learning, and the importance of metacognitive, or self-regulatory, skills is increasingly being recognised (Anderman, Sinatra, & Gray, 2012). Motivated students with strong and well-organised subject knowledge can learn a great deal from a pedagogically skilled expert in lecturing mode. The skilled lecturer engages learners' minds and gets them to think about the subject matter in ways that cause them to activate prior learning and form new links with presented material. This approach does however rely on learners having a high level of metacognitive awareness so that they can monitor their own understanding and know when to ask questions or seek supplementary tuition—that is, lecturing assumes learners have both the ability and intention to take a major share of the responsibility for learning. There is much that can go wrong with this approach to teaching (see Chapter 10) and it is not suitable as a primary approach to instruction when teaching less-motivated students or those who have not developed skills of monitoring their own learning.

It is well recognised then that effective teaching with most school classes relies on adopting 'active learning'—activities which provoke students to engage with and mentipulate presented ideas to actively explore their meaning and how they relate to prior learning. To be effective, then, learning activities should not just engage students in thinking about the lesson content, but also about their own understanding. Students should share in the lesson objectives to the extent that they are able to evaluate their own learning—to what extent they are making sense of new ideas, and being successful in applying them. There are certainly limits to which the learner can make such evaluations (again, see Chapter 10), but they can still be a valuable source of information to support the teacher in their work (see Chapter 11).

Informal Science Learning

The focus of the present volume has largely been on formal science learning, but learners will also learn from their own self-directed learning experiences: nature walks, fossil collection, sky gazing, visiting museums and science centres, reading for interest, and watching documentaries, for example. In these situations interest is often high and there is likely to be much spontaneous learning where the learner may both commit much time to an activity and be highly engaged. The term 'flow' has been used to describe the experience of getting lost in an activity when we are so engrossed that we have little awareness of the passing of time and pay little attention to distractions (Csikszentmihalyi, 1988). We know that students are *not* experiencing flow in lessons when they keep looking at the clock or asking 'how long' before the end of the lesson.

Although engagement in activities due to an intense personal interest may lead to a good deal of learning related to science topics, this may not always align well with target knowledge as set out in the formal curriculum. So a student obsessed with dinosaurs may know the names of many more types of dinosaurs than his or her science teacher, and may have a focus on learning facts about different dinosaurs (How tall or heavy were they? What did they eat? How fast could they move?), whereas science education is less concerned with specific facts and more with general principles and theories. The learner's personal wealth of factual knowledge can however be a valuable resource to help engage them in learning about adaptation and habitat and food webs and ecosystems, or about the geological timescale (for example).

Autodidactic Science Learning

Where informal learning is primarily following an interest rather than having a preplanned learning scheme, it is of course also possible for individuals to set about a formal programme of self-directed learning without an external teacher. The extent to which secondary-age learners can do this effectively varies, but traditionally students have been expected to take more responsibility for their own learning as they progress through the education system. Research students (once they have completed their research training) undertake projects with supervision, rather than following any external syllabus or attending taught courses. Academics themselves are expected to develop their own programmes of scholarship.

Teachers may have heard adages along the lines that 'one only really understands a subject when you have to teach it', and new teachers preparing for classes soon discover that they need a confident grasp of their subject that allows them to be flexible and respond to students' questions, many of them unpredictable, and indeed some quite bizarre. Teachers may rely for support on textbooks or websites, but know they have to think deeply about the subject matter and how it links together—to have the 'bigger picture'—often much more so than was ever the case when preparing for their own school or college examinations.

Teachers not only have to have the 'right' knowledge, but they have to know how and when to simplify, and what kinds of metaphors, analogies, models, and other kinds of representations can be considered to convey the essence of key ideas—and they need to make immediate judgments about how to respond to students' own takes on teaching (something discussed in more detail in Chapter 11) to advise them whether their partial and often noncanonically framed interpretations of teaching are on 'the right lines' or 'the wrong track'. This level of interrogation of understanding requires flexibility of thinking about subject matter that goes well beyond what is needed to compose written responses to largely conventional questions in the quiet of a formal examination.

Teachers therefore need very high levels of metacognition so that they are able to critically test out the robustness of their own understanding of subject matter—before it is publicly tested in the classroom by groups of students.

It seems reasonable to suggest that, in general:

- sophistication of metacognitive thinking increases with age;
- sophistication of metacognitive thinking will vary between individuals in a class;
- development of metacognitive sophistication can be encouraged by education that supports learners in taking more responsibility for their learning and gives them opportunities to engage and evaluate their own metacognition.

Students Thinking About Their Science Learning

As teachers we may assume that secondary-level science students will be aware of the importance of reflecting upon their own learning, and increasingly schools are considering themes such as 'study skills' or 'thinking skills' as an important part of the curriculum. It has long been assumed that students are expected to develop such skills through learning curriculum subjects, but it has increasingly been recognised that for many students this does not happen as well as it might unless they are given explicit guidance in these areas.

When I taught in a further-education college (an institution which teaches a mixture of 16–19-year-olds and adults, across academic, vocational, and professional courses) we used to have A-level revision classes. A-level is the standard English academic qualification most widely used for judging candidates for university degree courses. Most commonly students take two-year courses often immediately after completing the compulsory school curriculum (that is, many students are 16–18 years old). The college where I taught had such classes, but also one-year 'revision' courses for those who had previously taken the course but not achieved the grades they required. Many of the students on these revision courses were highly motivated (for example, aiming for medicine and related subjects where only candidates with the top grades were considered).

With my first class of an A-level revision course I would get the students to draw a concept map of a core topic to act both as a gentle return to studying, and to allow me to get a notion of where the students were in their learning. For A-level physics classes I would (having explained and given an example of concept mapping) ask the students to produce a concept map of the core concept of energy. Concept maps can be used as diagnostic assessment tools (or research tools) to explore student thinking (diagnostic assessment is discussed in Chapter 11). However, concept maps are also useful study tools as they require students to actively process and represent their existing knowledge (cf. Chapter 3), and help students to spot both 'gaps' in their current understanding (cf. Chapter 8), and how different ideas can be related (cf. Chapter 9).

Some examples of student responses on being introduced to concept mapping are presented in Textboxes 8.2, 8.3, and 8.4. These comments demonstrate aspects of the students' metaknowledge, and also suggest that the concept mapping activity itself supported the activation of this knowledge. So the comments in Textbox 8.2 suggest students are able to recognize the adequacy of their knowledge of the topic, and those comments in Textbox 8.3 indicate students appreciate something of the potential to organise subject knowledge, and are able to evaluate the current state of their own learning in these terms.

The comments presented in Textbox 8.4 are particularly interesting as they demonstrate how students are able to think about their own learning processes and evaluate their performance on the set task. The second comment here includes the phrase 'I could have carried on writing', which could even indicate that the iterative nature of constructing a concept map—with each new concept or link added suggesting possible further candidates for inclusion—may have provided this respondent with something approaching the experience of 'flow' where

---

"Textbox 8.2: Students are able to assess the extent of their own learning.

"I feel a little disappointed that I can't remember that much more to put on."

"I think this exercise was useful as it let me know exactly how much I know about energy, which I can now see is not enough."

(18-year-old students commenting on being introduced to concept mapping as a study tool)

Source: Taber, 1994.

Textbox 8.3: Students are able to judge the degree of organisation of their learning.

"My knowledge of physics is very un-organised at present."

"brings back memories; good to see how well topics relate or how well you can interrelate them"

(18-year-old students commenting on being introduced to concept mapping as a study tool)

Source: Taber, 1994.

> Textbox 8.4: Students are able to reflect on their own thinking processes.
>
> *"I found I was digging around, trying to put fragments of things I could remember together. I found I could remember only scraps of information, but when doing the drawing, saw how things pieced together, and linked with other things."*
>
> *"At first I did not know where to start but as I began putting ideas down, it reminded me of other points. I could have carried on writing."*
>
> *(18-year-old students commenting on being introduced to concept mapping as a study tool.)*
>
> Source: Taber, 1994.

engagement in a task comes to dominate thinking to the exclusion of distractions and the artificial nature of the school or college timetable.

It is important to reiterate that these comments came from a particular group of students—at the top end of the secondary age range, and generally highly motivated after previous disappointments in their performance in examinations. What I found especially valuable about this activity was that it not only provided information to me on the existing state of the learners' knowledge and understanding, but that it often seemed to engage learners in a more metacognitive approach to their own studying. It seems that even when students have acquired the necessary metacognitive abilities to support them in critically interrogating and evaluating their own learning, they have not always been encouraged to see that this is something that they should be doing in their science learning.

Learners' Epistemological Beliefs

So past educational experience can lead learners to have particular expectations about the extent to which they should engage metacognitively in the learning process. Similarly, research also suggests that learners may develop ideas about the nature of scientific knowledge and how it is developed.

The Nature of the Scientific Disciplines

A teacher of a particular school subject, or someone working professionally in a particular academic discipline, is likely to have given considerable thought over time to the nature of that subject, and the related demarcation question—of where that subject stops. Teaching about *the nature of* science is now a major feature of secondary science education. Within science we also expect that learners will develop an appreciation of the distinct nature of the specific science subjects they are taught (biology, chemistry, and physics, for example), as well as appreciate how they can be considered part of science.

Yet actually these are not straightforward matters. It is difficult to actually offer simple yet authentic definitions that will mean anything to a novice (Kuhn, 1977). Although we often have glib definitions in science, we only tend to come to understand what those definitions actually mean once we have worked with the associated ideas in some depth. So we might suggest, for example, that chemistry is the science that studies the nature and properties of substances, and how those substances react. Whilst this might arguably be considered an accurate definition, it is only genuinely meaningful to someone who already understands chemistry well enough to know what is meant by the term 'substance' and how the term 'reaction' is specifically used in chemistry. To most people, milk, brass, and seawater would probably seem reasonable examples of substances, but they would not be considered substances in chemistry.

Perhaps we should not be surprised then that students who attend science lessons in school do not always have very clear ideas about the nature and range of the subjects they study. Textbox 8.5 presents a comment from a student who had elected to study physics after completing compulsory schooling. Although he had attended lessons labelled 'physics' for several years previously, and had made a positive choice to study the subject further, he was not able to offer any clear notion of what was particular about physics as a subject.

Students may not always share the science teacher's assumption and expectation that science should seek a coherent understanding of the world, and where possible limit the number of fundamental principles needed to make sense of that world. This was brought home to me when I was teaching an advanced-level chemistry class where a student was struggling to make sense of atomic energy levels and ionisation energies. As I taught Sonia for physics as well as chemistry I was aware that just a matter of days earlier she had undertaken a practical observing the emission spectrum of a sodium lamp, and calculating the frequencies of the different spectral lines. I suggested she think about how that practical activity related to what she was studying in chemistry. Sonia—who was a mild-mannered and very courteous student—responded with what appeared to be panic laced with something of a sense of minor outrage (see Textbox 8.6). The implication was that it was hard enough trying to make sense of chemistry concepts—but to be asked to then deal with physics concepts at the same time really was 'out of order'.

Textbox 8.5: A physics student attempts to make explicit his notion of 'what physics is'.

"Physics, I don't know what Physics is. I suppose it's more looking like . . . I don't know. Erm . . . you study all sorts of things in Physics . . . you study like things you can't see and things you can see in Physics."

(Adrian, 16-year-old studying advanced physics as an elective course)

Source: ECLIPSE project website; see www.educ.cam.ac.uk/research/projects/eclipse/.

> Textbox 8.6: Students may compartmentalise learning rather than seek conceptual integration.
>
> *"I can't think about physics in chemistry, I have to think about chemical things in chemistry."*
>
> *(Sonia, advanced-level student studying chemistry and physics, c. 17 years old)*
>
> Source: Reported in Taber, 1998.

Chemistry certainly does have its own domain of concepts (for example, acidity, oxidation, and so forth) that are understood in their own terms rather than being 'reduced' to physics, but the suggestion that chemistry should be seen as an encapsulated subject dealing only with 'chemical things' is not a good reflection of how science often relies on interdisciplinary approaches. In particular the teacher's (my) assumption that thinking in terms of prior learning in another, related subject might be helpful seemed to be alien to the way Sonia compartmentalised her thinking.

The Role and Nature of Models

Models and modelling are ubiquitous in science and science teaching (Gilbert, 2004). Clearly, science teachers use many models that are specifically intended to be simplifications, to act as starting points for students to think about scientific concepts. These models are often presented with the assumption that they are 'just' models and should be understood as such. Perhaps as science specialists we are so used to working with various kinds of models that we do not always think to make this point explicit to learners.

Science uses a wide range of types of models and does so for different reasons. Sometimes models are primarily thinking tools for the scientists looking to find a way to understand some phenomena. Sometimes they are developed for use in science communication to better explain ideas to others (a more direct parallel with models used in teaching) and sometimes models are more like hypotheses that are set up to be tested and see how well they reproduce patterns observed in nature.

Scientific models may be physical—that is, materially built—or purely conceptual. They may be mathematical models—effectively of the form of equations. Some physical models actually look to reflect the physical structure of what is modelled—but that is not always so. An appreciation of the nature and roles of different types of models is something that scientists working with them will have developed—although this may be largely 'taken-for-granted' knowledge rather than something they explicitly think about.

Secondary-science teachers will also have significant familiarly with these issues through their own undergraduate studies and teacher preparation. There has been a strong emphasis on models and modelling in the science education literature over a number of years, and an understanding of the nature and roles of models in science and science teaching is now considered an important part of science teachers' pedagogic subject knowledge (that is, their specialist knowledge about teaching science). Science teachers need to be explicit about the models they present to students in teaching both to ensure students do not misinterpret particular models (and some examples of this happening will be found in the book) and to model for students this important aspect of the nature of science (Taber, 2010).

Student Understanding of Models in Science Education

There has been research into how students understand models they meet in science (Driver, Leach, Millar, & Scott, 1996; Grosslight, Unger, Jay, & Smith, 1991). In general, it is found this understanding is usually of quite limited sophistication, especially in the earlier secondary years. Students tend to predominantly think of physical models to the exclusion of more abstract kinds of models. Students also generally fail to appreciate that building and testing models is an important part of scientific work. In particular, students tend to think of models as scale replicas of things that are too large, small, or inaccessible to observe directly. Typically, students think of such teaching models as a model solar system, a model cell, or a model of the human body where various tissues or organs can be removed to examine anatomy.

Interpreting Teaching Models

I observed a trainee teacher present a model of the solar system to a secondary class. The teacher had carefully chosen a range of spherical objects to represent the different planets, and arranged then with various spacing across the front of the classroom. As an observer with a reasonably high level of subject knowledge, I was aware that whilst the model represented the relative sizes of the different planets quite well, it presented them (as some textbook illustrations do) in a single line out from the sun—a most unusual alignment. A more experienced teacher might have realised that it was important to make the point that the planets did not all sweep around in a line as they orbited the sun.

Moreover, the student teacher had actually used two distinct scaling factors in presenting his model, as in order to fit the model in the classroom he had used a scale for the distances between the planetary orbits which was considerably different from the scale he had used to represent the relative sizes of the planets themselves. (The alternative would have been to use models of the planets that would have been too small for most of the class to see.) The novice teacher had not considered that by not making this explicit to the students he might mislead them. After all, if a teacher presents a scale model (and stresses how the scaling shows the relative sizes of the planets), students may readily assume that all aspects of the model use a single scale unless informed otherwise.

Students often misinterpret or fail to interpret teaching models. Textbox 8.7 reports some comments made to me by a student in Y12 of the UK system. Amy was telling me that she was learning about the mass spectrometer and two of her comments about this experience are presented in the textbox. In the first extract, Amy seems rather unimpressed by the teacher demonstrating how he could knock one matchbox off a board duster by throwing another matchbox at it. Out of context this would seem a rather odd thing to be doing in a science class. However, Amy was aware that the teacher was using this to model how an electron gun in a mass spectrometer could ionise atoms. Despite Amy seeming to lack confidence that she had understood the lesson, she was able to offer quite an extended account of the basic principles of the mass spectrometer.

When Amy told me about the teacher's demonstration I immediately thought what a good idea it was. There is clearly a teaching point to be made here—how does a 'gun' firing negative electrons manage to produce positively charged ions? Although the demonstration was a limited representation of the process involved I thought it offered a good visual analogy of how a fast moving electron can displace another electron from an atom through imparting some of its momentum. However, Amy reported how her teacher used 'these analogies' but with 'no disrespect to our teacher'—in the same way a student might qualify a claim that a teacher did not know their subject or could not explain ideas well. No disrespect

---

Textbox 8.7: Student response to a teacher modelling ionisation in a mass spectrometer.

"Erm—I dunno if it's that I'm not convinced, it just sounds weird, because it's like, erm—I dunno, well it's like it's not something which you can see, and it's like, I dunno, he did this sort of example using a duster and two matchboxes, and, which wasn't very good, so . . . Like no disrespect to our teacher but he uses these analogies, a duster being an atom with matchboxes being the electrons or something, and them being knocked off, because, yeah."

"If you had like a piece of iron and then you put it through this machine thing . . . You need all the atoms to be free, so you'd like heat it until it becomes like vapour, like a gas, and then it goes into like this other thing, which is an electron gun, which has a filament, so it has electrons which are being attracted to this plate underneath it, and as the electrons from the filament are attracted to the plate they hit the iron atoms causing an electron to be knocked off the iron atom making it into an iron positive ion. And then it passes through these sort of plates, and it's deflected, and then there's like an electromagnetic field which—depending on like the direction and the strength—the beam of ions that you've got will be deflected a different amount and so you can somehow measure."

(Amy, 16 years old)

Source: ECLIPSE project website; see www.educ.cam.ac.uk/research/projects/eclipse/.

intended, *but* Amy seemed to think that such 'analogies' were not an appropriate part of science teaching at upper-secondary level—perhaps failing to realise how such modelling processes are central to science itself.

References

Abrahams, I. (2011). *Practical work in school science: A minds-on approach.* London: Continuum.

Abrahams, I., & Millar, R. (2008). Does practical work really work? A study of the effectiveness of practical work as a teaching and learning method in school science. *International Journal of Science Education, 30*(14), 1945–1969. doi: 10.1080/09500690701749305

Anderman, E. M., Sinatra, G. M., & Gray, D. L. (2012). The challenges of teaching and learning about science in the twenty-first century: Exploring the abilities and constraints of adolescent learners. *Studies in Science Education, 48*(1), 89–117. doi: 10.1080/03057267.2012.655038

Black, P., & Wiliam, D. (1998). Assessment and classroom learning. *Assessment in Education, 5*(1), 7–74.

Collins, H. (2010). *Tacit and explicit knowledge.* Chicago, IL: University of Chicago Press.

Csikszentmihalyi, M. (1988). The flow experience and its significance for human psychology. In M. C. Csikszentmihalyi (Ed.), *Optimal experience: Psychological studies of flow in consciousness* (pp. 15–35). Cambridge: Cambridge University Press.

Driver, R. (1983). *The pupil as scientist?* Milton Keynes, Buckinghamshire, England: Open University Press.

Driver, R., Leach, J., Millar, R., & Scott, P. (1996). *Young people's images of science.* Buckingham: Open University Press.

Gilbert, J. K. (2004). Models and modelling: Routes to more authentic science education. *International Journal of Science and Mathematics Education, 2*(2), 115–130.

Grosslight, L., Unger, C., Jay, E., & Smith, C. L. (1991). Understanding models and their use in science: Conceptions of middle and high school students and experts. *Journal of Research in Science Teaching, 28*(9), 799–822.

Keller, E. F. (1983). *A feeling for the organism: The life and work of Barbara McClintock.* New York, NY: W. H. Freeman.

Koffka, K. (1967). Principles of gestalt psychology. In J. A. Dyal (Ed.), *Readings in psychology: Understanding human behavior* (2nd ed., pp. 9–13). New York, NY: McGraw-Hill.

Kuhn, T. S. (1977). Preface. In *The essential tension: Selected studies in scientific tradition and change* (pp. ix–xxiii). Chicago, IL: University of Chicago Press.

Necker, L. A. (1832). LXI. Observations on some remarkable optical phenomena seen in Switzerland; and on an optical phenomenon which occurs on viewing a figure of a crystal or geometrical solid. *Philosophical Magazine Series 3, 1*(5), 329–337.

Polanyi, M. (1962/1969). The unaccountable element in science. In M. Greene (Ed.), *Knowing and being: Essays by Michael Polanyi* (pp. 105–120). Chicago, IL: University of Chicago Press.

Taber, K. S. (1994). Student reaction on being introduced to concept mapping. *Physics Education, 29*(5), 276–281.

Taber, K. S. (1998). The sharing-out of nuclear attraction: Or 'I can't think about physics in chemistry'. *International Journal of Science Education, 20*(8), 1001–1014.

Taber, K. S. (2010). Straw men and false dichotomies: Overcoming philosophical confusion in chemical education. *Journal of Chemical Education, 87*(5), 552–558. doi: 10.1021/ed8001623

9
INTEGRATING KNOWLEDGE AND CONSTRUCTING CONCEPTUAL FRAMEWORKS

Conceptual Integration in Cognition

There seems to be an inherent imperative in human cognition towards greater integration of our conceptual resources. The previous chapter discussed the importance of metacognition in allowing learners to reflect upon, and seek to develop, the state of their knowledge and understanding about a topic area. We do make links intrinsically, and indeed this seems to be tied to our capacity for creativity, but students do not always make the links a science teacher might expect and hope for.

Consolidation of Learning

Studies on brain functioning suggest that learning new conceptual material occurs in two distinct stages. When we first learn new material it will be linked to perceived relevant material already represented in the brain. Understanding of the way the brain represents and recalls memory is still uncertain, but research suggests that declarative memory is largely dependent upon representation in the neocortex, but that formation of memories depends upon structures in the medial temporal lobe, and in particular the hippocampus. Despite some reports of people having particular neurons claimed to be associated with very specific stimuli (such as a neuron found in one subject that was said to fire when the person was shown any image of Marilyn Monroe, but not in response to other images), it seems likely that representations involve arrays of connected neurons, and that at least sometimes these arrays may not all be physically located at the same place in the cortex. When new learning takes place representations are formed that have indirect links to other representations via the hippocampus.

These connections through the hippocampus are not permanent, but are lost over time. However, they can be replaced by direct connections between the different representations in the neocortex. That is, the hippocampus provides an interim indirect link, and sufficient activation of this indirect linkage seems to trigger the development of more permanent and direct connections. It is often considered (although this has not been settled) that much of the consolidation process of establishing and strengthening the direct connections occurs during sleep, but whether this is the case or not, it seems many (indirect) links that are present on first learning are not consolidated into strong permanent links. This would explain the importance of teachers reinforcing new 'fragile' learning, so it can become more robustly established (Alvarez & Squire, 1994; Vertes, 2004; Walker & Stickgold, 2004; Wiltgen, Brown, Talton, & Silva, 2004).

Seeking Coherence and Rewriting History

However, this does not seem to be the only type of preconscious process that occurs in terms of reorganising material represented in memory. Our brains seem to have the ability to 'automatically' review current understanding of the world as represented in memory in order to make new links and increase the coherence of representations. 'Automatically', here, refers to how this is a process that occurs without conscious or deliberate effort, and indeed takes place away from conscious awareness (although it has been suggested that dreaming may be some kind of by-product of this process).

As suggested in Chapter 3, the pressures on evolving human cognition appear to have selected for memory function that is not necessary complete or accurate, but rather supports decision-making. Humans are often better at making judgments and decisions and committing to them, than offering logical arguments for their decisions—and presumably this had survival value for most of human history (if not optimal for supporting the intellectual development of young scientists). Memory seems to be better considered as *an organ for developing a coherent understanding of past experience that supports decision-making in situations faced now*, rather than as a means to develop a full and accurate record of experience.

This is significant for science education because sometimes students appear to learn new material even though this is inconsistent with their prior knowledge and understanding, but then later revert to earlier ways of thinking. So students' well-established alternative conceptions may be challenged by classroom teaching that seems to have persuaded them of the scientific perspective. However, if the new learning is not subsequently strongly reinforced, then over time the preexisting way of thinking will likely again come to predominate. Moreover, memories of the teaching that challenged that thinking may even have become distorted and recruited to support that perspective.

This was seen where students who expected current to drop around a series circuit appeared to have been persuaded by teacher demonstration that current was conserved, yet some time later the students reported seeing the demonstration confirm their previous expectation that the current was reduced after each circuit component (Gauld, 1989). They had not forgotten the teacher's demonstration, but rather their memory had (without their conscious awareness) been adjusted to fit better with their strongly held conception of what was going on in a circuit.

An Example of Conceptual Shifts Over Time

In some of my own research I followed the development of a student's thinking about one topic area (chemical bonding) over a two-year course through an extensive series of in-depth interviews. Tajinder came to his advanced-level chemistry course from school science thinking that chemical bonding occurs to allow atoms to fill their electron shells, and applied this principle widely across examples. During his study at advanced level (that is, ages 16–18) he developed two other explanatory principles for bonding based on instruction: that bonds formed because of forces between charges, and that bonds formed to minimise the energy of the system. Although these two principles might be seen from the scientific perspective as closely linked, Tajinder tended to consider he had three alternative complementary principles he could call upon to explain bonding phenomena—as shown in the example in Textbox 9.1.

Textbox 9.1: A student offers three alternative explanations for bonding in the oxygen molecule during the same interview.

"To become stable it wants an octet state, well it wants eight electrons in its outermost shell to become stable, as it were . . . a way for it to bond together, for both the atoms to have full outer shells or eight electrons in this outer shell, is to share two electrons . . . The other oxygen atom is in the same situation so it can share an electron with the other, with another atom, so it thinks it's got a full outer shell."

"And to become more stable, or at a lower energy, it can gain two electrons, to move down in the energy state, therefore becoming more stable, and so because there's a gap there, there's a tendency for covalent bonding to occur, as in the case of O_2, where electrons can be shared, so therefore . . . the atom can be at a lower state in energy terms, and therefore more stable, and that's why anything takes place in bonding, or any species takes place in bondings in order to lower the energy state or become more stable."

"The orbitals are a sort of a guide roughly to . . . where we think electrons exist . . . where they spend most of their time due to attractions, repulsions between . . . other charges in the atom, or in the species, so there's a plus six charge, and there's six electrons in the outer shell . . . and that plus six charge can attract electrons from another species to pull into there, or just to gain an attraction for it . . . and they form a bond."

(Tajinder, c. 17 years old)

Source: Taber, 2000.

The full-shells explanatory principle is a very common alternative conception (see later in this chapter) that is widely used by students to explain covalent bonding and ionic bonding. However it proves less useful to explain bond polarity, dative bonding, hydrogen bonding, van der Waals' forces, solute-solvent interactions, bonding to ligands in complex ions, bonding in higher oxidation states (for example, sulphur in SF_6) or bonding in compounds of noble gases (for example, XeF_4).

During his two-year advanced course, Tajinder came to rely increasingly on explanations based around the interactions of charges, and to a lesser extent on minimising energy, and less on his full-shells explanatory principle which had a more limited range of application. However, he did not come to reject this alternative conception, and considered his three different explanations as complementary narratives from which to select in particular contexts. So Tajinder retained manifold conceptions, but over time there was a shift in the profile of use of these different explanations.

I later met and interviewed Tajinder when he was well into his university course, almost four years after the research on his high-school-level learning. When he was shown images of various chemical species (molecules, etc.) and asked to comment on any bonding present, he tended primarily to try and explain the bonding in terms of his full-shells explanatory principle: he had reverted to primarily drawing upon the alternative conception that had been his only way of thinking about bonding when he had started his advanced-chemistry course. After several years away from studying chemistry, the explanation that he most readily brought to mind was the one he had first learnt in school, even though it had proved inadequate for much of his advanced-level study.

However, there was also something new in his responses that had not been present in the earlier research interviews. During the original research, Tajinder had tended to draw upon his three forms of explanation as though these were alternatives and not directly linked. Yet when interviewed some years later he now seemed to support his full-shells explanations by linking this to minimising energy (see Textbox 9.2). That is, where he had seen the drive to fill shells, and the drive to minimise system energy, as distinct principles, now he saw filling electron shells as a means to minimise energy. Tajinder told me he had not had reason to revisit the topic of bonding since going to university, so it seems that in the intervening period a preconscious process had been at work which had started to integrate what he had previously seen as distinct ideas. Despite having integrated a more 'physical' principle (systems tend to evolve spontaneously to lower energy states) with his full-shells explanatory principle, this retained a strong anthropomorphic frame (see Chapter 6) where atoms can be happy, have reasons, think, have likes, and try to achieve outcomes.

Chunking, Problem-Solving, and Making Creative Links

This ability of the human brain to forge new links between represented knowledge and to work at making more coherent sense of the world 'in the background'

> Textbox 9.2: An explanation relating two ideas that had previously been treated as alternatives.
>
> *"They come to a more stable energy level, is it, where they're happier to be in that state, which is a lower energy. So therefore they've got no reason to go back to being where they were, if they drop down a level. . . . they form something called a covalent bond, which entails that the oxygen atom thinks that it has a full outer shell of electrons therefore it makes it less reactive . . . There has to be another oxygen atom for it to join to, and they sort of come together, and where there's six electrons in the outer shell, so then two of the electrons would form a covalent bond where they'd share . . . so sort of they would they'd come together so . . . therefore it would think it has eight electrons in its outer shells . . . all atoms would like to have a full outer shell, and therefore be the most stable atom they could be. And therefore they try to do this by either bonding with something, or reacting with something, which is the same sort of thing . . . to have a full outer shell of electrons and therefore be at lowest energy."*
>
> *(Tajinder, interviewed some years after completing his study of chemistry)*
>
> Source: Taber, 2003.

without our conscious effort or awareness could be disconcerting. The things we felt we knew when we woke up this morning may not all be the same as the things we thought we knew when we went to bed last night. It is a bit like our account of the world is slowly being worked over by an editor who is charged with seeking to increase connectivity and where possible eliminate contradictions. There is no malicious intent, but our memories of the world are subject to being modified to offer a more coherent and better-integrated working model to support us in facing the world.

Although this is a preconscious process, it is one that is made use of both in creative work and problem-solving. Creativity involves making new links between things previously seen as unconnected. This creativity may be cultural or personal—that is, we all make new links that are novel for us, and sometimes these prove to be novel to others as well. We may associate such creativity with the arts, but it is also essential in science that relies on forming creative new ideas that can then be developed, explored, and tested (Taber, 2011). Meitner and Frisch's liquid-drop model of the atomic nucleus would be one example and Darwin's representation of life as a branching bush showing the relatedness of all life on earth would be another.

Creative people often give their preconscious thought processes time to work on problems in the background, and report later having moments of insight whilst out for walk or taking a bath (most famously Archimedes). Kekulé claimed to have solved the problem of the structure of benzene (a cyclic molecule) when he dozed and visualised a snake biting its own tail. Of course these preconscious processes can only be effective when they have material to work with—as Pasteur noted, 'chance favours the prepared mind'. Equally, such processes do not produce result to order—and sometimes there may be a long wait for insight. Barbara McClintock (see the previous chapter) relied on her mind to 'integrate' in this way and solve scientific problems for her, and could become quite distressed when no solutions were forthcoming.

The integrative tendency in human cognition is also reflected in the phenomenon of chunking. Human working memory is extremely limited in terms of the number of items that it can mentipulate at once (see Chapter 3), but an 'item' can be quite extended. It seems that as material gets consolidated into memory by being integrated with other existing representations, it gets embedded into frameworks that can be considered as single items for the purposes of mentipulation in working memory. This is sometimes referred to as chunking.

In teaching we have to consider material from the learner's resolution—that is, how many chunks of information does it appear to involve to the novice learner, rather than to the expert teacher? This is important in scaffolding (see Chapter 6). Complex information and procedures may overload working memory for learners unless we find ways to scaffold learning (in effect acting as add-on memory units for learners) through structuring tasks and information in suitable 'learning quanta'. However, as learners get experience working with new material and begin integrating it into their existing cognitive frameworks (that is, as learning becomes consolidated) they can increasingly work with more complex material without help, and the teaching scaffold can be 'faded'. Multimodal teaching—teaching with images as well as words, and various kinds of representations—provides learners with multiple forms of representations of core ideas, and is considered to support the learning of new material providing additional scope for integrating material into existing mental representations (Cheng, 2011).

Conceptual Integration in Science and Science Education

Science is by its nature an activity that puts a premium on coherence and conceptual integration. One aim of scientists is to explain great amounts of data with a minimal number of laws or principles. Theories and models are considered more useful when they have wide explanatory scope, rather than very curtailed ranges of application. New findings are considered more sceptically when they do not seem to fit with widely accepted principles, and new theories are expected to be consistent with existing well-trusted scientific ideas. For example, the claim that it is possible to produce nuclear fusion in a small amount of material in a test tube at room temperature was widely received with disbelief, despite initial reports of replications in other laboratories, because the results were inconsistent with existing ideas about how and under what circumstances nuclear fusion can occur. In contrast, the 'Piltdown man' fossils, now widely recognised as a hoax (and indeed considered a somewhat crude hoax), was for some time seen as credible evidence of a form of hominid because it *did* fit with expectations about likely intermediate forms between man and nonhuman ancestors.

The ideal, for science, is to produce explanations for all aspects of the natural world that are as coherent and well integrated as possible. Although the extent to which that can ever be achieved is arguable, many working in science would expect science to make progress in that sense. It will never be possible to simply reduce all other sciences to physics, as complex systems bring emergent properties. It may *in principle* be possible to one day describe—for example—the mating display of the peacock in terms of physics, yet that level of description will not be the most useful one for understanding the phenomenon. Despite this, a biological account of the mating display that was *inconsistent with* the laws of thermodynamics (for example) would not be considered acceptable.

Students may not appreciate how coherence is considered highly important in science (across topics, across disciplines), and how being able to subsume different phenomena under a limited number of fundamental principles is so highly valued. I have suggested, only partially tongue-in-cheek, that conceptual integration should be seen as a demarcation criterion for science education (Taber, 2006). That is, science teaching that presents isolated facts and ideas, and does not support learners in seeing the links between topics and concepts, is failing to offer an authentic reflection of a key aspect of the nature of science. Good science teaching emphasises the links within, and across, topics (Scott, Mortimer, & Ametller, 2011).

In the previous chapter, I quoted Sonia who had to focus on chemical things in chemistry (see Textbox 8.6). Sonia perceived being asked to make links between different science subjects as an additional demand, rather than something that might support her learning. This is similar to those students who struggle to apply mathematics when in science that they can do perfectly well in mathematics lessons. Perhaps working memory becomes overloaded, perhaps the contextual aspects of learning undermine such transfer, or perhaps there is something about the way learners compartmentalise different lessons and school subjects.

For example, one study reports how Gavin was working with another student in a class of 13–14-year-olds on a bridge-building exercise. Gavin worked out that he needed 3,000 mm of string for his bridge, and knew that 'the string cost $1.00 for every 300 mm'. Gavin 'had difficulty doing the proportional problem to work out how much he had to pay' (that is, $X:3,000::$1.00:300), and his teacher had to carry out the calculation for him. However, after being shown the calculation Gavin then acknowledged that they 'do those all the time in mathematics' (Rennie, Venville, & Wallace, 2012, p. 82). However, this episode did not occur in a mathematics lesson, but in a technology studies class.

Such failures to apply what is learnt in one topic elsewhere happen a lot. A teacher might assume that a student who had confidently reported that 'there is particles in everything' would apply this knowledge in other topics, but this is not always so (as suggested in Textbox 9.3). A teacher might also assume that it was clearly obvious that atoms and molecules—if fundamental units of matter—must

> **Textbox 9.3: A student suggests that everything is made of particles—although perhaps not chlorophyll.**
>
> *Bill on particles: "Solids they stay same shape and their particles only move a tiny bit . . . [particles are] the bits that make it what it is . . . you can't see them . . . they're very, very tiny . . . they are microscopic . . . there is particles in everything."*
>
> *Bill on plants: "They produce their own food . . . inside, it has leaves, inside it, there is chlorophyll, which stores sunlight, and then it uses that sunlight to produce its food . . . in the leaves it is chlorophyll which is a green substance, so that would give it its colour.*
>
> *Do you think chlorophyll is made of particles?*
>
> *Hm, don't know."*
>
> *(Bill, c. 11 years old)*
>
> Source: ECLIPSE project website; see www.educ.cam.ac.uk/research/projects/eclipse/.

> **Textbox 9.4: A student suggests that a cell is somewhat larger than an atom.**
>
> *"A cell, I'd have thought it was bigger than the atom . . . they're both really microscopic so, I couldn't really say how much bigger they are than each other . . . I'd say, I'd probably go with ten times bigger."*
>
> *(Bert, c. 14 years old)*
>
> Source: ECLIPSE project website; see www.educ.cam.ac.uk/research/projects/eclipse/.

be very much smaller than more complex structures like cells, but it may not be so obvious to students (see Textbox 9.4). Another example is reported in Textbox 9.5. In the same interview Amy (a) told me how she had been taught in her physics classes about *conservation* of energy—but (b) described learning in biology lessons about how energy could be *produced*.

A 17-year-old advanced-level student I spoke to was unable to explain the party trick where a balloon is made to 'stick' to a wall after rubbing on a jumper. Yet in the same interview Alice was able to explain how van der Waals forces ('strong enough . . . intermolecular forces holding things together') operated in terms of 'an electron cloud between, surrounding . . . each molecule' which 'don't stay in one fixed place, there's always going to be sort of momentary areas of dipole—and that's where you get your positive and negatives attracting each other again'. Alice understood how induction could occur at the molecular level, but did not make a link between this mechanism and the phenomenon of the balloon apparently defying gravity.

> Textbox 9.5: A student reports what she has been taught in biology and physics classes.
>
> "[Respiration is] converting oxygen and glucose into energy and carbon dioxide . . . it produces energy which like in humans your body needs . . . [trees are] living and they need to produce energy and when they photosynthesise they produce like energy."
>
> "There's like different types of energy . . . [energy] cannot be made or destroyed, only converted."
>
> (Amy, c. 14 years old)
>
> Source: ECLIPSE project website; see www.educ.cam.ac.uk/research/projects/eclipse/.

> Textbox 9.6: A student recognises the interconnectedness of physics concepts.
>
> "I didn't realise how much the different areas interlinked."
>
> (18-year-old student commenting on being introduced to concept mapping as a study tool)
>
> Source: Taber, 1994.

In the previous chapter, I also reported on comments of some of my own advanced-level physics students asked to concept map their associations for 'energy'. All of the students in this group had previously completed the two-year physics course but some seem not to have realised how so much of what they had been taught linked to the core idea of energy until they were asked to draw the concept map (for example, see Textbox 9.6).

At the other end of the secondary age range, Textbox 9.7 presents a quote from an 11-year-old trying to explain why her teacher had suddenly launched into work on magnets during a unit of work on electricity. Sophia suggested tentative links between these two apparently discrete topics, but also considered it was just the teacher's desire to break up the work on the electricity topic with something different. To the science teacher, magnetism is an electrical effect, and electromagnetism is one of the fundamental forces in nature. The unification of electricity, magnetism, and electromagnetic radiation is seen as a major integrative step forwards in science—but our students are not going to see the connections without some help.

Creating Noncanonical Links

These examples show how learners may fail to spot the links that can help make science knowledge a highly coherent and strongly interlinked body of knowledge.

> Textbox 9.7: A lower secondary student attempts to understand why she has been taught about magnets during the electricity topic.
>
> *"It's not that much to do with electricity but, yesterday we done magnets. I think we're still doing electricity. I don't know if it was just something—so we know what electricity will flow through, and maybe it's something to do with—'cause magnets like stick to other things—I'm not sure, I think we might just have had a break from it, I don't know."*
>
> **(Sophia, c. 11-year-old student)**
>
> Source: ECLIPSE project website; see www.educ.cam.ac.uk/research/projects/eclipse/.

This is unfortunate both because this means they are missing something important about the nature of the subject, and because such links can support effective learning. However, as suggested earlier in the chapter, human cognition includes a natural tendency to see links and connections, and to fit new learning with existing understanding. Sometimes successful students do this very well. Yet, just as students can sometimes miss the connections the teacher might hope they will make, the natural tendency towards conceptual coherence can also lead to students developing links that are less helpful in supporting learning of the science in the curriculum.

Textbox 9.8 reports one 11-year-old's notion of why a Bunsen burner's safety flame will cause glassware to go black. Jim had learnt how the flame was adjusted by closing or opening the air hole (that allows air to mix with the methane), but interpreted this as allowing 'dirt' carried in the gas stream to escape into the air, and so saw closing the air hole as retaining dirt in the gas stream.

Textbox 9.9 offers an older (about 14 years of age) student's suggestion for why atoms can bond together—as an ability they have evolved over time. Presumably to Bert the idea of atoms evolving bonding ability was not so different from giraffes evolving long necks or birds evolving the ability to fly. Bert had learned

> Textbox 9.8: A student's explanation for how 'dirt' gets into a Bunsen flame.
>
> *"A flame . . . can either be yellow, orangey-yellow, or . . . like a, bluey colour, bluey-purple . . . the yellow one has a lot of . . . if you touch it with glass or something, . . . will go black, because with the Bunsen burners, if you are twisting the knob, open, the dirt gets out, and you get the nice clear blue flame, but to get the orange flame, you have to have it closed, don't you, and then that doesn't let the dirt out."*
>
> **(Jim, c. 11 years old)**
>
> Source: ECLIPSE project website; see www.educ.cam.ac.uk/research/projects/eclipse/.

> Textbox 9.9: A student's notion of bonding having evolved.
>
> *"A bond is . . . something to hold, hold two atoms together . . . it could have been like evolution, like . . . the atoms evolved so that they could hold on to each other."*
>
> *(Bert, c. 14 years old)*
>
> Source: ECLIPSE project website; see www.educ.cam.ac.uk/research/projects/eclipse/.

about an acceptable scientific notion, evolution, but applied it outside its appropriate range of application.

Developing an Alternative Conceptual Framework

Where students have developed an alternative conception of some topic area that is inconsistent with scientific accounts, this can provide a suitable 'anchor point' for new learning just as well as prior knowledge that fits with scientific accounts. In some of my own research I reported what I described as an alternative conceptual framework from chemistry education, the octet framework (Taber, 1998, 2013). The framework consists of conceptions that are related. Among the (alternative) conceptions that I found in interviewing mostly 16–19-year-old students studying chemistry were the following ideas:

- Chemical reactions occur so that atoms can obtain full outer electron shells (or octets of electrons).
- Chemical bonds form to allow atoms to obtain full outer electron shells (or octets of electrons).
- Ions with full outer electron shells (or octets of electrons) are more stable than the neutral atoms.
- Atoms can form bonds by sharing or transferring electrons so that they obtain full outer electron shells (or octets of electrons).
- An ionic bond is the transfer of an electron from a metal atom to a nonmetal atom.
- In an ionic lattice, an ion is only bonded to the ion(s) it has transferred electrons to or received electrons from.
- In an ionic lattice, the number of counterions an ion can bond with is limited by its electrovalency or charge.
- In an ionic lattice, there are ionic bonds between some counterions, but just forces between others.
- A hydrogen bond is a covalent bond to a hydrogen atom.
- An atom can only undergo successive ionisation until it has a full outer electron shell (or octet of electrons).

- Polar bonds are a subclass of covalent bonds.
- An excited chlorine atom that has an electron promoted from an inner shell to the outer shell will be more stable than the ground-state atom.

Each of the previous ideas is an alternative conception because it does not match the scientific account. In some cases, the statements are clearly contrary to the science, and in some cases we can be kinder and just say they do not match the scientific account very well. Some of these conceptions seemed very common—to be held by most of the learners I talked to. Others were only presented by some learners. However all of the students in my sample seemed to hold a common key idea (or explanatory principle) that was applied widely, and could be seen as the core of a structure of conceptions.

Different students used different language to describe their ideas, but they tended to all agree that atoms wanted or needed to fill their outer electron shells (or to gain octets of electrons, or to achieve noble gas electronic configurations) and that chemical processes—reactions, bond formation, and so forth—tend to occur as a means for this to be achieved. This is quite at odds with the canonical models of chemistry that tend to employ explanatory principles related to electrical charges and forces, energy states, and entropy.

An Example of Coherent Alternative Thinking

There is a logical network of ideas built around this central explanatory principle. So, for example, the ionic bond is seen as either an electron-transfer process to allow atoms to get full outer shells, or as the outcome of such a process. As the focus is on the needs of atoms, NaCl (sodium chloride) would be considered to be formed from sodium atoms and chlorine atoms (rather than sodium metal and molecular chlorine gas, or—more likely—solutions of sodium hydroxide and hydrochloric acid). The central principle was applied here in terms of a bond being formed between one sodium atom or ion and one chlorine atom or ion, as that allows the atoms to complete their electron shells. The conception that a sodium ion could only bond to one chloride ion followed from this central principle. If the bond was an electron transfer (or the result of such an electron transfer) that led to a full electron shell then the number of bonds formed would depend upon how many electrons an atom had in excess of, or short of, a full outer shell. This determines how many electrons can be transferred from, or to, that atom. The implication here then was that when NaCl formed, it was composed of ionically bonded NaCl units (that is units of a single sodium ion bonded to a single chloride ion which tend to be considered as molecules).

As the NaCl lattice holds together as a solid this suggested there must be two types of interaction—the ionic bonds between the ions that had been involved in an electron transfer process, and some kind of other interaction, that held these 'molecule' type units together (a bit like in solid iodine where covalent molecules are held together in a crystal lattice). These other interactions did not count as bonds (according to the students) as they did not lead to atoms obtaining full outer electron shells, but rather were 'just forces'. So the conception that there were different types of interaction in the ionic lattice was linked back directly to the central principle.

It is certainly not the case that all the students I spoke to had built up precisely the same framework of ideas. So when it came to thinking about what held a metal lattice together my participants had quite different views. Some would suggest covalent bonding, or something very much like covalent bonding (where atoms could get full shells by sharing electrons). Other suggested metals had ionic bonding where electrons were transferred between atoms—perhaps in more sophisticated and dynamic ways than was the case with NaCl. Others suggested the bonding in metals was some kind of hybrid between covalent and ionic bonding. Others could not see how the bonding in metals could allow atoms to have full outer shells, and so drew the conclusion that metals did not actually have chemical bonding, but were rather just held together by forces. Although learners had different conceptions here, they still often linked back to the same core principle (that bonding is about atoms obtaining full outer shells).

The range of application of the full-outer-shells principle was extensive—as students attempted to apply the principle to the wide range of different examples presented to them. I consider the term 'alternative conceptual framework' useful here because students clearly developed a series of related conceptions about an area of knowledge that were logically linked together. The octet framework does not simply involve one alternative conception, but many, and it is not simply a series of discrete conceptions, but rather *an extended conceptual structure*. Findings of this kind seem to offer very good evidence that learners' alternative ideas *can* indeed be theory-like in important senses. The students I interviewed were able to consistently apply a principle across a wide range of contexts.

However, this is certainly not to suggest that all ideas elicited from learners are of this kind. This octet framework derives from interviewing older students, studying at what is called 'advanced level' in England, who were mostly studying with the aspiration of going on to university—often to study science-related subjects.

The argument here is that *sometimes* learners' conceptions are built into extensive and coherent frameworks—but clearly that is not always so. As the various examples presented in this book suggest, students sometimes make the links we anticipate and hope for; they sometimes make alternative and less helpful links we did not expect; and sometimes they learn new material in relative isolation from other knowledge.

References

Alvarez, P., & Squire, L. R. (1994). Memory consolidation and the medial temporal lobe: A simple network model. *Proceedings of the National Academy of Sciences, 91*, 7041–7045.

Cheng, M. M. W. (2011). *Students' visualization of scientific ideas: Case studies of a physical science and a biological science topic* (Doctoral thesis, King's College, University of London, London).

Gauld, C. (1989). A study of pupils' responses to empirical evidence. In R. Millar (Ed.), *Doing science: Images of science in science education* (pp. 62–82). London: Falmer Press.

Rennie, L. J., Venville, G., & Wallace, J. (2012). *Knowledge that counts in a global community: Exploring the contribution of integrated curriculum.* Abingdon, Oxon.: Routledge.

Scott, P., Mortimer, E., & Ametller, J. (2011). Pedagogical link-making: A fundamental aspect of teaching and learning scientific conceptual knowledge. *Studies in Science Education, 47*(1), 3–36. doi: 10.1080/03057267.2011.549619

Taber, K. S. (1994). Student reaction on being introduced to concept mapping. *Physics Education, 29*(5), 276–281.

Taber, K. S. (1998). An alternative conceptual framework from chemistry education. *International Journal of Science Education, 20*(5), 597–608.

Taber, K. S. (2000). Multiple frameworks? Evidence of manifold conceptions in individual cognitive structure. *International Journal of Science Education, 22*(4), 399–417.

Taber, K. S. (2003). Lost without trace or not brought to mind? A case study of remembering and forgetting of college science. *Chemistry Education: Research and Practice, 4*(3), 249–277.

Taber, K. S. (2006). Conceptual integration: A demarcation criterion for science education? *Physics Education, 41*(4), 286–287.

Taber, K. S. (2011). The natures of scientific thinking: Creativity as the handmaiden to logic in the development of public and personal knowledge. In M. S. Khine (Ed.), *Advances in the nature of science research: Concepts and methodologies* (pp. 51–74). Dordrecht: Springer.

Taber, K. S. (2013). A common core to chemical conceptions: Learners' conceptions of chemical stability, change and bonding. In G. Tsaparlis & H. Sevian (Eds.), *Concepts of matter in science education* (pp. 391–418). Dordrecht: Springer.

Vertes, R. P. (2004). Memory consolidation in sleep: Dream or reality. *Neuron, 44*(1), 135–148. doi: 10.1016/j.neuron.2004.08.034

Walker, M. P., & Stickgold, R. (2004). Sleep-dependent learning and memory consolidation. *Neuron, 44*(1), 121–133. doi: 10.1016/j.neuron.2004.08.031

Wiltgen, B. J., Brown, R. A. M., Talton, L. E., & Silva, A. J. (2004). New circuits for old memories: The role of the neocortex in consolidation. *Neuron, 44*(1), 101–108. doi: 10.1016/j.neuron.2004.09.015

SECTION 3
Diagnosing Student Thinking in Science Learning

10
A PROVISIONAL SYNTHESIS: LEARNING, TEACHING, AND 'BUGS' IN THE SYSTEM

Consideration of how learning occurs, and the possible different influences on learners' thinking discussed in previous chapters, suggests that classroom teaching is a complex and challenging activity. This chapter seeks to build a synthesis of ideas presented earlier in the book by considering classroom teaching and learning as a 'system'. As a complex system there is much that can go wrong in classroom teaching—where intended learning does not happen. However, understanding the 'system' and being aware of the kinds of 'bugs' it is prone to can empower teachers to analyse 'system errors' and 'engineer' system adjustments to bring about better learning outcomes. The present chapter emphasises what can go wrong in science teaching, as preparation for a discussion of the 'science-teacher-as-learning-doctor' approach to responding to these challenges in the following chapter.

Development and Learning

The human cognitive system has evolved to provide us with an apparatus which can be considered to simultaneously carry out two key functions:

- to make sense of current experience in terms of existing understanding of the world;
- to learn from current experience to develop existing understanding of the world.

There is clearly a tension here. The first function would seem to privilege our existing understandings, as these provide the resources that we have available for making sense of the world. Yet the second function seems to privilege the potential of current experience as a resource for developing our understanding of the world, to better support future interpretations of experience. The set-up of our cognitive processes, and in particular the limited capacity of working memory to deal with unfamiliar information (compared with the ability to mentipulate very complex structures that have been previously established—see Chapter 9), suggests that the system has a conservative bias such that existing patterns of thought are not readily shifted by limited exposure to apparently disconfirming examples. Humans tend to have a confirmation bias that means that once we are committed to a way of thinking about something that works well for us, we do not readily 'change our minds' (Nickerson, 1998).

Presumably the nature of our cognitive system is a successful outcome of natural selection: our cognitive processes proved adaptive in relation to the environments in which humans evolved. However most of us now live our lives in highly technological built environments, in societies numbered in millions rather than dozens, and we are educated largely through formal systems of education. This is all quite different from the conditions in which human cognition developed, and perhaps our cognitive apparatus is not optimised for teaching and learning in science classes.

In addition, the apparatus that proved effective in making sense of the natural world (at least effective enough for us to have survived and learned to live in many parts of the world) has led to us commonly adopting conceptions which—although they work well in everyday life—are inconsistent with the abstract concepts that have allowed science to progress.

The key message from what we understand about human cognition is that learning is highly contingent—what is learnt is very much dependent on how the learner is able to make sense of learning experiences (see Figure 10.1). New learning is contingent on prior learning. As classroom experience interacts with (being interpreted through, and building upon) existing ways of thinking, learning is clearly also contingent on the way the teacher explains ideas, including the choice of language and the selection of models presented; the ways other students in the class interpret and talk about teaching; the nature of the scaffolding built into learning activities; and so on.

Rote and Meaningful Learning

The interaction between (a) our current experiences of the world, and (b) the ways of understanding the world constructed from prior experience, occurs both ways (see Figure 10.1). All our current experience of the world depends upon perception filtered by our existing models of the world, and those models can also be modified by that new experience.

A key idea about learning that is often emphasised is the distinction between rote and meaningful learning (Ausubel, 2000). Meaningful learning occurs when we can link a new experience to our existing ways of understanding, so we can make sense of that new experience. When this does not happen, and there is no existing mental structure to 'anchor' new experience to, then meaningful learning is not possible, and the best we can achieve is rote learning.

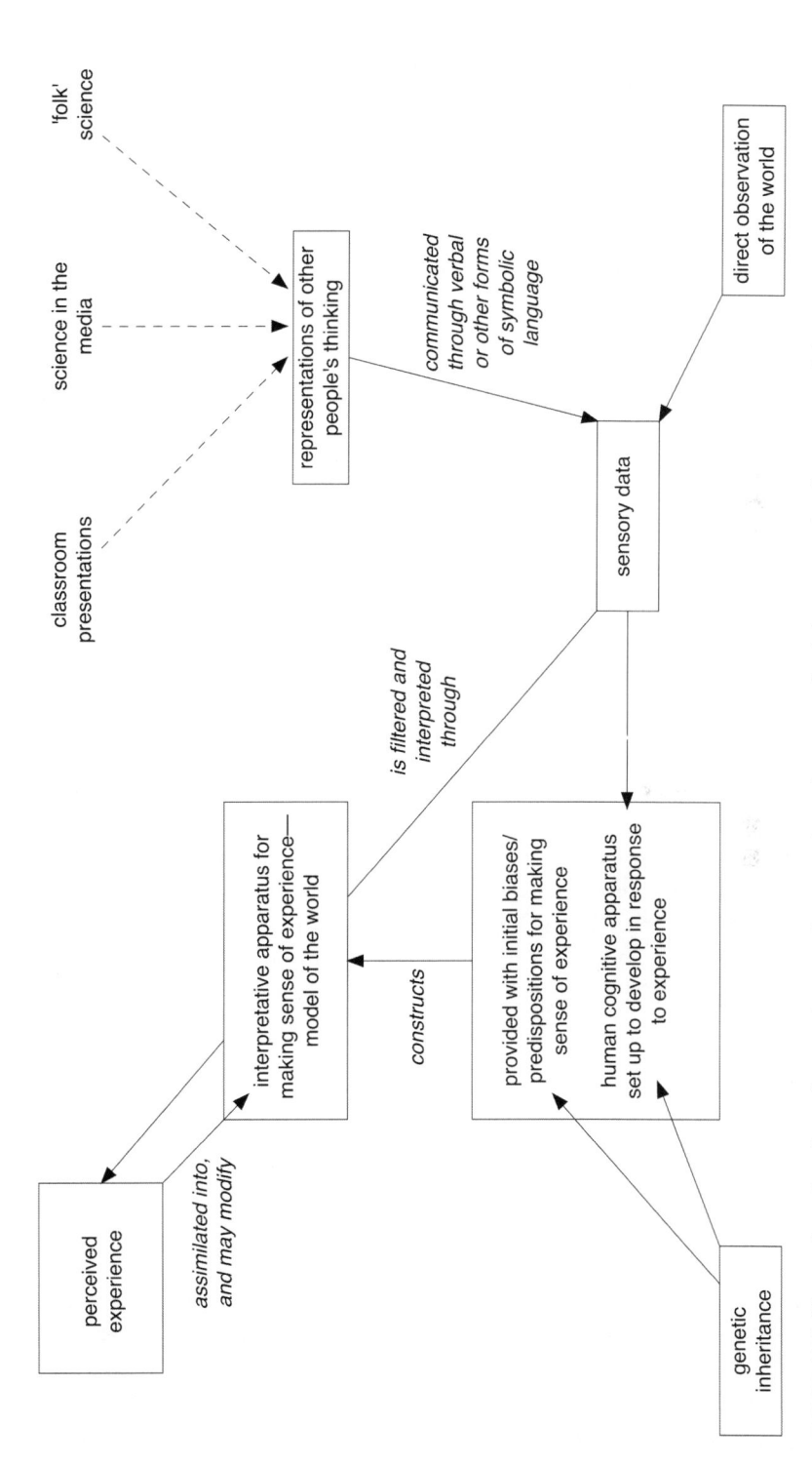

FIGURE 10.1 Human learning depends upon interpreting experience in terms of existing ways of making sense of the world.

Now the alert reader may spot an apparent inconsistency here between this idea of 'rote learning' and the model of learning being used to develop the arguments in this book. According to the constructivist model of learning discussed in Chapter 3, all new learning depends upon making sense of experience in terms of the existing cognitive structures we have developed through past experiences. That would seem to suggest that rote learning should not be possible!

Rote learning does rely upon being able to process sensory information to produce something 'sensible', but not necessarily something that makes good sense. So, for example, if a teacher asked a lower-secondary science class to learn the phrase 'reaction types can be explained in terms of overlap of frontier molecular orbitals' or to learn that 'Mollicutes are Firmicutes' it is very unlikely that any of the class would have sufficient knowledge and understanding to make much sense of the ideas being represented. However, at the least, their mental 'language module' would likely allow them to recognise that these were verbal phrases and to appreciate the function of the everyday words, and recognise that unfamiliar terms referred to some kind of entities.

The students could commit the phrases to memory if they rehearsed them enough, although this would require deliberate effort. Strictly, this is only possible because at some level the learners made some minimal sense of the information—if only to understand it was a verbal phrase. Yet this would not involve any understanding of the conceptual ideas represented, so this would be considered to be 'rote' learning rather than meaningful learning. It seems that the notion of 'rote' versus 'meaningful' learning is a useful one, although it is perhaps not an absolute distinction, as material to be learnt can be *more* or *less* meaningful to learners. Figure 10.2 represents 'rote learning' as an *ideal* type in the sense that purely rote learning is a useful reference category whereas real learning will be meaningful to a greater or lesser extent.

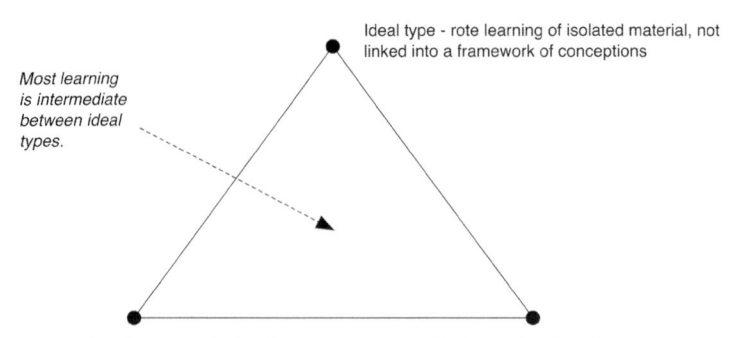

FIGURE 10.2 Ideal categories of learning (modified from Taber, 2013a, p. 163). Reproduced by permission of the Royal Society of Chemistry (RSC).

Assimilation and Accommodation

Figure 10.2 does not show a single category of meaningful learning; rather, meaningful learning is represented by the side of the triangle (the base) opposite the rote learning apex. The terms 'assimilation' and 'accommodation' are sometimes used to describe how new learning fits into existing conceptual structures. These terms derive from Piaget's theory of cognitive development (see Chapter 4). Assimilation implies that new learning just fits into existing conceptual structures as they are, and accommodation refers to when existing frameworks have to be modified before new learning will fit. Piaget himself seemed to think that all learning involved what he called a 'disequilibrium' because it required some kind of compromise with existing understanding, and that learning would be assimilated, but put a strain on existing structures which would then have to accommodate the new learning (providing a new 'equilibration').

However, researchers in science education have often emphasised a distinction between those situations where new learning can be readily fitted without any major upheavals in thinking, and those cases where conceptual change requires the students to significantly modify their way of thinking (Vosniadou, 2008). Sometimes the labels 'assimilation' and 'accommodation' are used for these two situations. Figure 10.2 suggests that in real classroom learning we normally have some degree of modification of existing thinking when new learning occurs.

Knowledge Representation in Curriculum and Teaching

Learning science in school is a process that involves a series of interpretations and representations of material. Arguably, knowledge only exists in minds, so books and other objects can only be said to contain representations of the ideas (Taber, 2013b). The accounts of scientific knowledge in research journals and review articles are already one step away from the actual knowledge of scientists. These accounts have to be interpreted by readers who make sense of them in terms of their own knowledge and understanding. In higher education, students may well read primary research literature, but in school this is seldom the case.

School teaching is usually informed by some form of target knowledge that is set out in curriculum documents, such as national education standards, national curriculum frameworks, examination specifications, and schemes of work. These documents are produced to offer a simplified account of scientific knowledge (as understood by the curriculum developers) considered to be suitable and appropriate for learners at a particular stage of their learning.

Some school and college learners might use such curriculum documentation extensively to organise, plan, and evaluate their own learning, if only when revising for high-stakes tests. However, usually in school the teacher has a major role in mediating the curriculum, interpreting the documents (in terms of their own knowledge and understanding), and planning instruction that they feel will best support the learning of the target knowledge set out in the curriculum.

In general then, and often exclusively in the early secondary years at least, the student does not often meet primary accounts of scientific knowledge, but rather experiences instruction designed to bring about learning that matches what the teacher understands to be the curricular models of scientific knowledge represented in curriculum documents (see Figure 10.3).

```
┌──────────────────────┐
│ canonical scientific │
│      accounts        │
└──────────┬───────────┘
           │  Scientific knowledge is selected and simplified for curriculum documents.
           ▼
┌──────────────────────┐
│ curricular account of│
│       science        │
└──────────┬───────────┘
           │  Teacher interprets curriculum documents in terms of his or her own
           │  subject knowledge.
           ▼
┌──────────────────────┐
│ teacher's understanding │
│  of target knowledge    │
└──────────┬───────────┘
           │  Teacher draws upon pedagogic expertise to plan classroom presentations
           │  and activities to bring about intended learning.
           ▼
┌──────────────────────┐
│  teacher's design of │
│  learning experience │
└──────────┬───────────┘
           │  Teacher teaches lesson in the light of constraints (student motivation and
           │  interest, classroom facilities, external distractions, etc.).
           ▼
┌──────────────────────┐
│teacher's implementation│
│      of lesson        │
└──────────┬───────────┘
           │  Student interprets lesson in terms of existing predisposition, as well as
           │  aspects of existing knowledge and understanding perceived as relevant.
           ▼
┌──────────────────────┐
│ student's interpretation│
│      of lesson        │
└──────────┬───────────┘
           │  Interpretation of lesson may lead to new learning assimilated into, or even
           │  modifying, existing knowledge and understanding.
           ▼
┌──────────────────────┐
│   student learning   │
└──────────────────────┘
```

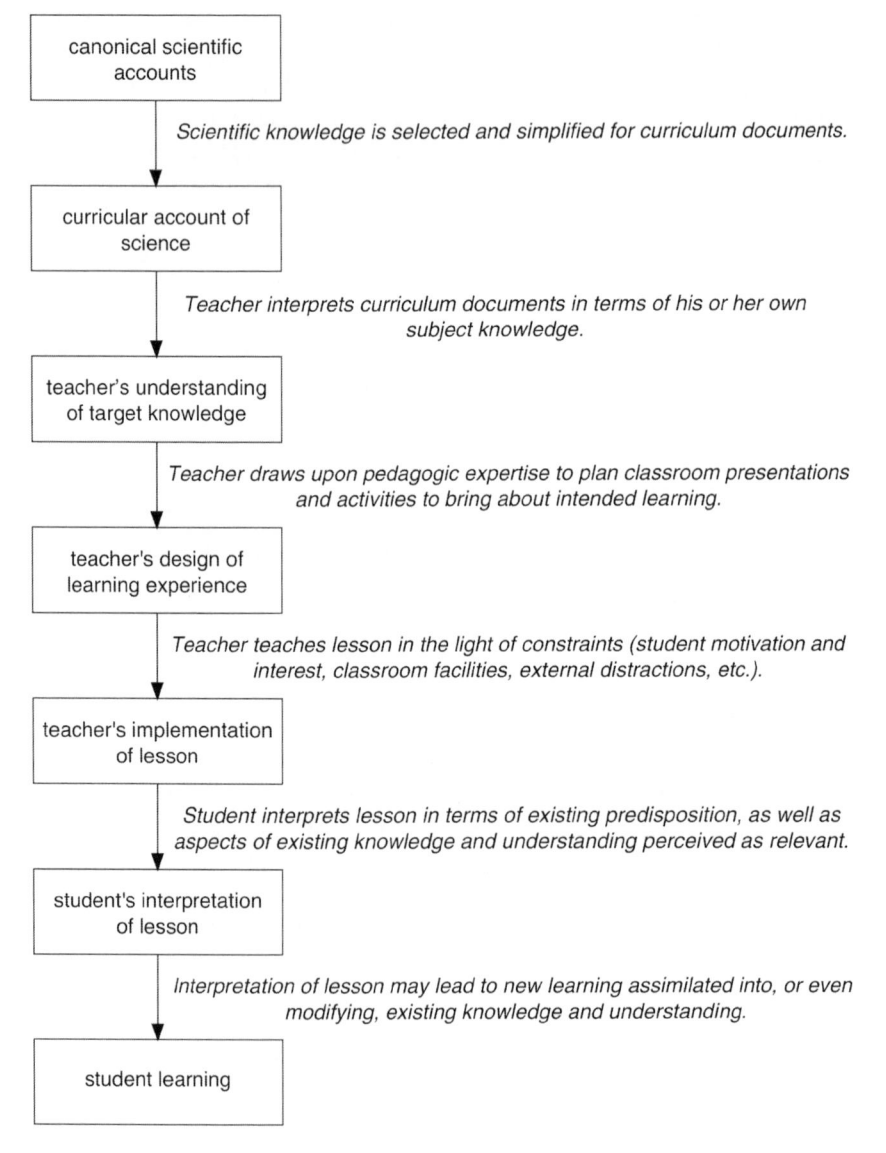

FIGURE 10.3 From formal scientific knowledge to personal understanding: a series of interpretations and representations.

Students may also use textbooks—as a main focus of lessons in some educational contexts, as an occasional supplementary resource in others. The textbook author acts as additional teacher—someone who is interpreting target knowledge represented in curriculum documents, and offering a presentation based on that target knowledge considered suitable for their readership. Textbooks are also indirect sources of scientific knowledge—like teachers, only less flexible. The teacher can hone lessons for particular classes, where the textbook is intended to meet the needs of a great many different students in a variety of classrooms.

It was suggested earlier in Chapter 3 that learning was incremental, interpretative, and iterative. Science teaching has to respect and fit these characteristics if we wish to teach effectively through instruction that best supports learning.

Teaching for Contingent Learning

The previous sections of the book have explored the nature of learning in science, and have discussed a range of examples of student comments that offer us insight into their thinking. By the time students come to class to learn particular science lessons they are anything but blank slates on which the teacher can metaphorically write the canonical ideas of science. Rather, learners will interpret teaching in terms of the mental resources available to them for making sense of the world (see Figure 10.1), resources that have developed iteratively from the action and reinterpretation of genetic predispositions, direct physical experience, and various cultural and social sources.

The teacher then teaches a lesson in a particular physical setting, within a particular institutional and curriculum context, to learners operating in a particular social and language community, with the hope that this learning experience with lead to something like a canonical understanding of the science. When presented in those terms it may seem incredible that any of our students ever learn anything close to what their teachers intend.

However, good teaching is not a one-way process of the teacher representing his or her thinking (in words, diagrams, gestures, etc.) and then simply hoping for the desired interpretation. Teaching is an interactive process (see the next chapter). Teachers set up learning opportunities that can scaffold learning in view of students' current knowledge and understanding. Teachers use mental models of students' current knowledge and understanding, to select explanations to link to current understanding, and they feed out new information in manageable 'learning quanta' that do not swamp students' working memories (see Figure 10.4).

Clearly such a one-shot conception of teaching relies on the teacher's own mental model of the learner and the learning processes being good enough to allow teaching to be interpreted as intended, so to modify the learner's existing knowledge and understanding in the desired ways. Given that even researchers who have more time to focus on modelling learners and their learning find this a highly challenging task (Taber, 2013b), it is unreasonable to expect teachers' own

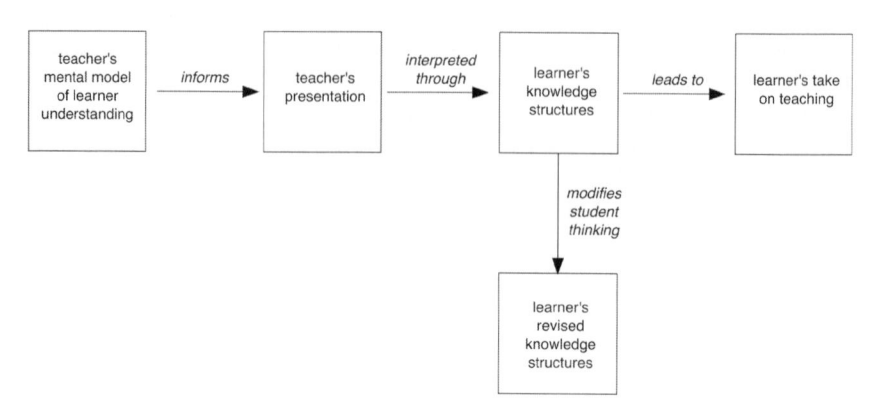

```
teacher's                          interpreted
mental model  → informs →  teacher's  → through →  learner's  → leads to →  learner's take
of learner                 presentation           knowledge              on teaching
understanding                                     structures
                                                      ↓
                                                  modifies
                                                   student
                                                   thinking
                                                      ↓
                                                  learner's
                                                   revised
                                                  knowledge
                                                  structures
```

FIGURE 10.4 Teaching as one-way process of acting in response to a predetermined plan based on the teacher's understanding of the learner prior to the lesson.

models to always support effective teaching—especially when most teachers are working with a number of different classes, each made of many learners. It is no mystery why there is often a 'mismatch' between the teacher's mental model of how learning will occur and what actually happens in the class itself!

Impediments to Intended Learning: Bugs in the Teaching Learning System

Clearly teaching is a highly challenging process, which depends upon both classroom skills and expert knowledge to support decision-making. The best teachers are highly skilled, and do have a great deal of expertise—relating to science, to pedagogy, to the constraints and affordances of the teaching context, and of their students. Yet it is clear that even with the most motivated students and highly skilled and dedicated teachers, there is much to go wrong.

Effective science teaching relies on a strong match between

1. the teacher's *expectation* of how particular classroom experiences will relate to and build upon the learners' current conceptual knowledge and understanding; and
2. how those enacted experiences will *actually* be interpreted in terms of the learners' *actual* prior conceptual knowledge and understanding.

Planning an effective lesson starts to seem akin to preparing for a sports contest or a political campaign—where planning one's own actions is informed by incomplete knowledge of the capacities of others and how they might respond to our actions.

Drawing upon the examples of student thinking in earlier chapters in the book it is possible to compile a typology of possible learning impediments, the different ways in which there might be a mismatch between the model of student knowledge and understanding informing lesson planning, and the ways a particular learner's actual knowledge and understanding will shape interpretations of classroom experiences to bring about new learning.

A Typology of Learning Impediments

The purpose of having the typology is to help us understand the different ways something can go wrong when learning does not occur as we intended, as this can be used as a tool for modifying and improving our teaching (and this will be considered in more detail in the next chapter). In formalising the typology it is useful to have labels to describe its different categories, and this can make it seem rather technical. However the labels are only intended to act as shorthand for distinctions that may help inform our future teaching.

The typology is based upon distinctions made at two levels. The first level distinguishes between (a) situations where a student does not make sense of teaching, and (b) situations where the student does make sense of teaching—but not as the teacher intended.

Null and Substantial Learning Impediments

In planning teaching, the teacher intends the ideas and activities included in the lesson to connect with aspects of students' existing conceptual knowledge and understanding. Even in informal communication in everyday life we make an implicit assumption about others' knowledge such that we use language to represent ideas we expect them to understand. In everyday life we do this automatically to some extent: shifting our language register when addressing a young child, or someone we know has limited English, or someone we know will not have technical vocabulary when we are talking about specialised subjects. These abilities depend upon our 'theory of mind' (which was introduced in Chapter 3). Teachers go beyond these automatic processes to deliberate about learners' existing knowledge in planning their lessons.

A *null learning impediment* occurs when the student does not make a meaningful link between what is presented in science teaching and his or her existing knowledge and understanding. Without such a link the best that can be achieved is rote learning (cf. Figure 10.2). It was intended that new learning would be built upon relevant existing knowledge and understanding—but as the link is not made, this cannot happen.

A *substantive learning impediment* occurs where the learner is able to interpret instruction in terms of existing knowledge and understanding, and make sense of it accordingly—but in a way significantly differently to that intended by the teacher. In this situation the learner certainly forms a new understanding based on teaching, but understands differently to the canonical interpretation represented in the curriculum. A link is made, but from the teacher's perspective, this is an 'unproductive' or 'flawed' link.

Two Types of Null Learning Impediments—Deficiency and Fragmentation

Null learning impediments can occur for two rather different reasons. Often the knowledge and understanding the teacher expects the learner to have does not exist—that is, there is a *deficiency learning impediment*. Perhaps the teacher is assuming knowledge and understanding that is part of the curriculum learners should have already studied. Perhaps the teacher is assuming familiarly with some feature of culture considered to be common ground and suitable for use as the basis of an analogy or example, but the students lack that familiarity. I well remember how during the 1970 Association Football ('soccer') World Cup Finals there was much talk in the media about the effect of the 'rarified air', a potential reference point for talking about the compressions and rarefactions that occur when sound passes through air. Unfortunately, by the time I became a school teacher the oldest pupils in the school would only have been four at the time of the competition and so did not share this cultural referent. The youngest had not even been born at the time.

However, not all null learning impediments relate to expected prior knowledge that is 'missing'. We all have represented an immense amount of past experience in our brains and can potentially recall vast quantities of material. However, at any one moment we are only aware of a minuscule fraction of what we actually know. Some material is more readily accessed; some less so. What we bring to mind at any time is often contingent on contextual factors—including our current lines of thought. In my extended interviewing of students there have been many occasions where they initially do not seem to know some particular scientific information, but then on probing suddenly bring it to mind.

So as well as failing to make a link because expected prior learning is not present, there are many occasions where learners simply fail to appreciate what background knowledge they are expected to see as relevant, and so do not bring to mind what the teacher thinks is obviously relevant prior learning. Sometimes these *fragmentation learning impediments* reflect how the knowledge structures of novices (such as students) tend to be much less well organised and integrated than those of experts (such as teachers)—so connections that seem very obvious to teachers need to be made explicit before learners will make them (cf. Chapter 9).

Two Types of Substantive Learning Impediments—Grounded and Associative

Just as failures to make sense of teaching can reflect two quite different things that have gone 'wrong' in teaching, there are also two main ways in which students make inappropriate sense of teaching so that they come to understand teaching differently than intended. Substantive learning impediments occur when students interpret teaching in terms of their existing knowledge and understanding, but in such a way that the intended meaning of instruction is distorted. That is, teaching is misinterpreted and learners develop new understandings quite at odds with target knowledge. Either teaching is made sense of in terms of existing alternative conceptions that are inconsistent with the scientific account, or students make inappropriate links with their existing knowledge.

Grounded learning impediments occur when students already hold alternative conceptions of a particular topic, and so when they meet new teaching about the topic they make sense of it in terms of preexisting nonscientific ways of thinking. *Associative learning impediments* occur when students bring to mind prior learning that from the scientific perspective is unrelated, but which seems relevant to them. They may consider something presented in teaching as an example of some existing category or application of some known principle that does not actually apply, or they might make a creative but unhelpful analogy with a source concept that encourages them to think about the new concept in a noncanonical way.

Sources of Grounded Learning Impediments

Grounded learning impediments occur because existing understanding is inconsistent with accepted scientific thinking. As we have seen earlier in the book there may be different sources of learners' alternative ideas. There may be 'intuitive' learning impediments where the students have developed models based on their interpretations of previous experiences (see Chapter 5). There may be 'life-world' learning impediments where folk beliefs—commonly held scientifically dubious ideas—may be acquired from friends, family, the media, and so on (see Chapter 7).

There may also be 'pedagogic' learning impediments due to limitations of previous teaching, such as oversimplification, use of poor analogies and unhelpful models, and so forth. We have seen that teaching involves simplification of scientific ideas and models so that they are accessible to learners, and it may be very difficult to judge an optimal level of simplification (Taber, 2000) that allows students to understand an account that retains enough of the essence of the scientific concepts to be an authentic simplification.

Sources of Associative Learning Impediments

Associative learning impediments occur because the student makes an unintended link with prior learning. These may also have various sources, as different kinds of cues can activate prior knowledge that is perceived as relevant to instruction. There are 'linguistic' learning impediments, where a student is cued by a word's 'everyday' usage, or the similarity of a word with the label for an existing concept (see Chapter 6). There are also 'creative' learning impediments where the learner spontaneously forms an inappropriate analogy. Analogies can be very productive, but may also mislead when surface similarities may be salient but there are significant differences in the underlying structure of the analogue and the target concept.

Also, as with grounded learning impediments, some associative learning impediments may derive from teaching itself. Students may overinterpret models and metaphors presented in class when what are intended as casual comparisons are understood as significant guides to how to understand a new concept. As teachers are charged with making the unfamiliar familiar, they will build up a repertoire of 'entry points' in the form of comparisons that can act as potential starting points for thinking about some abstract new concept. This is, in principle, good pedagogy, but brings the risk that if students form a strong association they may then become committed to the link. Students may not appreciate that something is intended only as a starting point, and simply assume this is a core aspect of the concept they are being taught.

This is what often seems to happen with the use of anthropomorphic language (see Chapter 6), where 'weak' anthropomorphism (that is, anthropomorphism used by the teacher to offer a way to start thinking and talking about a new abstract ideas) is readily adopted by learners as strong anthropomorphism—where talking about, for example, the *needs* of atoms is seen as a sufficient form of explanation in science. Forms of language that are intended to be 'fluid' and readily drain away as they become superfluous, instead condense into something more rigid and permanent.

So there are 'epistemological' learning impediments when students lack the epistemological sophistication to appreciate the nature and limitations of models, analogies, and metaphors used in science teaching (see Chapter 8), and so come to interpret teaching in a too literal and absolute sense. This is not a reason to abandon the use of models, analogies, and metaphors as these can be productive in science teaching (as in science itself), but rather shows the importance of making explicit the central role of models of different kinds—their affordances and their limitations—as part of science education.

Classification of Learning Impediments

These different types of learning bugs—different impediments to intended learning—are listed in Table 10.1. The terminology used to label the different categories is less important than the recognition that there are different ways in which students coming to class can fail to understand teaching in the way we intend, given how effective learning requires a good match between the teaching and the ways learners perceive instruction in terms of their existing learning and understanding of science topics.

This might appear to be a very negative message for teachers. Science is difficult to learn (see Chapter 1), and teaching requires teachers to match instruction to the existing conceptual structures of learners—which are often at odds with scientific accounts of the world, and may be quite idiosyncratic. There is certainly a lot to potentially go wrong, and common experience is that students in science classes can often fail to learn as intended.

TABLE 10.1 A typology of learning bugs.

A learning 'bug' can occur when ...		
... students do not make sense of teaching ... *(a null learning impediment)*		
	... because they lack expected prior knowledge ... *(a deficiency learning impediment)*	
	... because they do not perceive the relevance of, and so do not bring to mind, prior knowledge ... *(a fragmentation learning impediment)*	
... students understand teaching differently from how intended ... *(a substantive learning impediment)*		
	... because their existing knowledge and understanding includes alternative conceptions ... *(a grounded learning impediment)*	
		... based upon their implicit understanding of the world ... *(an intuitive learning impediment)*
		... drawing on folk beliefs with currency in society ... *(a life-world learning impediment)*
		... drawing upon misleading prior teaching ... *(a pedagogic learning impediment)*
	... because they make inappropriate links with existing knowledge ... *(an associative learning impediment)*	
		... forming a creative but unhelpful analogy with prior knowledge ... *(a creative learning impediment)*
		... drawing upon unintended cues in language ... *(a linguistic learning impediment)*
		... failing to appreciate the limitations of models, analogies, metaphors, and so forth used in teaching ... *(an epistemological learning impediment)*

However, it is not the purpose of this book to tell science teachers and others working in science education what we already know: effective science teaching is challenging. Rather this book offers an analysis to help teachers adopt strategies to best respond to and overcome these difficulties. The next chapter then considers how science teachers can use an understanding of the sources of learning 'bugs' to inform and develop their own classroom teaching. In particular, the next chapter sets out the 'science-teacher-as-learning-doctor' perspective to thinking about classroom teaching.

References

Ausubel, D. P. (2000). *The acquisition and retention of knowledge: A cognitive view.* Dordrecht: Kluwer Academic.

Nickerson, R. S. (1998). Confirmation bias: A ubiquitous phenomenon in many guises. *Review of General Psychology, 2*(2), 175–220.

Taber, K. S. (2000). Finding the optimum level of simplification: The case of teaching about heat and temperature. *Physics Education, 35*(5), 320–325.

Taber, K. S. (2013a). Revisiting the chemistry triplet: Drawing upon the nature of chemical knowledge and the psychology of learning to inform chemistry education. *Chemistry Education Research and Practice, 14*(2), 156–168. doi: 10.1039/C3RP00012E

Taber, K. S. (2013b). *Modelling learners and learning in science education: Developing representations of concepts, conceptual structure and conceptual change to inform teaching and research.* Dordrecht: Springer.

Vosniadou, S. (Ed.). (2008). *International handbook of research on conceptual change.* London: Routledge.

11
THE SCIENCE TEACHER AS LEARNING DOCTOR

The previous chapter spelt out in some detail how teaching can go wrong. The nature of the teaching process was analysed in terms of how effective teaching requires teachers to anticipate how instruction will interact with, and be interpreted through, students' existing knowledge and understanding. The different perspectives on aspects of student thinking considered earlier in the book suggest a diversity of ways in which this process can break down because of how students make sense of instruction in terms of their actual knowledge and understanding. The present chapter considers how science teachers can respond to these challenges to teach more effectively in the light of what we can learn about learners' thinking about scientific topics. In particular, the chapter discusses the 'science-teacher-as-learning-doctor' perspective.

Diagnostic Assessment as Part of Teaching

Teachers undertake diagnostic assessment to check for essential prerequisite learning and for the presence of common alternative conceptions that may impede learning of science. In particular, teachers talk to and with, not just at, their students. Good teachers maintain a conversation in the class—constantly asking questions to test out whether students are following arguments, and whether they are interpreting teaching as intended. In Chapter 6 some of the limitations of language as a medium of communication were considered, but, as the lauded educationalist Jerome Bruner (1987, p. 87) pointed out, conversation allows us to draw upon 'constant transactional calibration'. That is, through dialogue, we can constantly check on whether our intended messages are getting through without too much distortion.

In a sense, good teaching often reflects the so-called Socratic method, where a learner is brought to knowledge by an ongoing sequence of questions. However, that pure form of Socratic method runs into both philosophical and practical difficulties in the science classroom. The philosophical difficulty is that the method assumes that we all have the knowledge to be learnt somehow already available to us, and that it just needs to be accessed by clever questioning. The constructivist model (see Chapter 3) drawn upon in this book (and indeed widely adopted in science education) does not accept that learning is about uncovering something buried deep in our minds, but sees it more as constructing something new by building upon existing knowledge in (what are for the learner) novel ways. The Socratic method is very powerful, and can help learners see how their existing knowledge can be used to draw new conclusions or make new links, but can only work with the resources a learner has available. Sometimes in teaching we need to offer new experiences as the basis for new learning.

A practical problem is that the Socratic method rather assumes that we are working with one student at a time. That was fine for Alexander the Great—his parents could afford to employ Aristotle to give him tuition with undivided attention. Most of us these days are working with much larger group sizes, and can only give each individual learner limited time for one-to-one instruction. Nonetheless, effective science teaching resembles conversation more than soliloquy. Mortimer and Scott (2003) described how effective science teaching shifts between different phases of eliciting and exploring students' ideas and views, and presenting the scientific narratives. The purpose of including student perspectives is not to suggest they are given equal status with canonical science, but to allow the teacher to engage with student thinking, helping students see how the scientific narrative differs from their own understandings, and why it is the preferred account in science.

A challenge here is ensuring all learners are engaged in the conversation. Even the best teacher finds it difficult to include all learners' voices in the classroom dialogue within each lesson. There are useful methods involving group work—such as asking students to work in pairs, then asking adjacent pairs to share, or envoying where groups have to share ideas through nominated students who move between groups. Group activities take time but tend to be useful when there are likely to be diverse views within a class; the exposure to different views and discussion of their relative merits can be very productive in getting students to question their own thinking.

Surveying students with quick paper-and-pencil diagnostic probes may be more useful when testing for the presence of well-established and often tenacious alternative conceptions known to be common among the age group taught. The identification of known major sticking points may indicate the need for the teacher to set up specific activities or arguments that have been demonstrated to challenge the particular conceptions. Clearly, getting pedagogy right can be a nuanced matter, but classroom diagnosis of student ideas is an important tool (Taber, 2001) given how readily students will interpret new learning in terms of their existing ideas.

Diagnostic Assessment Probes

There are many instruments available to teachers to help them diagnose student thinking, and in particular common alternative conceptions. One of the most well known is the Forces Concept Inventory which is especially suitable for college-level students (Savinainen & Scott, 2002). The processes of designing and refining diagnostic instruments that are valid and reliable enough to provide information suitable for research have been explored by David Treagust (1988), and have been applied in the development of various research instruments that can also be used by classroom teachers.

Whilst these research instruments can be applied in teaching, there are also many other probes that are useful for classroom teaching, including some intended as a basis for group work and classroom discussion rather than to collect data from individual learners. When such probes are used in this way they should not be considered to be tests, but rather to be teaching and learning activities that also provide diagnostic information to the teacher. This fits with the now commonly accepted notion that most classroom assessment should be formative in nature, supporting rather than just evaluating teaching and learning (Black & Wiliam, 1998).

Some years ago I worked on a project funded by the UK's Royal Society of Chemistry (RSC) to provide a set of resources for classroom teachers (Taber, 2002) that would allow them to probe student understanding in a number of secondary-level chemistry topics where common learning difficulties and alternative conceptions were recognised (Figure 4.2 in Chapter 4 is taken from one of the probes). Most of these probes would be considered underdeveloped as research instruments that can allow researchers to draw firm conclusions from response patterns. That is usually only assured by cycles of instrument development including interviews with students about their interpretations of questions and why they gave particular responses (Tan, Goh, Chia, & Taber, 2005). However, the RSC probes were not primarily intended to provide precise data on the proportions of students holding particular ideas, but rather to provide contexts for learners to reveal their thinking, and so to give the classroom teacher insight into the ways students understood key ideas. Teachers who used the probes and supporting materials found this a 'very useful tool' for planning teaching and for improving students' learning (Murphy, Jones, & Lunn, 2004).

There are other sources of useful diagnostic probes that teachers can incorporate into their teaching. For example, concept cartoons offer students several views to consider and discuss. Stuart Naylor and Brenda Keogh (2000) produced an extensive collection of such cartoons relating to a good many of the concepts learners meet in lower-secondary science classrooms. Each cartoon offers a picture showing some phenomenon of interest, and a number of individuals offering their views and interpretations—including both suggestions that fit with the canonical science, and alternative suggestions reflecting those revealed by research into learners' thinking and conceptions. An adaption of this approach to considering an aspect of the nature of science is shown in Figure 11.1.

194 Diagnosing Student Thinking in Science Learning

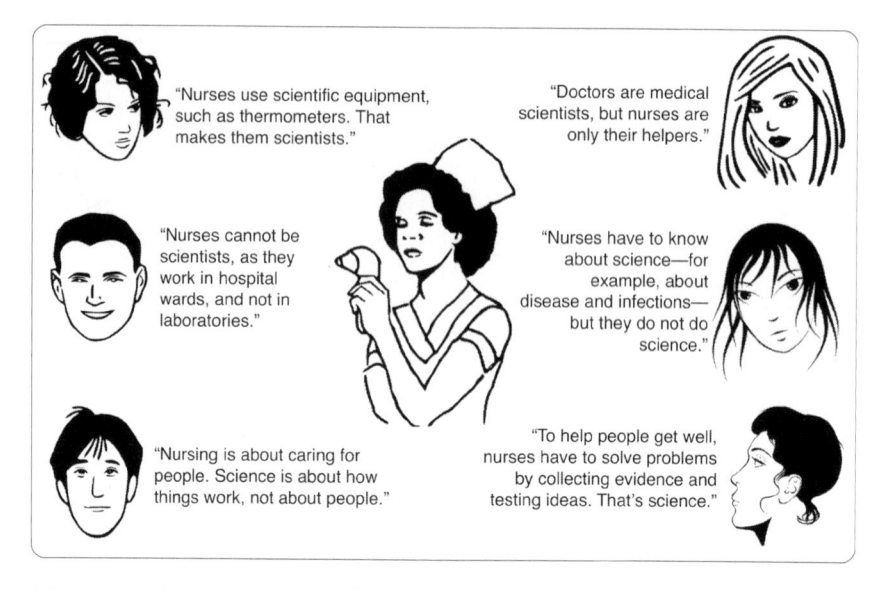

"Nurses use scientific equipment, such as thermometers. That makes them scientists."

"Doctors are medical scientists, but nurses are only their helpers."

"Nurses cannot be scientists, as they work in hospital wards, and not in laboratories."

"Nurses have to know about science—for example, about disease and infections—but they do not do science."

"Nursing is about caring for people. Science is about how things work, not about people."

"To help people get well, nurses have to solve problems by collecting evidence and testing ideas. That's science."

FIGURE 11.1 A concept cartoon designed to elicit learners' notions of the nature of science (activity designed for the epiSTEMe project, www.educ.cam.ac.uk/research/projects/episteme/).

There is a good deal of material now available, either commercially or shared by researchers and teachers through websites, that can be used as the basis for diagnostic activities in science. This material is often designed in the light of research which shows that learners commonly hold—or are inclined to develop—particular notions, and so provides contexts where students with such ways of thinking are likely to make their ideas explicit, allowing the teacher to become aware of them.

A reader of this book will have realised that in many science topics there are common alternative conceptions or at least predispositions to developing those conceptions likely to be shared by at least some learners in many classrooms. Yet, by no means are all alternative conceptions widely shared by students. Time spent talking to learners about their ideas leads to the identification of both common themes and unique features of the thinking of individuals. Indeed most students seem to have idiosyncratic ideas in some topic or other. This is perhaps not surprising: each individual has unique experiences that feed the iterative interpretation process of human learning (see Chapter 3).

What this means is that whilst specific probes may be useful for checking for common alternative ways of thinking, it is not possible to have a comprehensive set of probes which are likely to capture all aspects of student thinking likely to be significant for learning in science. It still makes good sense to adopt diagnostic assessment probes designed to reveal common alternative conceptions within teaching schemes, as this allows teachers to know when they need to explore, challenge, or develop particular ideas within the class. Yet diagnostic assessment of this type can only 'catch' known common conceptions.

Thinking Like a Science Learning Doctor

This suggests that the effective science teacher needs to always be on the alert for indicators of student thinking that might imply alternative conceptions, or the inappropriate application of implicit knowledge (intuitions) where not scientifically appropriate. Every time students communicate about their ideas in science (whether through talk, writing, drawing, modelling, etc.), they offer the teacher a modest window into their way of thinking. In classrooms where students have rich opportunities to communicate their ideas (rather than mostly listening, reading, or taking down notes), teachers have regular opportunities to become aware of how learners are thinking. These are the classrooms where learners are challenged to process and question their knowledge, to make it explicit enough to explain it to others, and to justify their thinking to others. Working in such classrooms offers the teacher the possibility of practising as a 'science learning doctor'.

Bugs in the System

The idea of the learning doctor draws on a medical analogy that sees part of the role of the teacher to be to 'diagnose' and 'treat' bugs in the teaching-learning process. As in the work of medical doctors, bugs are considered somewhat inevitable. The complex nature of human beings living alongside biota that has coevolved with us makes us susceptible to a wide range of medical problems. Sometimes we can understand these well enough to put preventative medicine in place. Often however we instead have to rely on good diagnosis and treatment when problems occur.

Teaching science requires the teacher to communicate complex and often abstract ideas to classes of learners, each of which brings his or her own somewhat unique set of cognitive resources as the basis of interpreting that teaching. We have seen earlier in the book just to what extent learning involves making personal sense of teaching by interpreting someone else's ideas represented in language, diagrams, and so on in terms of existing knowledge and understanding. Clearly a lot can go wrong in this process (see the previous chapter), even if we can take for granted that students are present, and paying attention, and wish to learn (which is sadly not always the case).

Figure 11.2 offers a simple representation of this complex system. The teacher draws upon his or her own understanding of the science, plus his or her knowledge of subject-specific pedagogy (for example, useful teaching models and metaphors, etc.), and then considers his or her understanding of the particular class (What do they already know and understand? What kind of activities engage them? What kind of examples might interest them? etc.), and the teaching context (What are the norms in the school? Is there a fume cupboard or sinks? Can the tables and chairs be rearranged? What habitats can be readily visited from the classroom? etc.),

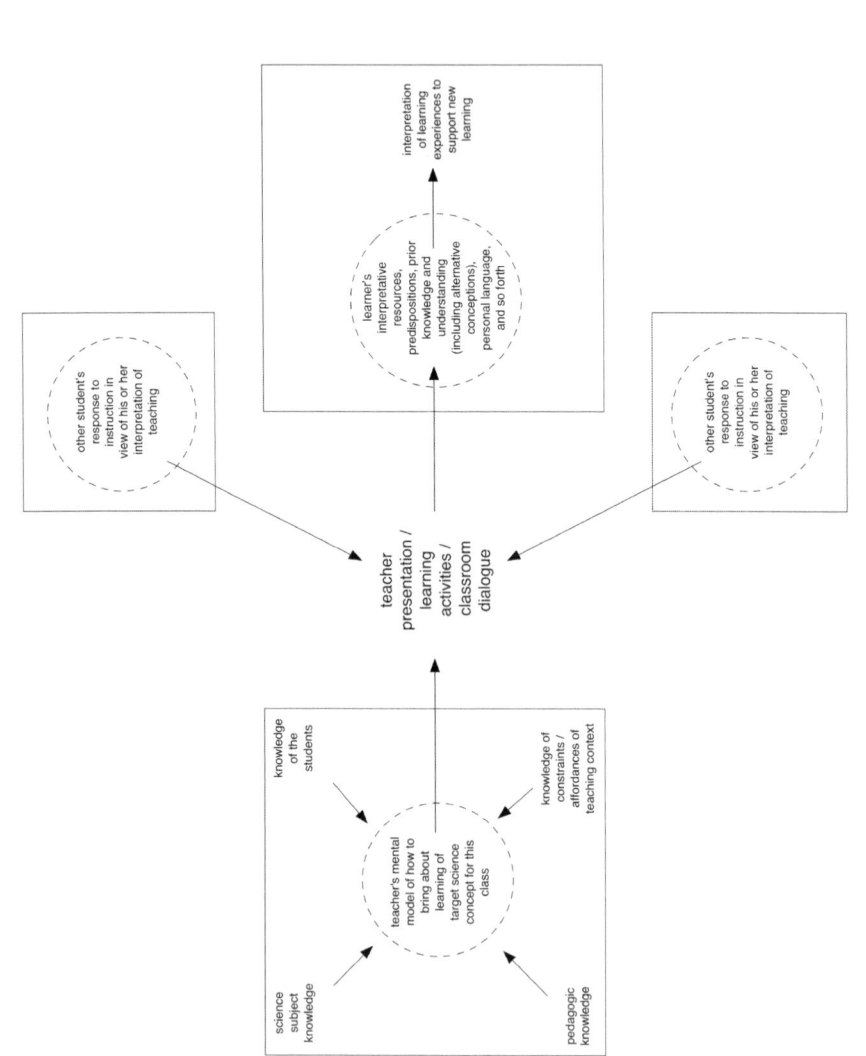

FIGURE 11.2 Teaching-learning can be considered as a system that involves the teacher anticipating how learners will interpret teaching.

and so produces a mental model of the way that teaching can bring about learning in this class. Each individual learner then experiences that lesson through the interpretive goggles of his or her existing knowledge and understanding, using his or her own individual takes on language, (preconsciously) assigning salience to particular features of demonstrations or activities, giving weight—or not—to the comments of other students in the class as they make their own sense of the science, and giving emphasis to particular terms or analogies that find resonance in his or her own thinking, and so on.

Just as getting ill is not generally the fault of the either the patient or the doctor, failures to learn as intended are not helpfully considered to be the fault of the learner or teacher. Teaching requires the teacher to have a good enough mental model of the learners' existing conceptual knowledge and understanding to present ideas in ways that will be understood as intended, and it is not reasonable to expect that can be possible all of the time. As Figure 11.2 (and Chapter 10) suggests, there is a good deal to go wrong.

Prevention, Diagnosis, and Cure

The science learning doctor, like the medical doctor, adopts a two-pronged approach to this situation. One aspect of the work is prevention—to avoid learning bugs as much as possible. This requires the teacher to have good pedagogical knowledge and good knowledge of learners.

Pedagogical knowledge would include such features as:

- understanding the difficulties of learning science concepts 'from the learners' resolution' (where they often seem more complex than they appear to the expert);
- understanding what amounts to optimal levels of simplification—where ideas are simplified enough to make sense to (particular groups of) learners, whilst maintaining the essential aspects of authentic scientific concepts;
- having a repertoire of relevant narratives, models, metaphors, and so forth that are likely to make sense to learners and that be used to help make the unfamiliar familiar.

Knowledge of the learners will include:

- appreciating the conceptual level at which learners are working;
- being aware of the prior knowledge available from earlier teaching;
- being aware of common alternative conceptions students may hold (in part from the use of diagnostic probes, discussed previously);
- being aware of students' levels of motivation, concentration span, personal interests, and preferred learning styles.

So the teacher-as-learning-doctor seeks to fine tune teaching to particular classes aware that how learners will interpret teaching is just as important to what is learnt as what is actually taught. However, given that the teaching-learning system is so complex (see Figure 11.2) the teacher-as-learning-doctor will also be aware that only so much prevention of learning bugs is possible by tuning of teaching *at the preparation stage*. The difficulty was summarised in Figure 10.4 (in Chapter 10), which presents teaching as a 'one shot' process, where the teacher's model informs classroom actions that will be interpreted by the learner, potentially leading to some change in his or her thinking.

So good preparation is important, but much of the work of the learning doctor takes place in the classroom itself where the teacher constantly seeks feedback on how teaching is being interpreted and made sense of by giving learners the opportunity to express and apply their developing understanding. This provides myriad opportunities for learning bugs to become clear where students are unable to answer questions, or offer scientifically inappropriate responses. The teacher-as-learning-doctor does not simply consider 'wrong answers' as failures to understand or learn, but rather opportunities to put things right by exploring student thinking and helping learners shift towards scientific understandings.

This sounds rather idealistic. When teaching complex, abstract material (see Chapter 1) to large classes of students with different levels of background knowledge, each with his or her own set of alternative conceptions, and perhaps different degrees of formal operational thinking available, it may be unreasonable to expect that all students will effectively understand all the presented science concepts in canonical ways. The experience of many science teachers is that in some classes many students fail to achieve an acceptable understanding of many of the taught concepts across a good many topics. This can easily lead to a defeatist attitude and low expectations—where getting some students to understand some of the material taught becomes the norm and is seen as 'good enough'.

However, being a science-teacher-as-learning-doctor then means adopting a stance towards those occasions when learners have not 'got' the science. Rather than simply label these occasions as 'failures to learn' (or perhaps 'failures to teach') the science learning doctor conceptualises them as 'bugs' in a complex system, which are in principle capable of being diagnosed, and corrected. The science-teacher-as-learning-doctor, whilst well aware of the complexity of teaching-learning, adopts the attitude that where motivated students fail to learn as intended from well-prepared teachers with good subject knowledge, it is possible *in principle at least* to diagnose where the failure occurs in the teaching-learning system, and to seek to respond by modifying the teaching input.

That is, just as learning is inherently iterative—where all new learning is interpreted through prior learning—effective teaching is iterative, too. Our initial presentations and learning activities are starting points from which we then precede through a dialogic approach. This is represented in a simplified schematic way in Figure 11.3.

Figure 11.3 ignores the very real complication that teaching and learning normally involves more than two minds and their voices, and so is usually much more

The Science Teacher as Learning Doctor 199

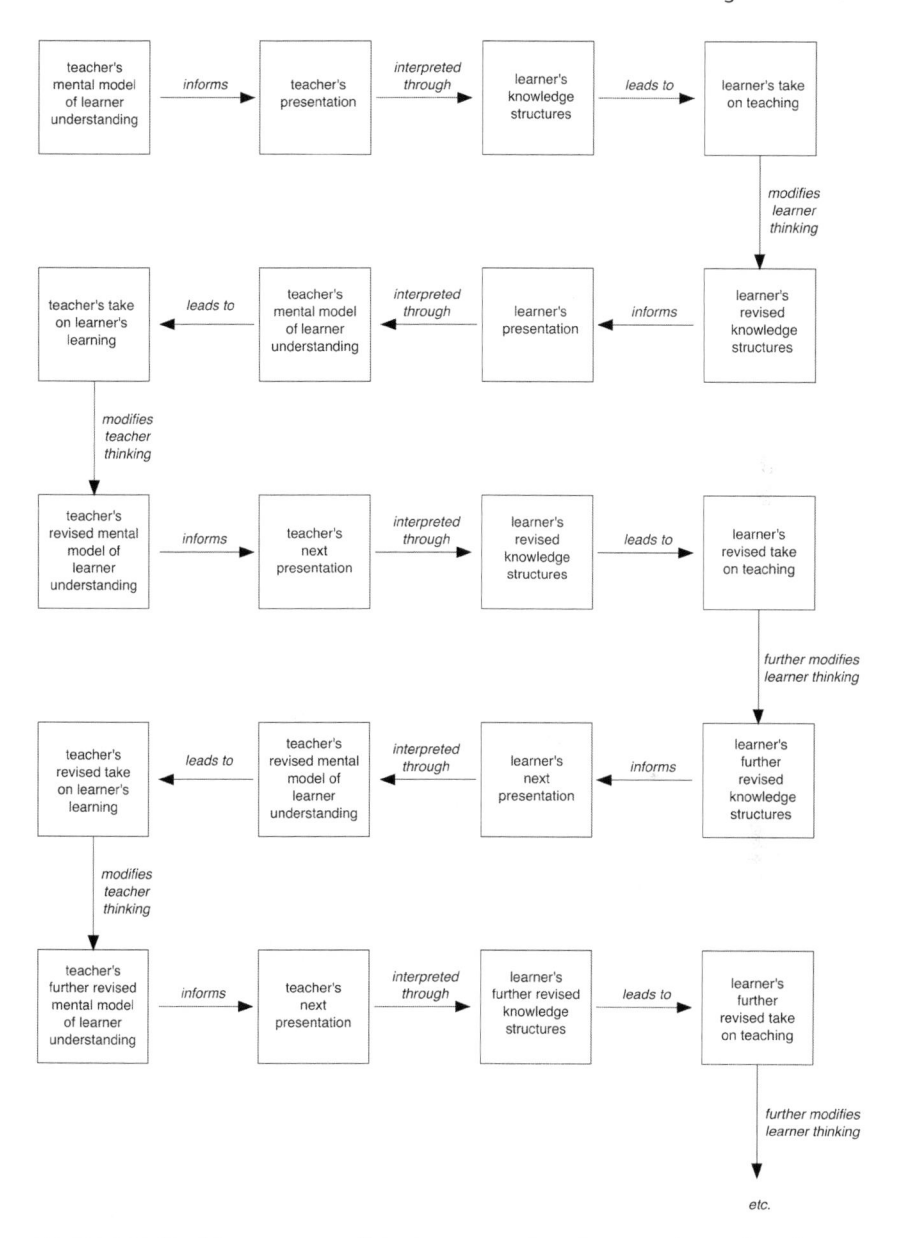

FIGURE 11.3 Teaching seen as a dialogic process that allows teacher and student to better understand each other (cf. Figure 10.4).

complex than a simple two-way conversation, but rather just focuses on how a dialogue allows two parties to come to a better understanding of each other. The 'presentations' in Figure 11.3 refer to different kinds of actions that a person might undertake to represent aspects of their own private mental experience, their ideas, in the public space that others can access. Such presentations could sometimes be traditional conversasional turns where each person offers an utterance in response to the other's utterance. However, Figure 11.3 is meant to be much more inclusive than this: a presentation might be an extended utterance, a simple gasp of incredulity, a gesture, a drawing of an image, the building of a physical model, the suggestion of a possible analogy, and so forth.

There is symmetry in Figure 11.3 as we might expect in a genuine dialogue—where two people seek intersubjectivity by seeking to share and compare their thinking. In many situations people hold such dialogic conversations in a symmetrical way—both parties are prepared to share their thinking and keen to learn about the other's ideas. However many human interactions are less symmetrical—where one person is keen to persuade another, or where the views of one person can be seen as more authoritative. An example might be a church sermon where it is assumed the preacher has a privileged perspective and it is not usually expected that members of the congregation will interrupt with alternative views or interpretations.

This is worth highlighting because teaching is traditionally considered to be an asymmetrical process where the teacher has authority. Some more progressive approaches to education seek to be student-centred, and to value the student voice, although sometimes such approaches are considered in some quarters as suspect (perhaps reflecting lazy teaching or lack of teacher authority). For example, some critics of constructivist approaches to science education have suggested that it is a way of teaching which negates the need for science teachers to have a good understanding of science, as it is all about children having and expressing ideas, and not about learning canonical science (Cromer, 1997). That is nonsense, and certainly the approach taken here assumes that it is important to present canonical target knowledge in school and college science, and that good science teachers need strong subject knowledge (cf. Figure 11.2). There are aspects of the science curriculum where different views are welcome (when considering sociocultural issues, for example), and authentic enquiry work is open-ended so that students are genuinely finding out something new rather than just reproducing textbook conclusions. Yet when students are learning about the periodic table, the circulatory system, transverse waves, or the orbits of comets, we wish to harness their creativity in supporting the learning of canonical science, not in producing their own alternative schemes inconsistent with scientific models. It is great if students can offer novel analogies or models to help themselves understand and learn accepted science, but we look to recruit these to help shift their thinking towards the 'accepted' scientific 'right answers'.

The symmetry in Figure 11.3 does not then relate to a democratic approach to science content—where perhaps the class gets to vote on whether to accept Newtonian mechanics or to carry on holding an impetus notion—but to the way that effective teaching depends upon both teacher and student developing a better understanding of each other's thinking. The student wants to understand the teacher's thinking about science because that will help them progress towards better understanding of canonical scientific ideas (and better grades)—and the teacher wants to better understand the student's way of thinking because that will help him or her refine his or her teaching so that it makes better sense to the student, and is more likely to be interpreted as intended. Both wish to learn from the other, but they seek to learn different things for different purposes.

Noticing the Symptoms and Signs of Learning Bugs

Medical doctors are helped in their work by signs and symptoms that give them clues to diagnose disease. The science learning doctor can also look for the symptoms and signs of learning bugs.

Not Making Sense as a Symptom of a Teaching-Learning System Bug

Symptoms are subjective, and experienced by the learner him- or herself. As teachers we are presenting science in ways that we believe students should be able to make sense of in terms of their existing knowledge and understanding. Students may complain that they are confused or do not understand, that they do not 'get it', or that something we have said must be wrong or cannot possibly make sense.

It is possible that we may overestimate student prior learning, so that the essential prerequisite knowledge we are assuming is missing. We may expect learners to make sense of what they hear and see in terms of background knowledge that is missing. As a result, the student does not make sense of the learning experience.

Even when students do have the required prerequisite knowledge, this does not ensure it is activated when we might expect. Sometimes it seems obvious to the teacher that what we are talking about *now* is related to what we discussed in a previous lesson. However, as David Ausubel (2000) explained, meaningful learning does not only require the learner to have potentially linked material in their cognitive structures, but also to actually perceive this as relevant to what they are learning now so they (intuitively, or through deliberate reflection) interpret the new learning in terms of what they already know and understand.

So our teaching may fail to make sense to learners either because the expected prior learning is missing, or simply because it has not been triggered by our presentation of material. We can hope to avoid this by careful sequencing of teaching, by pretesting to check for essential prerequisite knowledge, and by using suitable scaffolding 'planks' (see Chapter 12) to help students to bring the required prior learning to mind. Such techniques can considerably reduce incidences of students failing to make sense of our lessons, but given the complexity of the teaching-learning process, there are likely to still be some bugs in the system requiring 'patching' through the interactive nature of classroom teaching (see Figure 11.3).

Failure to understand teaching is not, however, always caused by the absence of, or failure to connect to, students' knowledge (see Chapter 10). It can also result from forming inappropriate connections. These can be of two rather different kinds. Students may interpret teaching through existing alternative conceptions—so what we teach may not make sense to them in terms of their existing ideas. It is also possible that students may form inappropriate associations with sound prior knowledge.

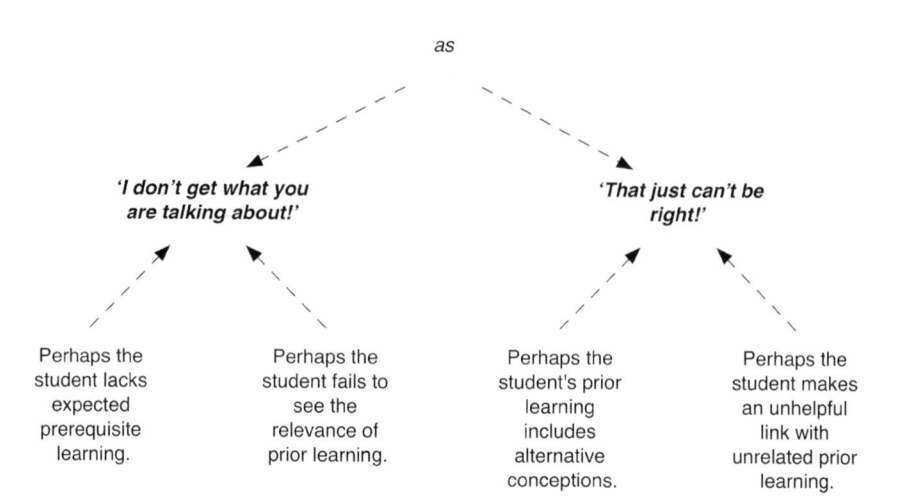

202 Diagnosing Student Thinking in Science Learning

'I do not understand. It does not make sense.'

as

'I don't get what you are talking about!' *'That just can't be right!'*

Perhaps the student lacks expected prerequisite learning.

Perhaps the student fails to see the relevance of prior learning.

Perhaps the student's prior learning includes alternative conceptions.

Perhaps the student makes an unhelpful link with unrelated prior learning.

FIGURE 11.4 The symptoms of teaching-learning bugs.

Human cognition supports us to be creative by forming totally new conceptions through relating different ideas. For example, Lise Meitner's research group had obtained results from their experiments on atomic decay that did not make sense in terms of existing ideas about radioactivity. In talking the problems through with her nephew Otto Robert Frisch, Meitner had the idea of considering the atomic nucleus, with its neutrons and protons, as being like an unstable liquid drop which might split into two parts (Frisch, 1979). In this case the creative process led to the now well-accepted idea of nuclear fission (Meitner & Frisch, 1939), but probably the vast majority of creative ideas of this kind turn out to be unproductive. Science depends upon both having creative ideas, and the ability to then test them so we can decide which to develop and which to reject (Taber, 2011). Students may not only interpret teaching in terms of the prior knowledge we intended, but may perceive teaching presentations to be related to all manner of other ideas—many of which we may feel are unhelpful in understanding the science.

In simple terms then, there are at least four types of impediments here to student learning following the path the teacher had envisaged when planning the lesson (see also Chapter 10). These are shown in Figure 11.4.

The Problem of Understanding Differently

Due to the challenges of teaching and learning science (see Chapter 1), most science teachers regularly experience students expressing the symptoms of bugs in the teaching-learning system: the mystified stares and quizzical looks, and the explicit comments about 'not getting it', or things not making sense. However, due to the nature of the human cognitive system as a highly effective interpretive apparatus, a great many of the 'bugs' in teaching do not produce any symptoms as the students do manage to make sense of learning, but without developing an understanding which closely matches the target knowledge set out in the curriculum. As the student *feels* he or she understands (the student does form an understanding, but just not as the teacher intended), there are no symptoms of confusion or frustration to be expressed by the student. In these situations there is a potential for both student and teacher to feel that learning has been successful, and for the new learning to become consolidated and be reinforced over time (see Chapter 9), and even to be used as the basis for (mis)interpreting subsequent teaching. Possibly the first instance either teacher or student knows of a problem is when the student responds to questions in high-stakes tests with answers that are marked as 'wrong'—something that is frustrating for both student and teacher.

Looking for Signs

The science-teacher-as-learning-doctor therefore needs to ensure there are opportunities to test out student interpretations of teaching that can help spot and address learning bugs as they occur (that is, as in Figure 11.3). So the science-teacher-as-learning-doctor looks to provide extensive opportunities for learners to express their developing understanding of the topic to check on their thinking, and diagnose learning bugs. This allows the teacher to spot signs of learning bugs even when there are no symptoms.

Of course, recognising problems is all very well, but the teacher then has to act to address them. The nature of the 'cure' depends upon the diagnosis of the system bug. Some problems are difficult to address. Some alternative conceptions have been found to be very tenacious, and in some cases specific teaching approaches have been designed to address them. In one example, a 'bridging analogy' has developed to help learners appreciate that a supported body is subject to an upwards-acting normal force (Clement, 1993). In situations such as this, research tells us that many students draw upon deep-seated intuitive thinking that is not readily put aside (see Chapter 5). This specific teaching strategy helps learners see how the situation where an object 'just' seems to rest on an inert support is analogous to other situations where it is more obvious force is acting.

However, other problems may be much easier to address. Missing prerequisite knowledge can be put in place through remedial work—which may sometimes be as straightforward as referring a student to a page in a textbook that provides key background that can make all the difference. Failures to make links may sometimes be even more readily addressed, as once we realise that the student is not thinking in terms of the core scientific idea, we can simply point out how it applies to the current situation. Similarly, when a student makes an unhelpful connection, an early intervention to explain why the concept does not apply here, or why that analogy or metaphor does not work well, can often redirect the student's focus before he or she develops a commitment to that way of thinking about the target concept.

Some Examples of Learning Bugs

To illustrate how this diagnostic tool can be useful in thinking about learning difficulties, I will revisit some examples of student thinking earlier in the book. As suggested at the start of the book, our interpretations of learners' thinking are always open to misreadings, and so the diagnoses we make should be considered as conjectures—as hypotheses to be tested out in our further work with learners. However, having some kind of hunch about what is going wrong is an important starting point for attempting to move the learner's thinking on.

Deficiency Learning Impediments

One example where I suggest a lack of specific scientific knowledge acted as a learning block relates to some dialogue in Textbox 5.1, presented in Chapter 5. Sophia, in her first year of secondary school, was telling me what she had learnt about space in her primary-school science classes. She had suggested that:

- stars were not as 'little' as planets;
- but they seemed little because they were a long way away;
- but the stars were easier to see than planets;
- so they might be closer to us than the planets.

Clearly there is something of a contradiction here. I think this was linked to Sophia's uncertainty over whether the sun was a planet. Indeed, when I asked her which planet was nearest to her she initially suggested the sun, before realising the earth was closer. Sophia lacked a rather major piece of scientific knowledge which would have clarified this—and the conundrum of why stars that were a long way away might still be easier to see than planets. Stars are visible because they are hot enough to emit their own light, whereas planets are only visible due to light they reflect. Realising that would have made it clear that the sun was a star, and allowed her to appreciate why other stars could often be more easily seen than much nearer planets.

Fragmentation Learning Impediments

Students often fail to make the links we expect in teaching, and as teachers we need to make explicit connections between concepts and topics if we wish students to appreciate them. A number of examples of fragmentation learning impediments were presented in Chapter 9. So although Bill has learnt that that everything is made up of particles, we cannot assume he thinks chlorophyll would contain particles (Textbox 9.3); and when Amy tells us that she has learnt energy cannot be created, we should not be surprised that she also talks of how oxygen and glucose can be converted into energy (Textbox 9.5).

Grounded Learning Impediments

Grounded learning impediments (see Chapter 10) occur when students' existing thinking leads them to interpret new teaching in noncanonical ways. That existing thinking may be due to the learner's intuitions about the world. Assuming that water that is soaked up into soil may not register weight (see Textbox 4.1, in Chapter 4), or that a smaller object experiences more force than a large object it is interacting with (see Textbox 5.5, in Chapter 5) would seem to be examples of such *intuitive learning impediments*.

Alternatively, prior knowledge may derive from ideas that have currency as everyday folk beliefs—the idea that fuel just gets 'used up' (so there is no issue of where it has gone) would seem an example of such *a life-world learning impediment* (see Textbox 7.2, in Chapter 7), reinforced by common ways of talking about using fuels. A third possibility is that previous teaching has led to noncanonical learning, such as when students explain chemical reactions in terms of atoms wishing to fill their shells (see Textbox 9.2, in Chapter 9)—something that seems unlikely to have origins outside formal instruction. Studies certainly suggest that teachers sometimes share learners' alternative conceptions (for example, see Textbox 11.1).

The distinctions here are nuanced; so, for example, the everyday notion of fuel being used up probably taps into intuitive thinking, and indeed many pedagogical learning impediments may be perpetuated over generations of students because they fit well with intuitions about the world.

Associative Learning Impediments

Associative learning impediments (see Chapter 10) occur when a student forms a link that is not intended by the teacher, and which is inconsistent with canonical scientific thinking. Some associative learning impediments appear to be quite *creative* in that the learners makes an original and sometimes quite idiosyncratic link—such as suggesting evolution as the means by which chemical bonds acquired their characteristics (see Textbox 9.9 in Chapter 9). Associative learning

---

Textbox 11.1: Teachers may share students' alternative conceptions.

"Specifically, most middle school students do not have a clear understanding of the terms 'ultraviolet' and 'infrared'. Additionally, almost half of the high school physics students and some teachers had alternative conceptions that were similar to those held by middle school students. Nearly 80% of all students in the study were unclear that humans cannot see in the presence of UV light alone, supporting the idea that 'light' to most students is a singular concept."

Source: Libarkin, Asghar, Crockett, & Sadler, 2011, p. 8.

> Textbox 11.2: The nucleus 'comes under' both biology and chemistry.
>
> *"There are lots of atoms in you. And we did about the nucleus which we've been doing about in Biology. I'm not sure if there's a link between it, but . . . 'cause we did about plant and animal cells in Biology, so it's got a nucleus. . . . [the nucleus]'s kind of like the brain of the cell kind of. It's what gets the cell to do everything, it's like, the core of the cell . . . we were doing, we were doing in Chemistry about the nucleus has the—neutrons and the protons in the nucleus, then around it is a field of electrons . . . the nucleus comes under both of them [biology and chemistry].*
>
> *So is it the same thing?*
>
> *I wouldn't have thought so, but because when I think of electrons and neutrons I think of electricity, which I don't really think of in our bodies, but it could be perhaps."*
>
> *(Bert, c. 14 years old)*
>
> Source: ECLIPSE project website; see www.educ.cam.ac.uk/research/projects/eclipse/.

impediments may have linguistic origins, as when a student tries to make sense of whether the nucleus in a cell is the same thing as the nucleus in an atom (see Textbox 11.2)—after all, would we not use a *different word* if they are different things?

Associative learning impediments can also occur when learners draw upon teaching models and analogies, taking them too literally, without appreciating their nature or limitations. Amy understood the analogical model of electrical current flow as water passing through pipes, but then transferred the idea of constrictions in the pipe as resistance to the molecular level. So she explained the high resistance of wood in terms of limited space for electricity to flow between molecules (see Textbox 11.3) and quite reasonably expected air, where particles were 'not as dense as a solid', would readily allow electricity to pass.

Textbox 11.4 presents an extract from an interview where a 14-year-old told me about the model of the atom he was just learning in school science. Ralph refers to orbiting neutrons, which he had clearly got wrong, but this seemed to relate to his compounding two different models. Ralph referred to the 'atom is like a tiny solar system' analogy (Gentner, 1983) which needs to be used carefully in teaching because of its limitations (Taber, 2013), but had also learnt that the electrons were in a 'cloud'. With the electrons accounted for by the cloud metaphor, Ralph assigned neutrons to the role of the orbiting bodies. It was not clear if Ralph was confusing two models being presented in his current lessons, or trying to make sense of new teaching in relation to having previously been taught a different model, but his response seemed to be an attempt to consolidate features of both models into a coherent understanding—an epistemological learning

> Textbox 11.3: Making sense of the structure of electrical conductors and insulators in terms of an analogical model.
>
> *"[Electrical] resistance is anything which kind of provides a barrier which the current has to pass through, slowing down the current in a circuit. . . . we've been taught the water tank and pipe running round it . . . just imagine the water like flowing through a pipe, and obviously like, if the pipe becomes smaller at one point, the water flow has to slow down, and that's meant to represent the resistance of something."*
>
> Electricity does *"not very easily"* pass through a wooden bench *"because wood is quite a dense material and the particles in it are quite closely bonded."*
>
> (Amy, c. 14 years old)
>
> Source: ECLIPSE project website; see www.educ.cam.ac.uk/research/projects/eclipse/.

> Textbox 11.4: Confusing different models of the atom.
>
> *"There are lots of different types of atoms, and so I think they have a nucleus and like a cloud of electrons around them, and there's neutrons rotating round, circulating rotating, round the nucleus . . . neutrons in like an orbit about it . . . [the electrons] they're the cloud round it, I'm not sure why . . . the nucleus is kind of like the sun in our universe, it's like the thing everything orbits around."*
>
> (Ralph, c. 14 years old)
>
> Source: ECLIPSE project website; see www.educ.cam.ac.uk/research/projects/eclipse/.

impediment due to not appreciating how in science we may use alternative (and inconsistent) models to represent different features of the same target. This is not in keeping with the way most learners consider scientific models as intended to be realistic (see Chapter 2).

A Useful Heuristic

As a very simple summary heuristic, Figure 11.5 lists the four main classes of learning impediment—bugs in the teaching-learning system—and suggests the general kind of action a teacher needs to take to put things right. Of course, 'making good' missing subject knowledge or 'dissociating' unhelpful connections students have made simply sets out what has to be achieved. What the teacher actually has to say, or demonstrate, or ask the learners to do to achieve such outcomes will vary from topic to topic and sometimes from learner to learner. However, recognising

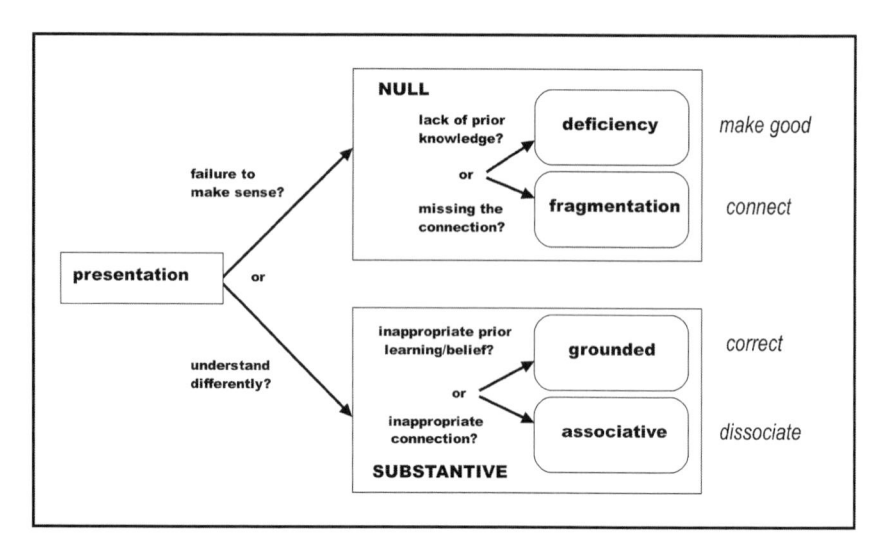

FIGURE 11.5 A simple tool for thinking about how teaching can go wrong.

the kind of thing that has gone wrong, and what needs to be done to put it right, represents an important stage in the process. This also reflects a mentality that teaching is fraught with things that can go wrong—*but* that these problems are in principle identifiable and correctable, even if this is not always easy in practice.

It is also useful to note that although every student is unique, and students often present somewhat idiosyncratic ideas (as some of the examples in this book suggest) there are often commonalities between students' ideas. Thinking and teaching like a learning doctor therefore brings iterative improvements in teaching over time. Familiarity with the quirks of this year's class, and with what did and did not help to treat identified learning bugs, informs our teaching of the topic with other classes. We can better anticipate, and sometimes avoid, learning bugs in future, and we build up a repertoire of better examples, arguments, thought experiments, and activities that prove successful in shifting student thinking in particular situations.

References

Ausubel, D. P. (2000). *The acquisition and retention of knowledge: A cognitive view*. Dordrecht: Kluwer Academic.

Black, P., & Wiliam, D. (1998). Assessment and classroom learning. *Assessment in Education, 5*(1), 7–74.

Bruner, J. S. (1987). The transactional self. In J. Bruner & H. Haste (Eds.), *Making sense: The child's construction of the world* (pp. 81–96). London: Routledge.

Clement, J. (1993). Using bridging analogies and anchoring intuitions to deal with students' preconceptions in physics. *Journal of Research in Science Teaching, 30*(10), 1241–1257. doi: 10.1002/tea.3660301007

Cromer, A. (1997). *Connected knowledge: Science, philosophy and education.* Oxford: Oxford University Press.
Frisch, O. R. (1979). *What little I remember.* Cambridge: Cambridge University Press.
Gentner, D. (1983). Structure-mapping: A theoretical framework for analogy. *Cognitive Science, 7*, 155–170.
Libarkin, J. C., Asghar, A., Crockett, C., & Sadler, P. (2011). Invisible misconceptions: Student understanding of ultraviolet and infrared radiation. *Astronomy Education Review, 10*(1), 12.
Meitner, L., & Frisch, O. R. (1939). Disintegration of uranium by neutrons: A new type of nuclear reaction. *Nature,* (3615), 239–240.
Mortimer, E. F., & Scott, P. H. (2003). *Meaning making in secondary science classrooms.* Maidenhead, Berkshire, England: Open University Press.
Murphy, P., Jones, H., & Lunn, S. (2004). *The evaluation of RSC materials for schools and colleges: A report.* London: Royal Society of Chemistry.
Naylor, S., & Keogh, B. (2000). *Concept cartoons in science education.* Sandbach, Cheshire: Millgate House.
Savinainen, A., & Scott, P. (2002). The force concept inventory: A tool for monitoring student learning. *Physics Education, 37*(1), 45–52.
Taber, K. S. (2001). Constructing chemical concepts in the classroom? Using research to inform practice. *Chemistry Education: Research and Practice in Europe, 2*(1), 43–51.
Taber, K. S. (2002). *Chemical misconceptions—prevention, diagnosis and cure: Classroom resources* (Vol. 2). London: Royal Society of Chemistry.
Taber, K. S. (2011). The natures of scientific thinking: Creativity as the handmaiden to logic in the development of public and personal knowledge. In M. S. Khine (Ed.), *Advances in the nature of science research: Concepts and methodologies* (pp. 51–74). Dordrecht: Springer.
Taber, K. S. (2013). Upper secondary students' understanding of the basic physical interactions in analogous atomic and solar systems. *Research in Science Education, 43*(4), 1377–1406. doi: 10.1007/s11165-012-9312-3
Tan, K.-C. D., Goh, N.-K., Chia, L.-S., & Taber, K. S. (2005). *Development of a two-tier multiple choice diagnostic instrument to determine A-level students' understanding of ionisation energy* (pp. 105). Singapore: National Institute of Education, Nanyang Technological University. Retrieved from https://camtools.cam.ac.uk/wiki/eclipse/diagnostic_instrument.html
Treagust, D. F. (1988). Development and use of diagnostic tests to evaluate students' misconceptions in science. *International Journal of Science Education, 10*(2), 159–169. doi: 10.1080/0950069880100204

12
SCIENCE TEACHING INFORMED BY AN APPRECIATION OF STUDENT THINKING

In this book I have discussed student thinking and learning from a number of perspectives, and presented, with my interpretations, a range of examples of the kinds of things students write and say relating to science topics. These examples could be multiplied many times, as the extensive literature into learners' ideas shows. Science education proceeds at two distinct levels. Academics and researchers develop theory, and collect evidence to test their ideas, to better understand in general terms how learners learn, how they think, and how instruction can best engage their thinking in ways which lead to the learning of canonical science. Inevitably, empirical research in science education involves particular learners, learning in specific institutional and curriculum contexts, with particular teachers. Research attempts to generalise from these specifics to find useful patterns that can inform teachers working in diverse contexts.

In this book I very much hope to have suggested both (a) that academic work has produced perspectives, findings, and ideas that can be useful to science teachers, but also (b) that the application of this abstract general knowledge requires skilled teachers who can relate these generalities to the specifics of their own teaching context. In particular, knowing something of the typical thinking of learners and of the range of ideas entertained by students of particular ages can prime the teacher to be aware of common alternative conceptions, and help the teacher to interpret the utterances of different students when they make comments that suggest their thinking does not quite fit with what we are trying to teach. However, for this to be possible, the teacher has to teach in a way that allows students to express their ideas, and be willing and able to engage with learners' ideas and find ways to support learning of more conventional scientific accounts.

Ultimately, successful science teaching leads to student learning that matches target knowledge set out in the curriculum, but a key message from research is that this is often only achieved by engaging with learners' ideas and setting up a dialogue that allows students to appreciate *how* their ideas are at odds with scientific accounts and *why* the scientific accounts have come to be preferred. Teachers' perfectly logical presentations of accurate subject knowledge that do not engage with student thinking often lead to disappointing learning outcomes. The science teacher as dictator or fax machine is likely to be disappointed in the learning that results. The science-teacher-as-learning-doctor will certainly not always be successful, but will achieve more and have a developing understanding of what is going wrong and how to fix it that will build year-on-year.

Representations of Teaching

There are many metaphors and models for what classroom teaching should be like. Teachers may envisage themselves as captains of the ship leading their crew on a voyage of adventure, or see their primary role as keeping students entertained, or see themselves as a resource to support student learning (Tobin, Kahle, & Fraser, 1990). The role metaphor adopted by a teacher is likely to influence his or her choices in how to go about teaching science. The challenge of teaching through what is sometimes labelled direct instruction (that is, telling, but supported with rationale, demonstrations, etc.) is reflected in Figure 12.1.

Teaching as Scaffolding Learning in a Class of Unique Learners

Figure 12.1 represents the teacher as a source of information to support student learning. Certainly teacher-talk from a knowledgeable and experienced teacher can be an effective tool, and can support active construction of student learning (Millar, 1989). However, the iconography of the figure is meant to imply that each student is unique. The symbols for students show two 'zones' drawing upon Vygotsky's (1978) notions of the zones of actual and next (or proximal) development. Each of the more central regions represents a student's current robust knowledge and understanding—what they already know and are able to confidently apply. The outer zones represent the potential for extending knowledge and understanding with suitable 'scaffolding' from the teacher.

In terms of the learning of new science concepts, teachers may provide learners with support in recognising relevant prior knowledge and helping arrange it in the most suitable way to support new ideas (scaffolding 'planks'), and may offer structured activities that support learners in working through new ideas that are currently too complex and unfamiliar to be tackled unaided (scaffolding 'poles'; for example, see Figure 6.2 in Chapter 6) but which they are ready to tackle with suitable support (Taber, 2002, 2003).

However, Figure 12.1 (which underrepresents the class sizes most teachers are commonly working with) suggests that scaffolding learning primarily through teacher-talk is often going to be problematic as the different students in any class

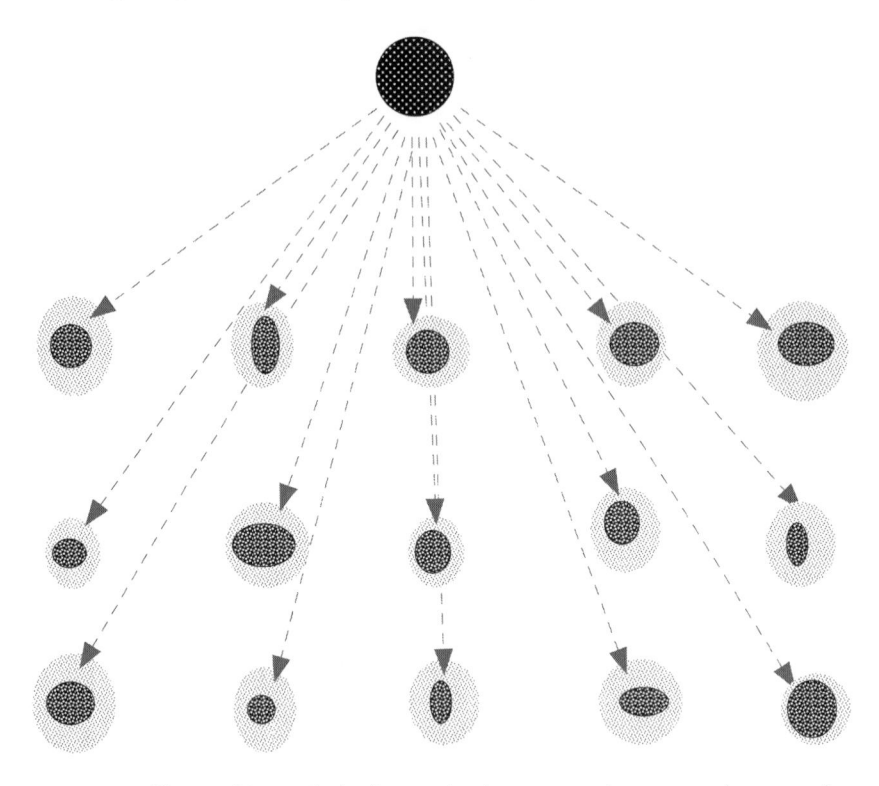

212 Diagnosing Student Thinking in Science Learning

FIGURE 12.1 Class teaching as aiming instruction into many unique personal construction zones (adapted from Taber, 2011).

differ in what they already can call upon as robust prior learning and therefore in what they are ready to tackle next. The symbolism here only reflects the extent of the zones, and does not indicate how the actual knowledge of each learner will fit a unique profile—often including idiosyncratic conceptions.

Teaching as Leading a Community of Participating Learners

The challenges of the 'teacher as source of information' model should be very clear to any reader who has considered the examples of students' ideas presented in this book—and possibly even more obvious to those readers who have adopted the suggestion (in the introduction) of keeping a record of the comments made by their own students that seem at odds with what is being taught in science lessons.

An alternative representation of teaching in the science classroom is presented in Figure 12.2. This draws upon sociocultural ideas about how learning occurs in human groups. This approach suggests a model that may seem to fit better with the notion of the inquiry classroom, where there is ongoing 'active' learning. In this model the teacher and learners are considered to be working together towards

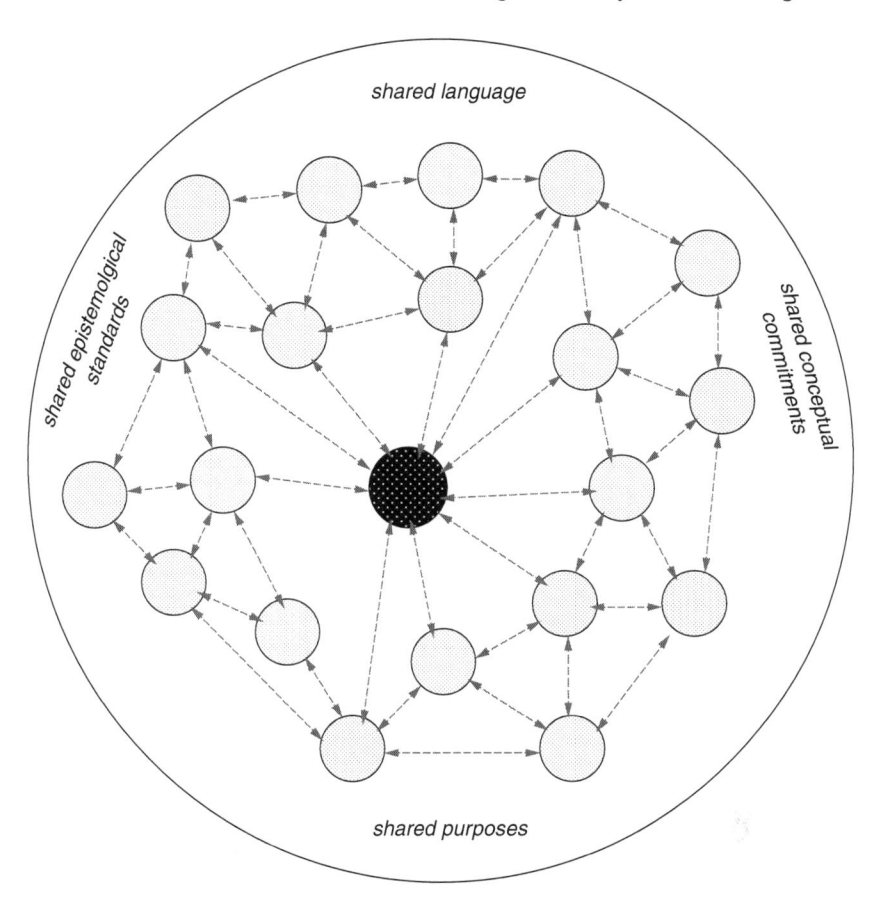

FIGURE 12.2 Teaching as leading participation in a community of learners.

a common goal as part of an interacting community, where responsibilities are devolved and where the roles of teacher and learner are distributed in a much more democratic way than in a more traditional classroom. The assumption is that different members of the community bring different levels of expertise (having been inducted into the practices and norms of the community to different degrees) that they can share with others within the learning community.

There are at least two reasons why we need to be careful about the adoption of such a model. For one thing, it is based on what *actually* seems to happen in professional communities and vocational learning—and the way things are is not always the best guide to how we might like them to be. That is, it is a descriptive model, and may not reflect the best prescriptive model.

More significantly, this pattern of learning normally assumes a community with learners at different stages of expertise. The novices initially have peripheral participation in the community, but will learn from more-advanced apprentices with some years of experience, and journeymen who have completed their training and are fully practicing, as well as the master. That is not what the typical school or college class is like (although bizarrely it was better matched by 19th-century classrooms using the monitorial system, where more-advanced pupils acted as teaching assistants).

The teacher may seek *to model* conceptual commitments, specialised language, and epistemological norms of the subject, but the earlier chapters of this book show well that learners will not initially share these norms. There is much value in a classroom that acts as a learning community, but it is unreasonable to expect a single teacher working with a class of novices to approximate the learning that goes on in, say, a research group with postgraduate students at different stages working alongside postdocs and faculty of different levels of experience.

The Dialogic Classroom

A very useful model of science classrooms was developed by Mortimer and Scott, who observed science teaching in real classrooms from a perspective that acknowledged both socio cultural ideas and the research on students' alternative conceptions (Mortimer & Scott, 2003; Scott, Mortimer, & Ametller, 2011). They identified the need for science teaching that flowed between activities with a focus on students' own ideas (inevitably the starting points of their new learning) and activities with a focus on the curriculum models of scientific concepts set out as target knowledge. They called this a communicative approach. A key part of this model is the dialogic nature of teaching, which encourages and invites the student voice, and then includes that in a conversation with the scientific account, designed to encourage the adoption within the class of that scientific account.

A teacher adopting Scott and Mortimer's communicative approach would be aware of the importance of learners' ideas to the teaching and learning 'system' (see Chapter 10), but does not lose sight of the aim of teaching the science set out as target knowledge. Such a teacher is highly skilled in both working with learners' ideas—showing them respect, testing out their strengths as well as highlighting their limitations, and comparing them with each other and with the scientific perspective—and leading students towards recognising the value of the canonical scientific approach. I feel that an important aspect of this work is the recognition that the question 'what does this science class look like?' will vary from lesson to lesson, and from activity to activity within the lesson. In particular, the class will sometimes reflect Figure 12.2 with all ideas being shared and explored, and at other times it will resemble Figure 12.1 with the teacher clearly leading from the front—although even when the class looks more like Figure 12.1 there will be phases when the teacher is representing and exploring the consequences of student ideas, and other times when the focus has moved on to privilege the scientific models.

Some teachers will elicit student thinking and explore different ideas largely through teacher-led dialogue with the class. Others will tend to use more small-group work that is structured to allow the sharing of ideas, and the exploration of the merits of different ways of thinking about topics. What is important though is that the teacher has access to student thinking, for if 40 years of research into learners' thinking about science has revealed anything, it is the folly of teaching learners science as if their existing thinking is irrelevant. Students have ideas of their own, and some of those ideas are strongly committed, and they are often not readily able to understand the scientific perspective, let alone recognise its advantages. Successful teaching is often, then, a highly dialogic process—where progress is iterative, as suggested in Figure 11.3 in Chapter 11.

The Informed Science Teacher

Adopting this approach to teaching requires high levels of teaching skills—in being able to adapt to different phases of teaching and various classroom organisations—which may not come 'naturally' to all teachers. There is clearly scope to find ways to organise teaching and learning within the general pattern of shifts between 'dialogic' (exploring all views) and 'authoritarian' (presenting the scientific account) phases of teaching. However, teaching in this way does rely on teachers who are interested in students' thinking, who are confident in working with learners' ideas, and who are able to utilise techniques for eliciting students' ideas.

I hope anyone who has read this far will have few doubts about the significance of learners' ideas for their further learning. Readers should also appreciate something of both the range and nature of learners' ideas about science, and how these 'alternative' ideas can come about. Those readers who have been able to keep a record of comments from their own students will have found that these learners have their own personal ideas about science topics. Your own students' ideas are likely to be as diverse and intriguing as the examples I have presented in this book. It is very easy to 'miss' the significance of learners' comments—for just as learners readily interpret teaching in terms of their existing ideas, it is easy for the teacher to interpret students' statements and questions as simply imprecise and inexpert reflections of teaching. That is sometimes the case—but as we have seen in this book, often students have developed understandings quite inconsistent with what we intend to teach.

The good science teacher has to work hard to shift students' thinking, and that usually requires having a good understanding of where students are now, and why they might be adopting particular ways of thinking (see Figure 12.3). This book provides the reader with the background to take on this challenge, illustrated with authentic examples from students I have worked with. I hope many readers will rise to the challenge of taking on the role of a science learning doctor and look to diagnose bugs in their own teaching that can be addressed by entering

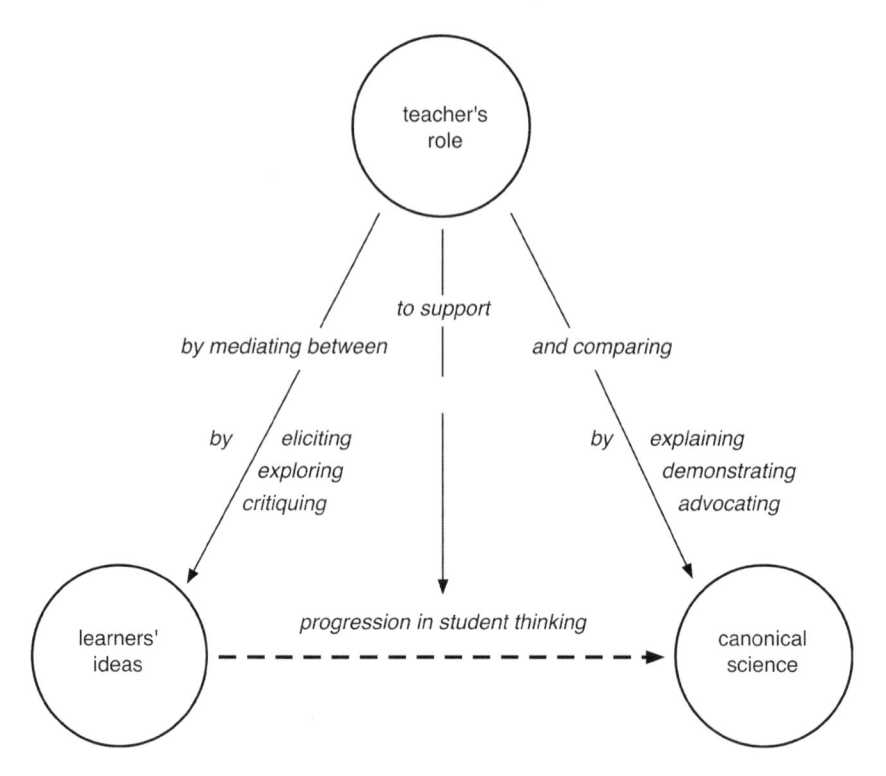

FIGURE 12.3 Dialogic science teaching.

into meaningful dialogue with learners about their ideas. This will always remain a challenging task, and sometimes a frustrating one, but ultimately it can also be a source of great satisfaction when we start to understand our students' perspectives, and engage in genuine learning conversations about the science we look to teach.

References

Millar, R. (1989). Constructive criticisms. *International Journal of Science Education, 11*(special issue), 587–596.
Mortimer, E. F., & Scott, P. H. (2003). *Meaning making in secondary science classrooms.* Maidenhead, Berkshire, England: Open University Press.
Scott, P., Mortimer, E., & Ametller, J. (2011). Pedagogical link-making: A fundamental aspect of teaching and learning scientific conceptual knowledge. *Studies in Science Education, 47*(1), 3–36. doi: 10.1080/03057267.2011.549619
Taber, K. S. (2002). *Chemical misconceptions—prevention, diagnosis and cure: Theoretical background* (Vol. 1). London: Royal Society of Chemistry.
Taber, K. S. (2003). Responding to alternative conceptions in the classroom. *School Science Review, 84*(308), 99–108.

Taber, K. S. (2011). Constructivism as educational theory: Contingency in learning, and optimally guided instruction. In J. Hassaskhah (Ed.), *Educational theory* (pp. 39–61). New York, NY: Nova. Retrieved from https://camtools.cam.ac.uk/wiki/eclipse/Constructivism.html

Tobin, K., Kahle, J. B., & Fraser, B. J. (Eds.). (1990). *Windows into science classrooms: Problems associated with higher-level cognitive learning.* Basingstoke, Hampshire: Falmer Press.

Vygotsky, L. S. (1978). *Mind in society: The development of higher psychological processes.* Cambridge, MA: Harvard University Press.

INDEX

Abrahams, I. 149, 150
abstract concepts 19–23, 32
accommodation 181
ACME (Acceptance-Connectedness-Multiplicity-Explicitness) model of conceptions 52–5
acquisition of knowledge 17–19
actions, schemas for 101–4
active learning 151–2
activity theory 104
agents 102, 116
agnosticism 140
A-level revision classes 153–4
alternative conceptions: culture and 135–6, 137; diagnostic assessment probes for 193–5; keeping track of 7; overview of 37–9; of teachers 205; technical and ethical notes on 7–9; understanding 4–6; *see also* alternative conceptions of learning
alternative conceptions of learning: aufbau principle 60–1; constructivist perspective 66–70; intuitive theories of mind and folk psychology 63–5; key messages 70; overview of 59–60; updating computers compared to teaching 62–3; Xerox model 61–2
alternative (conceptual) frameworks 47–8, 171–3
animism 102
anthropocentric framing 116

anthropomorphic language 115–16, 126–9, 188
anthropomorphism 102
argumentation: learners' explanations and 117–22; overview of 112–13
argument for scientific ideas, complexity of 23–7
assessment *see* diagnostic assessment
assimilation 181
associative learning impediments 187–8, 189, 205–7, 208
Atkins, Peter 140
aufbau principle of learning 60–1, 70
Ausubel, David 201
autodidactic science learning 152–3
axiology 138

beliefs: epistemological 48–50, 155–60; folk science and 135–7; knowledge and conceptions compared to 50; overview of 135; worldview and 137–44
border-crossing into discourses of science 112, 138
Boyle, Robert 115
bridging analogy 203
Bruner, Jerome 33, 191
bugs in teaching learning system: examples of 204–7; heuristic for 207–8; overview of 195–7; symptoms and signs of 201–4; types of 184–90
Burnell, Jocelyn Bell 147

canonical knowledge 33–4
CASE (Cognitive Acceleration through Science Education) project 85
causation, experiential gestalt of 101–4, 128–9
chemical bonding, conceptual shifts about over time 163–4, 165
Chemical Misconceptions (Taber) 36
chunking 166
cognition: assumptions from research about 84–5; brain development and 78–84; conceptual integration in 161–6; innate aspects to 75–8; mental modules and 85–9; role of implicit knowledge in 96; schematic of 109
Cognitive Acceleration through Science Education (CASE) project 85
cognitive dissonance 100
coherence: of alternative thinking 172–3; memory as seeking 162–3, 164–5; science and 166–7
commitment: to objectivity 13; to theory, levels of 43, 50
communication and sharing of ideas 65
communicative approach to teaching 214–15
communities of participating learners 212–14
concept cartoons 193–4
conceptions: ACME model of 52–5; formation of 106–7, 108; knowledge and beliefs compared to 50; manifold 50–1, 54; overview of 34–5; *see also* alternative conceptions
concept maps 154
concepts: abstract 19–23, 32; learners' ideas as 32–4; melded 108–9; simplification of 27
conceptual integration: in cognition 161–6; in science and science education 166–71
concrete operational thinking 79, 80–1
confirmation bias 178
connected nature of science 53–4
conservation, principles of 79, 81–2
consolidation of learning 161–2
constructivism: in Piaget's model 78; in science education 5–6
constructivist perspective on learning: learning as incremental 66–7; learning as interpretive 67–8; learning as iterative 68–70; overview of 60–1; rote learning and 180
contingent learning 178, 183–4

creationism 141
creative learning impediments 187, 189, 205
creative links, making 164–6
culture: alternative conceptions and 135–6, 137; discourse communities and 110–14; language, vicarious learning, and 107–9; traditional ecological knowledge and 138
curriculum: as filter, notion of 3–4; knowledge representation in 181–3

Dawkins, Richard 140
decision-making and memory 162
deficiency learning impediment 186, 189, 204, 208
demands and level of development 85
demonstrations: language and 113–14; of refraction 21–2
development: of brain and cognition 78–84; demands and level of 85; of explicit knowledge 106–7; genes and 75–6; of implicit knowledge 145–6; of intuitive knowledge 146–7; learning and 177–83; zones of actual and next development 211
diagnostic assessment: bugs in teaching learning system 201–7; overview of 191–2; probes 193–5
dialogic classrooms 214–15, 216
discourse communities, learning as participation in 110–14
diSessa, Andrea 94, 98
Driver, Ros 44

ECLIPSE project website 8, 9–10
ecological knowledge 138
epistemological beliefs 48–50, 155–60
epistemological learning impediments 188, 189
everyday beliefs *see* beliefs
evidence, interpretation of 23–7
evolution: cognitive apparatus and 69; natural selection and 15, 25–7; origins of species and 88–9; rejection of on religious grounds 141–4
experimental tests and theory 16
explanations: argumentation and 117–20; features of 120–2; general-purpose 101–4; *see also* pseudo-explanations
explicit knowledge, development of 106–7
explicitness of thinking 54–5

face recognition 76–8
falsification 24
fieldwork and spontaneous learning 146–9
flow 152
folk knowledge: of biology 87–8; influence of 135–7; of mechanics 89; of psychology 65, 87
Forces Concept Inventory 193
formal operational thinking 79, 80–2, 85, 86, 121–2
fragmentation learning impediments 186, 189, 204, 208
frameworks: alternative (conceptual) 47–8, 171–2; multiple 50–1, 54
Frisch, Otto Robert 202
F-v thinking 42, 92–4

Galileo Galilei 139, 141, 148
general-purpose explanations 101–4
genes and development 75–6
gestalt of causation 101–4, 128–9
gestalt psychology 147
grounded learning impediments 187, 189, 205, 208

hidden persuader, language as 114–15
hippocampus 162
history, memory as rewriting 162–3
Hooke, Robert 17
human brains 76, 162
human cognition *see* cognition
Huxley, Thomas 140

impediments to learning: examples of 204–7; heuristic for 207–8; overview of 195–7; symptoms and signs of 201–4; types of 184–90
impetus notions 42, 92
implicit knowledge: development of 145–6; explicit conceptions and 108; in learning science 96–104; p-prims 45–6; role of in cognition 96
imprinting 77
incremental, learning as 66–7
informal science learning 151–2
informed consent 8
instinct, intuition compared to 91, 92
integration of knowledge *see* conceptual integration
interpretive, learning as 67–8
interviews, semi-structured 8
intuition: artificial neural nets compared to 91–2; building from patterns in sensory experience 94–6; general-purpose explanations or schemas for action 101–4; instinct compared to 91, 92; rules, applying 98–100
intuitive learning impediments 187, 189, 205
intuitive theories/knowledge: activation of 107; development of 146–7; F-v thinking 92–4; overview of 41–5; theory of mind as 64
iterative: learning as 68–70, 199; teaching as 199–200

journal articles, argumentation in 112–13

Keogh, Brenda 193
knowledge: acquisition of 17–19; canonical and target 33–4; conceptions and beliefs compared to 50; ecological 138; explicit, development of 106–7; implicit 45–6, 96–104, 108, 145–6; of learners 27–8, 197; pedagogical 197; scientific, cognitive development and understanding of 84; scientific, production of 16–17; tacit 39, 55; *see also* conceptual integration; folk knowledge; intuition; intuitive theories/knowledge
knowledge construction 17–19
knowledge representation in curriculum and teaching 181–3
Kuhn, T.S. 110–11

laboratory work: learning from 149–50; spontaneous learning and 146–9
Lakatos, Imre 24
language: anthropomorphic 115–16, 126–9, 188; argumentation and learners' explanations 117–22; creating new entities through 113–14; culture, vicarious learning, and 107–9; explicit knowledge development and 106–7; as hidden persuader 114–15; as interpretive resource 67–8; learners' pseudo-explanations 122–32; learning and 106, 110–14; learning language 94–5; 'natural attitude' and use of language 112–13; teleological 117, 125–6; *see also* metaphors
language-acquisition device 86–7
learners' ideas: ACME model of conceptions 52–5; characterising and labelling 30; research on 30–1; taking into account in teaching 27–8; working to shift

215–16; *see also* alternative conceptions; terminology for learners' ideas
learning: active 151–2; applying implicit knowledge in 96–104; aufbau principle of 60–1, 70; autodidactic 152–3; consolidation of 161–2; contingent 178, 183–4; development and 177–83; as incremental 66–7; informal 151; as interpretive 67–8; as iterative 68–70; from laboratory work 149–50; language and 106, 110–14; as participation in discourse community 110–14; rote and meaningful 178–80; scaffolding 85, 118, 119, 166, 211–12; self-regulated 150–1, 152–3; spontaneous 145–9; thinking about 152–5; vicarious 107–9; *see also* alternative conceptions of learning; constructivist perspective on learning; teaching
'life-world' 20
life-world learning impediments 187, 189, 205
life-world thinking 40–1
linguistic learning impediments 187, 189
links between subjects *see* conceptual integration
Long, D.E. 143
Lorenz, Konrad 77

manifold conceptions 50–1, 54
McClintock, Barbara 147, 166
meaningful learning 178–80
Meitner, Lise 202
melded concepts 108–9
memory: chunking and 166; hippocampus and 161–2; as reconstructive 69; as seeking coherence and rewriting history 162–3, 164–5; theory of mind and 64–5; working 63, 69–70
mental models 48, 49
mental modules 85–9
metacognition 150–1
metaphors: for theory of mind 64–5; use of 13, 108, 110, 116
Millar, R. 149
Millikan, Robert 115–16
misconceptions 35–6
Modelling Learners and Learning in Science Education (Taber) 52
models in science education: interpreting 158–60; role and nature of 157–8; student understanding of 158

Mortimer, E.F. 192, 214
multiple frameworks 50–1, 54

'natural attitude' 100–1, 112–13
natural kinds 87–8
natural sciences, objectivity in 13
natural selection: case for 25–7; cognitive system and 178; evolution and 15
natural theology 14, 139, 143
nature of science: conceptions of 48–50, 83–4; teaching about 155–7
Naylor, Stuart 193
Necker, Louis Albert 147–8
Necker cube 147–8
neural nets, artificial 91–2
neutralisation reaction 114
Newton, Isaac 14, 17–18, 139–40
Newtonian physics 41, 92, 102–3
noncanonical links, creating 169–71
null learning impediments 185–6, 189, 208
nutrition, knowledge construction compared to 18–19

objectivity, commitment to 13
octet framework 47–8, 171–3
Ohm's p-prim 98
ontology 138

particle, use of term 115
particle theory 123–5
pattern recognition: building intuition from 94–6; faces and 76–8; perception and 147–8
Pavlov, I. 59–60
pedagogical knowledge 197
pedagogic learning impediments 187, 189
perception: as interpretive process 95–6; pattern recognition and 147–8
personal constructivist perspective 70
phenomenological primitives *see* p-prims
Piaget, Jean: assimilation, accommodation, and 181; criticism of model of 82–4; 'romancing' answers and 43; theory of cognitive development of 78–82
post-formal operational stage 83–4
postpositivism 33
p-prims 45–6, 94, 98
practicals 149–50; *see also* laboratory work
preconceptions 37
preconscious processes 162–6
preoperational stage 79–80
prior knowledge of students 27–8, 197

probes for diagnostic assessment 193–5
problem-solving 164–6
pseudo-explanations: anthropomorphic language 126–9; example of 121; limited explanations 129–32; overview of 122–3; tautology 123–5; teleology 125–6; types of 123

range of application of theory 44
refraction: as abstract concept 20; demonstration of 21–2; teaching analogy for explanation of 22–3
relativist interpretations of science 39, 84
religion and science 14, 139–44
research in science education 5, 6; *see also* terminology for learners' ideas
rewriting history, memory as 162–3
'romancing' answers 43
rote learning 178–80
Royal Society of Chemistry probes 193

scaffolding learning 85, 118, 119, 166, 211–12
schemas for action 101–4
schemata 46–7
Schmidt, Hans-Jürgen 114
school science and discourse communities 111–12
science: argumentation in 112–13; beliefs and 135–7; border-crossing into discourses of 112, 138; coherence and 166–7; as conceptual subject with abstract ideas 19–23; connected nature of 53–4; difficulty of learning 12–13, 17–23; interpretation of evidence in 23–7; relativist interpretations of 39, 84; religion and 14, 139–44; theory in 42–4; as way of understanding world 13–17; *see also* nature of science
science education: conceptual integration in 166–71; constructivism in 5–6; levels of 210; *see also* models in science education
scientific attitude and worldviews 140
scientific disciplines, nature of 155–7
scientific knowledge of world, production of 16–17
Scott, P.H. iv, 192, 214
scriptural literacy and rejection of science 141
self-regulated learning 150–1, 152–3
sense-making and teaching-learning system bugs 201–2
sequencing of teaching 27–8
simplification of concepts, optimum level of 27
Socratic method 191–2
Solomon, Joan 113
species principle 88–9
speech, transcription of 7–8
spontaneous learning 145–50
Stavy, R. 98
study skills 150–1, 153–5
substantive learning impediments 185, 186–8, 189, 208
symmetry, conceptions of 98–100

tacit knowledge 39, 55
Taming the Atom (van Baeyer) 116
target knowledge 33–4
tautology 123–5
teachers: alternative conceptions of 205; compared to medical practitioners 7; as learning doctors 195–201; metacognition of 152–3; *see also* teaching; teaching models
teaching: bugs in learning system and 184–90; as complex system 177, 195–7; conceptual integration and 167; for contingent learning 183–4; discourse practices and 112; as iterative 199–200; knowledge representation in 181–3; as making unfamiliar familiar 110, 113–14; representations of 211–16; updating computers compared to 62–3; *see also* learning; teachers; teaching models
teaching models: communities of participating learners 212–14; constructivism 60–1, 66–70; dialogic classrooms 214–15, 216; lecturing 151; limits of 21–3; scaffolding 85, 118, 119, 166, 211–12; Socratic method 191–2; Xerox 61–2; *see also* teachers; teaching
teleological language 117, 125–6
terminology for learners' ideas: alternative conceptions 37–9; alternative conceptual frameworks 47–8; conceptions 34–5; concepts 32–4; epistemological beliefs 48–50; intuitive theories 41–5; life-world thinking 40–1; making sense of 51–2; mental models 48, 49; misconceptions 35–6; multiple frameworks and manifold conceptions 50–1; overview 31–2; p-prims 45–6; preconceptions 37; schemata 46–7

theory: activity theory 104; of cognitive development of Piaget 78–82; commitment to, levels of 43, 50; experimental tests and 16; particle theory 123–5; in science 42–4; *see also* intuitive theories/knowledge

theory of mind (TOM) 64–5, 80, 87

thinking: about science learning 153–5; coherent alternative 172–3; concrete operational 79, 80–1; explicitness of 54–5; formal operational 79, 80–2, 85, 86, 121–2; F-v 42, 92–4; life-world 40–1

time, conceptual shifts over 163–4

Tirosh, D. 98

Toulmin, Stephen 119

transcription of speech 7–8

transfer of information (Xerox) model of teaching 61–2

Treagust, David 193

typology of learning impediments 185, 188–90

understanding world: evidence for 15–16; evolution as allowing 15; science as way of 13–14; scientific knowledge and 16–17; universe as deliberately created 14

United Kingdom, constructivism in 5–6

United States, constructivism in 6

vicarious learning 107–9

vocal sounds, perception of 94–5

Vygotsky, Lev 108, 211

Whewell, William 14

Wolpert, Lewis 115

working memory 63, 69–70

worldview: influence of 137–8; scientific attitude and 140; traditional ecological knowledge 138; *see also* religion and science

Xerox (transfer of information) model of teaching 61–2

zones of actual and next development 211